# Reassessing the 1930s South

# REASSESSING THE 1930s SOUTH

EDITED BY

Karen L. Cox

AND

Sarah E. Gardner

LOUISIANA STATE UNIVERSITY PRESS BATON ROUGE

Published by Louisiana State University Press

Manufactured in the United States of America
First printing

DESIGNER: Michelle A. Neustrom
TYPEFACE: Chaparral Pro
PRINTER AND BINDER: Sheridan Books, Inc.

LIBRARY OF CONGRESS CATALOGING-IN-PUBLICATION DATA
Names: Cox, Karen L., 1962– editor. | Gardner, Sarah E., editor.
Title: Reassessing the 1930s South / edited by Karen L. Cox and Sarah E. Gardner.
Description: Baton Rouge : Louisiana State University Press, [2018] | Includes bibliographical references and index.
Identifiers: LCCN 2017040225 | ISBN 978-0-8071-6921-6 (cloth : alk. paper) | ISBN 978-0-8071-6922-3 (pdf) | ISBN 978-0-8071-6923-0 (epub)
Subjects: LCSH: Southern States—Civilization—20th century. | Southern States—History—1865–1951.
Classification: LCC F215 .R425 2018 | DDC 975/.04—dc23
LC record available at https://lccn.loc.gov/2017040225

The paper in this book meets the guidelines for permanence and durability of the Committee on Production Guidelines for Book Longevity of the Council on Library Resources. ♾

## CONTENTS


1 Editors' Introduction
KAREN L. COX AND SARAH E. GARDNER

**PART I. LITERARY ALTERNATIVES**

13 Unveiling Black Labor: *Sterling Brown, Charles Johnson, and the Depression-era Critique of the Plantation Myth*
STEVEN KNEPPER

30 Time Is the Longest Distance: *Tennessee Williams, New Orleans Tourism, and the Long Shadow of the 1930s*
ANTHONY J. STANONIS

47 E. P. O'Donnell: *A Life in a Handful of Leaves*
BRYAN A. GIEMZA

**PART II. ART AND THEATER**

69 From Farm to Factory: *New Deal Murals Celebrating the Tennessee Valley Authority*
LISA DORRILL

87 Three Dramatic Southerners in Depression New York: *Stark Young, Tennessee Williams, and Horton Foote*
ROBERT W. HAYNES

**PART III. TOURISM AND MODERNIZATION**

107 Driving Southerners through the Great Depression
DOUGLAS E. THOMPSON

122 A Forward Glance: *TVA Modernism and the Regional Designs of National Progress*
TED ATKINSON

## PART IV. RURAL REPRESENTATIONS AND REALITIES

141 We Shall Not Be Moved: *Highlander Folk School's Cultural Radicalism in the Great Depression*
EMILY SENEFELD

154 A Fierce Contest Over Images: Collier's *Magazine and the Fight Against Documentary Reportage in Greene County, Georgia, during the Great Depression*
SCOTT L. MATTHEWS

172 Inside the Farmhouse: *Ruth Allen and Margaret Jarman Hagood Confront Rural Realities*
REBECCA SHARPLESS AND MELISSA WALKER

## PART V. RACE AND INTERRACIALISM

191 Redlining Georgia
ELLA HOWARD

210 Empire on Parade: *Public Representations of Race at the 1936 Texas Centennial Exposition*
NICHOLAS ROLAND

228 Interracialism, Socialism, and William R. Amberson's Vision for the Rural South
ROBERT HUNT FERGUSON

245 CONTRIBUTORS

249 INDEX

Reassessing the 1930s South

# Editors' Introduction

KAREN L. COX AND SARAH E. GARDNER

This collection of essays reassesses the South during the 1930s, a decade when the region's problems magnified those of the nation more broadly. At that time the South's literature and music flourished to give the Jazz Age its name and American letters new international purchase and resonance. Capitalist institutions, which had experienced tremendous expansion in the previous decade, teetered on the brink of collapse, and the democratic promise of America was extended to include many whom it had previously ignored and was ruthlessly and violently denied to others to whom it had long been foreclosed. Critics lamented the crassness and hollowness of American culture as well as celebrated many of the most significant cultural triumphs of the twentieth century. These developments played out against a backdrop of wrenching events—often spectacularly, and tragically, in the South.

Despite the decade's complex and contentious development, the popular image of the South is limited by an artificial binary that at once simplifies and distorts the region's place in the nation. Americans had grown so accustomed to the rhetoric of boundless opportunity in the 1920s that the Depression shook their confidence. In response, there was a desire to better understand all things American. The increased popularity of historical fiction, with weighty tomes such as *Drums Along the Mohawk* and *Northwest Passage* leading the way, is one manifestation of this impulse. The work of the Federal Writers' Project—with its life stories project, its State Guide Book series, and its collections of American folklore—was another. Yet none of these was as compelling to America's cultural consumers as those efforts that romanticized the region that seemed to embrace the country's pastoral traditions, the American South. Especially strong was the pull of the Deep South, a region of rustic landscapes that, despite its own social and economic problems, had held fast to an uncomplicated and preindustrial past often represented in popular culture by images of the antebellum South.

To say that Americans in the 1930s were fascinated by the idea of the Old South would be an understatement. This fascination's long history extended back to the antebellum era, when plantation novels came into vogue. As scholarly works by Jennifer Rae Greeson, Jeremy Wells, and K. Stephen Prince have recently documented, the popularity of plantation settings remained consistent throughout the century and was key to the success of Joel Chandler Harris's Uncle Remus tales.[1] Stories of the Old South were also made into popular songs; Americans tapped their toes to Stephen Foster's plantation melodies "Swanee River" and "Old Black Joe." In the early years of the twentieth century, the country's enchantment with the Old South reappeared in the Dixie songs of Tin Pan Alley, some of which were penned by such well-known composers as Irving Berlin and George Gershwin. The fascination with the Old South was also evident in modern advertising, which made Aunt Jemima one of the most recognizable advertising icons of the twentieth century.

Novels based on the plantation legend achieved popularity again during the 1930s. Among them were Stark Young's *So Red the Rose,* published in 1934 and set in Natchez, and, of course, Margaret Mitchell's Civil War epic *Gone with the Wind,* published in 1936. Films of the 1930s drew heavily from successful novels and plays as Hollywood, too, capitalized on the nostalgia surrounding the Deep South. In *Music in the Old Bones: Jezebel through the Ages,* Janet Howe Gaines estimates that there were seventy-five films set in the Old South during the decade. Beginning with *River of Romance* in 1930, to the highly successful Shirley Temple films *The Littlest Rebel* and *The Little Colonel,* both made in 1935, to film versions of *So Red the Rose* and *Gone with the Wind,* themes of the Old South proved their profitability with film audiences. It was as if all of American mass culture had conspired to sell the country on the romance and nostalgia of the Old South.[2]

Although the sentimentalized image of the Old South was ascendant during the 1930s, it faced stiff competition from grotesque images of the "Problem South," as Natalie J. Ring and Angie Maxwell have shown.[3] Challenging the dashing cavaliers, hoop-skirted belles, and faithful retainers were images of slack-jawed, pellagra-ridden, and morally and biologically stunted sharecroppers, depictions made popular by Erskine Caldwell, Margaret Bourke-White, and others. Rather than invite Depression-era consumers to participate in the fantasy of an Old South that never was, the pathologized South allowed those same consumers to see the region as the nation's whipping boy, the source of all its current ills. Even at the time, the nation's tastemakers knew that neither image was "the" South. But they also knew what appealed to a consuming public that hungered for simplicity and escape from the woes brought on by the Great Depression. As the nation faced its most significant crisis since the Civil War, its inhabitants needed a focal point on which to fix their attention. Whether genteel or violent, opulent or impoverished, the South became the region that at once embodied the nation's fantasies and gave rise to its worst nightmares. Today, a lucrative tourist industry that capitalizes on Katrina tours and plantation weddings, and a savvy entertainment industry that turns out *Swamp People* and *Snake Salvation* as well as *Sweet Home Alabama,* testify to the continued cultural currency of images of the pathologized and romanticized South.

This book of essays, therefore, offers an opportunity to reexamine the South of the 1930s by exploring the broader contours of travel, literature, theater, and the visual arts, in addition to more nuanced explorations of race. These essays also help us to better understand the region's rural identity, perceived and real, as well as how southerners grappled with modernity.

This project emerged from a panel we organized for the Southern Historical Association that attracted an audience of over one hundred people at a conference where the norm is an audience of less than twenty. It was then we realized that there is a broader audience for a book on this topic, one that speaks to historians as well as students of literature and American Studies.

As with any collection, there are challenges to providing a balanced volume. This is based, in part, on the response to the call for essays but also on what happens during the editing process. Still, we believe the essays that make up this volume represent a reassessment of the 1930s South by providing fresh analyses on familiar subjects and by exploring topics that are less familiar and yet help to complicate our understanding of the region.

Our volume is in conversation with scholarship that spans history, literature, and interdisciplinary works in southern studies. As editors, we have both delved into the milieu of the Depression-era South. Sarah Gardner's *Blood and Irony: Southern White Women's Narratives of the Civil War, 1861–1937,* examines the ways in which the cultural and intellectual climate of the postwar decades informed Civil War narratives of the Depression era. More recently, in *Reviewing the South: The Literary Marketplace and the Southern Renaissance, 1920–1941,* she explores how the book industry responded to an expanding market of readers, hungry for stories about the South. Karen Cox has also examined the 1930s South through films, music, early radio, and tourism in her book *Dreaming of Dixie: How the South Was Created in American Popular Culture.* As she notes, popular perceptions of the South were often shaped or influenced by entities beyond the region.

Books by Leigh Anne Duck, Tara McPherson, and Angie Maxwell certainly inform the essays in this volume. Duck's *The Nation's Region: Southern Modernism, Segregation, and U.S. Nationalism* and McPherson's *Reconstructing Dixie: Race, Gender, and Nostalgia in the Imagined South* are both concerned with constructed images of the region. Duck, in particular, is focused on literary constructions of the South in a nationalist perspective as she examines the work of Zora Neale Hurston, William Faulkner, Erskine Caldwell, and others. While McPherson, a media arts scholar, is concerned with more contemporary interpretations of the region, she still reaches back to the 1930s to demonstrate the long history of an idealized South. Angie Maxwell, in *The Indicted South: Public Criticism, Southern Inferiority, and the Politics of Whiteness,* looks at how the region came under increased public scrutiny and responses of white public figures to that inward gaze.[4]

Still, the essays in this volume, while built upon the work of previous scholars, also expand our understanding of the 1930s by pressing beyond the binary of a benighted versus romanticized region.

The volume is divided into five parts. The essays in Part I turn our attention away from clichéd literary images of the region to alternatives that gained critical, if not necessarily popular, traction during the decade. Steven Knepper examines powerful critiques of the plantation myth leveled by Sterling Brown, an African American poet and scholar who, for a brief time, taught at Nashville's Fisk University, and his colleague, the University of Chicago–trained sociologist, Charles S. Johnson. As Knepper demonstrates, both writers revealed the ways in which the plantation myth, with its emphasis on leisure, veiled black labor. Their critiques did more than expose the plantation myth's fallacies, however. At the most fundamental level, their work demanded an end to sharecropping and an overhaul of the region's agricultural sector. For these reasons, Knepper argues, Sterling and Johnson "were at the forefront of the southern renaissance," as well as leading social critics who deserve our attention.

Rather than uncover little-considered figures of the southern renaissance, Anthony Stanonis takes on a well-known figure of the southern literary scene, Tennessee Williams, but highlights an aspect of his career that has garnered little attention from biographers and literary scholars. Stanonis focuses on the centrality of the New Orleans tourism industry to Williams's work. According to Stanonis, Williams "recognized New Orleans as a universal place—a tourism destination with a global reach from which plots could speak to the common condition of humanity while appealing to public curiosity about the Crescent City." Whereas civic boosters exoticized New Orleans in order to attract tourists, Williams used the city to "celebrate age-old human struggles for expression and freedom." By situating specific places, such as Galatoire's and Antoine's in his plays—places that tourists had seen as iconic and singular—Williams linked the unique with the universal. An urban, cosmopolitan, and racially and ethnically diverse place like New Orleans, then, joined Faulkner's fictional Yoknapatawpha County as a significant locus of the southern renaissance.

The first section concludes with Bryan Giemza's wonderfully evocative essay on E. P. O'Donnell, a prize-winning novelist whose works fell by the wayside during the postwar period of canon formation. Yet Cleanth Brooks, one of the canon's architects, had at an earlier moment held O'Donnell's work up to Faulkner's. In this meditation on place and a life, Giemza examines the process by which literary culture is both made and unmade. Equally telling, Giemza's essay also reveals the making and unmaking of a man, an artist who never quite belonged, in the bayous of Louisiana, in New Orleans, or in New York. If we measure O'Donnell's life not by the conventions of literary fame or personal success, however, we emerge with a different portrait. A turn to O'Donnell's second novel, *The Great Big Doorstep,* provides us with that alternative measure.

Part II shifts our attention away from fiction and prose and considers other forms of artistic production. Lisa Dorrill's examination of the Tennessee Valley Authority's (TVA) courthouse and post office murals links the ways in which a diverse group of artists, none of whom hailed from the South, worked in service of the New Deal. As Dorrill demonstrates, muralists unequivocally supported the modernization of the South's agricultural sector. Their federally funded murals, then, unabashedly celebrated the New Deal's role in reforming the region and served to foster and solidify local support for the TVA's mission.

Robert Haynes's essay, "The Thirties in New York," considers the engagement of three southern writers, Stark Young, Tennessee Williams, and Horton

Foote, with Manhattan's theater scene during the Great Depression. Far removed from Caldwell's Tobacco Road and Faulkner's Frenchman's Bend, these southern transplants—one a critic and translator, the other two dramatists—were nonetheless familiar with and influenced by the same social realities as the more famous chroniclers of the American South. Haynes suggests throughout his essay that Young, Williams, and Foote spent much of the decade balancing the often competing demands of "serving their muses" and serving as spokespeople for their region. This tension was made all the more palpable by national discussions of the South's place in the nation.

Of course, cultural expression found its way in other forms, too. The essays in Part III examine the role of technology in fostering modernization. Douglas E. Thompson explores the growth and development of automobile culture in the South. He is especially concerned with the automobile's power to transform social structures, including racial dynamics. To be sure, novelists and social critics commented on the automobile's ability to destabilize place. Yet Thompson concludes that rural southerners, especially, were less concerned with mechanization's effect on their daily lives than they were with maintaining that way of life by adapting available technology. As Thompson writes, the automobile fit southerners' understanding of "independence, self-reliance, and freedom. Marketed to them in this way," he notes, southerners "believed they could control the process" of modernization.

Ted Atkinson makes a compelling case for reassessing the cultural productions of the Tennessee Valley Authority as part of a larger project to rethink southern modernism. Long subsumed by the Agrarians' origin story of southern modernism as a reactionary response of melancholic and alienated writers who feared the effects of mechanization, industrialization, and an expansive federal government, scholars have in recent years begun to explore other encounters with modernism in the region. In "A Forward Glance," Atkinson turns to two examples, Arthur Arent's 1937 play *Power* and Pare Lorentz's influential 1938 documentary *The River,* as emblematic of TVA modernism. Taken together, they offer alternative narratives to those articulated by Allen Tate and Donald Davidson and later endorsed by the New Critics of the post–World War II generation. Southern modernism could, Atkinson demonstrates, embrace the possibilities of material progress, regional rehabilitation, and national unification.

The essays in Part IV address public representations of the 1930s rural South versus the reality on the ground. Observers from journalists to sociologists, as well as southerners themselves, contributed ideas about regional identity. Emily Senefeld explores the strategies used by the founders of Tennessee's Highlander Folk School to promote their work training educational and cultural leaders within the context of the national labor movement. Senefeld specifically looks at a 1937 British Broadcasting Corporation (BBC) broadcast by the school in which a program of Appalachian folk culture (song, dance, and drama) was used to "build support for the school's radical ideology." By presenting traditional culture as a means of activism—labor songs performed in the folk tradition, for example—the school, Senefeld argues, sought to publicly connect its mission with the broader labor movement.

Scott Matthews's essay examines a 1938 article on Greene County, Georgia, in the popular magazine *Collier's*. Entitled "Devil in de Cotton," it was one of many documentary depictions of poverty in the rural South to appear in newspapers and magazines during the 1930s. The article used both image and narrative to suggest that federal intervention was the only remedy to the problem. While such documentary essays appeared with some regularity, they were rarely challenged. As Matthews's essay reveals, there was a backlash to the *Collier's* piece, as leading white citizens of Greene County mounted a robust response to protect the county's, and their own, reputation. From the local newspaper to the *Congressional Record,* Matthews asserts, the controversy exposed "the contentious political and cultural stakes involved in documentary expression in the Depression-era South."

Representations, whether generated from within the region or from without, always butted up against reality. Sociologists and economists, too, applied their skills to unraveling the real-world challenges of the rural South, a region whose economy was still largely agricultural during the 1930s. Economist Ruth Alice Allen and sociologist Margaret Jarman Hagood, in fact, pioneered studies of farming in the region. As historians Rebecca Sharpless and Melissa Walker demonstrate, both women established that gender analysis was critical to understanding the agricultural life of the South, given that women were essential to farming operations. Their exploration of farming in different states—Allen in Texas and Hagood in North Carolina—were revelatory. While both women studied white women's work, Allen also studied the significant role played by African American and Mexican women in their communities. As Sharpless and Walker show, Allen and Hagood's use of gender analysis proved significant to our understanding of farming practices but also to the respective fields of economics and sociology.

In Part V, the final essays of this volume focus on race and interracialism. Ella Howard writes about residential segregation and the practice of redlining, in which banks restricted where African Americans could live based on mortgage-lending practices. Using Georgia as a case study, Howard looks at the cities of Columbus, Macon, Savannah, and Atlanta to demonstrate how redlining shaped communities. Applying digital-mapping techniques, Howard demonstrates how redlining not only determined where African Americans could live but how this practice affected future mortgage practices and economic development.

From the late nineteenth through the first decades of the twentieth century, states and cities throughout the region hosted expositions to showcase their successes and present an image of progress. Nicholas Roland examines one of these events, the Texas Centennial of 1936, and how it purposefully sought to shape the state's image. As Roland notes, the centennial gave Americans an image of Texas that persists to this day. Cowboys, oilmen, and the heroes of the Alamo were used to emphasize "economic dynamism" and a message of progress. As Roland contends, the Centennial also marked the state as "Anglo-Texan." And while black participation was encouraged at the event, the intention was to suggest the existence of racial harmony, while detracting from the negative reality of racial discord and, in some cases, violence.

In the final essay, Robert Hunt Ferguson introduces us to William R. Amberson, a member of the American Socialist Party and radical visionary who helped create the Delta Cooperative Farm in Bolivar County, Mississippi, in 1936. Amberson had witnessed the flow of southern sharecroppers—black and white—into Memphis in the early 1930s. As he saw it, they were devastated not only by the Depression but by New Deal legislation. Amberson was particularly critical of the Agricultural Adjustment Act (AAA), which benefited large-scale farm production and led to the mass eviction of sharecroppers. In response, he penned an essay for the *Nation* outlining the devastation caused by the AAA. Amberson also envisioned relocating those farmers into collective, egalitarian communities, the basic tenet of which was interracial cooperation. As Ferguson concludes in his study of the short-lived Delta Cooperative Farm, Amberson, while well intentioned, was wrong in thinking that the future of the South lay in "socialist collectivism."

* * *

The 1930s South served as a region of study, of social experimentation, and of government-sponsored efforts at change. Its economy failed to modernize until World War II, when an influx of military spending, industrial expansion, and improved agricultural technology pushed the South to enter the modern age. And yet socially, culturally, and politically, many southerners still romanticized agrarian traditions, which included a defense of the racial status quo. Even when southerners envisioned a more progressive region, popular culture undermined it by presenting the South as the keeper of America's pastoral tradition, a tradition upheld by a pliable black servant class. As these essays illustrate, there are many ways to examine and reexamine the region of that decade. As editors, we know that the quest to understand the 1930s South continues.

## NOTES

1. Jennifer Rae Greeson, *Our South: Geographic Fantasy and the Rise of National Literature* (Cambridge: Harvard University Press, 2010); Jeremy Wells, *Romances of the White Man's Burden: Race, Empire, and Plantation in American Literature* (Nashville: Vanderbilt University Press, 2011); K. Stephen Prince, *Stories of the South: Race and the Reconstruction of Southern Identity, 1865–1915* (Chapel Hill: University of North Carolina Press, 2014).

2. Janet Howe Gaines, *Music in the Old Bones: Jezebel Through the Ages* (Carbondale: Southern Illinois Press, 1999).

3. Natalie J. Ring, *The Problem South: Region, Empire, and the New Liberal State, 1880–1930* (Athens: University of Georgia Press, 2012); Angie Maxwell, *The Indicted South: Public Criticism, Southern Inferiority, and the Politics of Whiteness* (Chapel Hill: University of North Carolina Press, 2014).

4. Leigh Anne Duck, *The Nation's Region: Southern Modernism, Segregation, and U.S.* Nationalism (Athens: University of Georgia Press, 2006); Tara McPherson, *Reconstructing Dixie: Race, Gender, and Nostalgia in the Imagined South* (Durham: Duke University Press, 2003); Maxwell, *The Indicted South.*

# I

# LITERARY ALTERNATIVES

# Unveiling Black Labor

## *Sterling Brown, Charles Johnson, and the Depression-era Critique of the Plantation Myth*

STEVEN KNEPPER

The plantation myth had a strong hold on US popular culture in the early decades of the twentieth century.[1] Romantic depictions of the plantation past appeared in novels, poems, songs, children's books, advertisements, and early films. In the words of George Tindall, these depictions often offered a "euphoric pattern of kindly old marster with his mint julep; happy darkies singing in fields perpetually white to the harvest or, as the case may be, sadly recalling the long lost days of old; coquettish belles wooed by slender gallants in gray underneath the moonlight and magnolias."[2] By focusing on leisure in an idealized countryside, these depictions offered a pastoral vision of the antebellum South. To sustain this vision, they had to veil the economics of the plantation and, in particular, the exploited black labor upon which it depended. While some depictions hid black labor altogether, most, as the passage from Tindall suggests, naturalized it, aestheticized it, or refigured it as leisure.

A few examples illustrate these different forms of elision. Consider the 1899 edition of Louise Clarke Pyrnelle's children's book *Diddie, Dumps, and Tot; or, Plantation Child-Life,* the cover of which is imprinted with cotton bolls. In the preface, Pyrnelle writes that her "little book" does not "pretend to be any defense of slavery. I know not whether it was right or wrong (there are many pros and cons on that subject)." Yet being "raised in the heart of the cotton section, surrounded by negroes from my earliest infancy, 'I KNOW whereof I do speak'; and it is to tell of the pleasant and happy relations that existed between master and slave that I write this story of 'Diddie, Dumps, and Tot.'" In this children's book, the plantation becomes a playground, with black slaves as playmates who provide frequent comic relief.[3]

Published a generation later, Dorothy Scarborough's 1923 novel *In the Land of Cotton* acknowledges that growing cotton is fraught with economic challenges. Her novel is critical of "King Cotton," who "may be cruel or benignant" but who nonetheless is "master" of all men in the South. Yet Scarborough describes black laborers enthusiastically flocking to the fields: "Into the 'cotton-patch' with shout and song and wild, barbaric mirth, troop the gay negroes, children of the sun, lovers of light and heat." She claims, "All join in the joy of the harvest with a state of mind peculiar to cotton-picking time." They work "in lazy languor" and stop "to gaze across the field, with many a pause to bandy words and jests or to incite some fellow-laborer to comic competition." The line between leisure and labor blurs, even in a novel with significant antipastoral elements.[4]

Early twentieth-century popular music also drew upon the familiar plantation myth. In Paul Whiteman's Rhythm Boys' 1927 rendition of "Mississippi Mud," Bing Crosby sings, "Just as happy as a cow chewing on a cud, when the darkies beat their feet on the Mississippi mud."[5] In his 1932 rendition of "Cabin in the Cotton," Crosby croons, "I get a feeling so sentimental / And I see a smile so gentle / When I think of Old Virginie / And those pickaninny days!"[6] Crosby would later sing "Dixie" in blackface in the 1943 film of the same name. In all of these songs, the familiar minstrel-show nostalgia for happier, carefree days on the old plantation is readily evident.

An intriguing example of the plantation myth's veiling of black labor is to be found in the 1939 film adaptation of *Gone with the Wind.* The opening sequence is a series of bucolic images accompanied by the film's soaring score: a sunset over a board fence, horses in a verdant pasture, a line of blossoming cherry trees, the columned big house. Interspersed with these images are equally idyllic scenes of slaves working on the plantation. The credits scroll over a landscape of slaves in a cotton field, a forest and mountain range unfolding in the distance, clouds like cotton bolls in the sky. As slaves herd cattle at dusk and the orchestra transitions into a mournful rendition of "Dixie," a legend scrolls across the screen: "There was a land of Cavaliers and Cotton Fields called the Old South . . . Here in this pretty world Gallantry took its last bow . . . Here was the last ever to be seen of Knights and their Ladies Fair, of Master and of Slave. Look for it only in books, for it is no more than a dream to be remembered. A civilization gone with the wind . . ."[7] The film's extended opening is a powerful evocation of the plantation myth, one in which black labor is absorbed into a bucolic tableau.

Contrast the opening sequence of *Gone with the Wind,* however, with the beginning of the film's second part, which opens (after the intermission) on a dark and war-torn Tara. Scarlett, her sisters, and Melanie are now picking cotton. What was an idyllic activity at film's beginning—with bolls as innocuous as cumulous clouds—has become real, back-breaking work. When aristocratic white women take to the fields, picking cotton becomes decidedly antipastoral.

There were also defenders of the plantation myth among intellectuals. In 1930, "Twelve Southerners," several of them affiliated with Vanderbilt University, published *I'll Take My Stand,* a defense of a beneficent Agrarian South against an insidiously encroaching industrial North. While many of their critiques of "industrialism" are trenchant, the depictions they offer of the agrarian South often advance the standard plantation myth. *I'll Take My Stand* makes few mentions of cash crops or sharecropping, for instance, even though the rural South was already deep in agricultural depression in 1930, and John Crowe Ransom claimed in his contribution that "slavery was a feature monstrous enough in theory but, more often than not, humane in practice; and it is impossible to believe that its abolition alone could have effected any great revolution in society."[8]

While the plantation myth continued to have significant popular appeal, it received increasing scrutiny during the Depression. The economic, ecological, and political climate of the late 1920s and 1930s led a number of scholars and artists to critique the myth. As some of the critical reviews of *I'll Take My Stand* made clear, the plantation myth could not address the problem of impoverished sharecroppers and exhausted soil, which were at least in part legacies of the plantation and its cash-crop monocultures.[9] Indeed, the myth diverted attention away from these harsh realities. One of those reviews came from Sterling Brown, a leading black poet and scholar who briefly taught across town from some of the Agrarians at Nashville's Fisk University. Writing in *Opportunity,* Brown entered into a dialogue with the Agrarians' claims about the Old South. Concerning their assertion that "the South has been non-acquisitive," Brown wrote, "With an oligarchy of planters ruining the past and future of their section!" And regarding the idea that the South "has been leisurely . . . kindly, serene," Brown commented wryly, "praises be for euphemism."[10]

Here Brown identifies the plantation myth's emphasis on leisure (and attendant veiling of black labor) as one of its chief features. The sociologist Charles Johnson, who was Brown's colleague at Fisk, made this same point in *Shadow of the Plantation,* a book-length critique of the plantation myth published just four years after *I'll Take My Stand.* Against the plantation myth's tendency to obscure or aestheticize black labor, both Brown and Johnson dramatize the plight of black sharecroppers, insisting on their hard work, exploitation, and frustration. Johnson and Brown thus often counter pastoral depiction with antipastoral critique. In this regard they were at the forefront of the southern renaissance, alongside writers as different as William Faulkner, Grace Lumpkin, and Erskine Caldwell. But they also joined influential social critics like Rupert Vance and Arthur Raper in kindling hopes for a transformation of the countryside, one in which sharecropping would give way to increased farm proprietorship and crop diversification.

Born into a middle-class black family in Washington, DC, Brown received an elite northern education at Williams College and Harvard University. He spent much of his early career, though, in teaching positions at southern black institutions such as Virginia Seminary and College, where he taught from 1923 to 1926, and Fisk, where he taught from 1928 to 1929. By the early 1930s, Brown had moved on to what would be a four-decade career at Howard University. Although he established himself as a poet with his 1932 collection *Southern Road,* Brown also emerged as an incisive scholar and social critic.[11]

Brown is, in particular, an underappreciated critic of the plantation myth. In a 1933 article, "Negro Character as Seen by White Authors," Brown claims, "The majority of books about Negroes merely stereotype Negro character." He identifies seven misleading stereotypes that white authors frequently draw upon in their depictions of blacks: "(1) The Contented Slave, (2) The Wretched Freeman, (3) The Comic Negro, (4) The Brute Negro, (5) The Tragic Mulatto, (6) The Local Color Negro, and (7) The Exotic Primitive." The contented slave is, of course, one of the plantation myth's stock characters. Brown analyzes this type of character by offering a genealogy of how literary depictions of the plantation came to "omit the economic basis of slavery." Brown argued that Eli Whitney's invention of the cotton gin had extinguished whatever nascent abolitionist sentiment had developed in the South by the late eighteenth century. "Up until this time," Brown continued, "the *raison d'être* of slavery had not been so powerful. But now there was a way open to quick wealth; Cotton was crowned King, and a huge army of black servitors was necessary to keep him upon the throne." Brown holds that new ethical and theological rationales were necessary to justify slavery, to present it as something other than the instrumentalization of human beings for economic profit. Literary depictions of contented slaves both reflected these new rationales and constituted a rationale in their own right.[12]

According to Brown, the stereotype of the wretched freeman often acts as "foil" to the contented slave. Slaves thrive on the paternalistic plantation but fall into squalor and vice when given independence. Brown aligns this stereotype with the common early twentieth-century historical narratives, associated with Claude Bowers and William Dunning, of Reconstruction's failure.[13] Together, these stereotypes provide a lens for reading the struggles of sharecroppers as the results of emancipation and Reconstruction rather than, at least in part, legacies of the plantation system.

At the end of his 1933 essay, Brown claimed that such stereotypes were increasingly being challenged by a new generation of writers, including white writers such as Julia Peterkin, Howard Odum, Eugene O'Neill, William Faulkner, and Erskine Caldwell. Brown was himself part of this new generation, of course. His poems depict plantations and sharecropping as exploitative institutions. His croppers' lives are defined by hard work for which they receive hardly any recompense. Far from contented or nostalgic, they are often acutely aware of the injustice of their situation. In the 1939 poem "Old Lem," for instance, the title character laments how sharecropping is set up to profit white owners and exploit black croppers.

> They weigh the cotton
> They store the corn
>     We only good enough
>     To work the rows;
> They run the commissary
> They keep the books
>     We gotta be grateful
>     For being cheated[14]

The very form of the poem, with its hanging lines that describe the croppers' proscribed roles, implies subordination.

The 1936 poem "Master and Man" suggests that life on the southern cotton farm can indeed seem bucolic from the white perspective. The first section is a cornucopian record of the plenty enjoyed by the "master" Mr. Cromartie and his family.

> The yellow ears are crammed in Mr. Cromartie's bin
> The wheat is tight sacked in Mr. Cromartie's barn.

> The timothy is stuffed in Mr. Cromartie's loft.
> The ploughs are lined up in Mr. Cromartie's shed.
> The cotton has gone to Mr. Cromartie's factor.
> The money is in Mr. Cromartie's bank.
> Mr. Cromartie's son made his frat at the college.
> Mr. Cromartie's daughter has got her new car.
> The veranda is old, but the fireplace is rosy.
> Well done, Mr. Cromartie. Time now for rest.[15]

This passage is decidedly pastoral. There is no work, only the results of a rich harvest. Mr. Cromartie's is a life of leisure on the veranda and by the fireplace. His farm and his family are seemingly ideal.

But after a break, Brown gives us "Uncle Ned's" perspective on this farm and its harvest. It is significant that the sharecropper's perspective appears second, below Cromartie's. Brown again uses form to suggest the hierarchies of the sharecropping system. This second stanza depicts the hard, exploitative work hidden beneath the record of plenty. It offers, in short, an antipastoral.

> Blackened sticks line the furrows that Uncle Ned laid.
> Bits of fluff are in the corners where Uncle Ned ginned.
> The mules he ploughed are sleek in Mr. Cromartie's pastures.
> The hoes grow dull in Mr. Cromartie's shed.
> His children have traipsed off to God knows where.
> His old lady sits patching the old, thin denims;
> She's got a new dress, and his young one a doll,
> He's got five dollars. The year has come round.
> The harvest is over: Uncle Ned's harvesting,
> Mr. Cromartie's harvest. Time now for rest.[16]

Here, the emphasis is on work. Uncle Ned has "laid," "ginned," and "ploughed." He has done the "harvesting," but after buying a new dress and a doll for his loved ones, he is left with only "five dollars," "blackened sticks," and "bits of fluff." His "rest" is not the idealized leisure of the pastoral but the weary rest of a man who has worked hard and well but who must stoically accept that another will reap most of the benefits of his labor. In this poem, Brown suggests the deservedness, competency, and kindness of Uncle Ned, contrasting his character with what comes to appear as the greed and decadence of Cromartie.

Charles Johnson, Brown's former colleague at Fisk, also focuses on how the plantation myth veils black labor. A native of Bristol, Virginia, he studied sociology at the University of Chicago with Robert E. Park and then moved to New York City in 1921. There he served as research director for the National Urban League and founded *Opportunity: A Journal of Negro Life,* which published work from many of the major figures of the Harlem Renaissance, including Brown. Yet he was eager to return to the South and to play a role in addressing its problems. In 1926 he accepted a position as chair of the recently established, Rockefeller-funded, sociology department at Fisk.[17]

His 1934 study *Shadow of the Plantation* was among the first fruits of his research at Fisk. A study of black sharecroppers in Macon County, Alabama, it also advanced a sustained critique of the plantation myth. Johnson offers a close look at Macon County croppers' lives and work, with a sociological study's characteristic charts, statistics, and detail. But his title suggests his broader aim—to show the poverty and exploitation of Depression-era sharecroppers as a legacy of slavery, to focus on the cash crops, exploited labor, and exhausted land that linked the antebellum and postbellum plantations.

In the opening pages of *Shadow of the Plantation,* Johnson paints some of the central images of the plantation myth: "In the romantic fiction, which has so largely supported the concept, [the plantation] is a far-flung, comfortably contained agricultural unit, crested by a spacious white mansion with imposing colonnades supporting cool and spacious verandas, and surrounded in ample and flower-laden grounds. In the background are the cotton fields stretching far and white into the distance. There are long rows of white-washed Negro cabins; sleek, contented slaves, laughing and singing as they work; little pickaninnies capering with the abandonment of irresponsible fledglings in the clearings of the cabins or on the smoothly clipped lawn." Johnson explains that these tropes have their origin point in antebellum southern writers like John Pendleton Kennedy, but they had since permeated popular culture. "The stage," he explains, "and particularly the minstrel, a long literary tradition, beginning no doubt with [Kennedy's] *Swallow Barn,* and warm memories of the past have helped build the conception most familiar to the present generation."[18]

Johnson levels two main charges at this romantic portrait of the plantation. One is suggested through his description of the "white mansion" and the "white-washed Negro cabins." He suggests that there is a bias in perspective in the plantation myth. It is itself whitewashed—a view from the veranda rather than from behind the plow. His second charge is more explicit. Johnson claims that the myth obscures the economics of the plantation and, in particular, the hard labor of growing cotton. There is little in his opening evocation of the plantation to suggest that it is a site of large-scale production. Work is present, but it is work subordinated to leisure, perhaps even work as leisure. The slaves laugh and sing as they work. There is a parallel between their work in the fields and "the pickaninnies capering." The cotton fields in this image are mainly aesthetic, stretching "far and white into the distance."

Johnson proceeds to offer a different picture of the plantation, one that would inform the rest of his study. He claims that "the actual plantation devoted to cotton was based on a rigorous and dull routine." Its year was defined by work: "In January there was ginning, sorting, and moting of cotton; in February more ginning and moting, ground-clearing, fence-mending, and ditching, picking joint grass, working cotton—the eternal hoe industry. In May, June, July, and August more hoeing and working and some picking; in September, October, and November more picking, clearing new ground; in December moting and ginning. There were tasks and punishments for falling short. Every detail of life was regulated not by any internal compulsions but by a system of physical punishments and rewards." He concludes that "life, on the whole, was a grim business. Such were the imperatives of the economic system."[19]

By emphasizing work in this second, revisionist description—hard, exploitative, factory-like work—Johnson contests the plantation myth's idealized and obfuscating leisure. The lives and labor of field hands are here disciplined by the regimented processes of mass cultivation of cash-crop monocultures for distant markets. Johnson's plantation was not the rooted cultural institution of myth. It relied on forced labor, and Johnson emphasizes how planters moved west as cash crops depleted the soil.[20] He thus argues that the exploitative labor arrangements and soil erosion of sharecropping were in important ways legacies of the antebellum plantation.

Johnson recognized the importance of cultural narratives like the plantation myth, with its evocative images and emotional resonance. He was aware that such narratives had to be challenged with counternarratives of similar rhetorical and affective power. *Shadow of the Plantation* is, therefore, not only a study of sharecroppers in a Black Belt county but also an attempt to craft such a counternarrative. It is grounded in scholarly research, but it is dramatized in literary fashion, with the use of striking photographs and legends, of pathos-stirring detail, of sharecropper testimony sampled and shaped into dramatic monologues.[21] The very title, with its figurative dimensions, suggests Johnson's rhetorical savviness, his awareness that pastoral images of the plantation must be countered with critical—but also culturally resonant—ones.

This awareness is evident even in the volume's front matter. Opposite the title page, acting as a frontispiece to *Shadow of the Plantation,* is a photograph, in side profile, of a sharecropper sitting on his porch. The cropper is blurred and shadowy in the foreground, perhaps suggesting a life that has been obscured in the shadow of the plantation. The caption reads "SEEM LAK' I AIN'T NEVER BREAK EVEN." It is a bleak photo, drained of any hint of romance, emphasizing that the economic realities of the plantation lead to degradation.

Immediately after the frontispiece, Johnson includes Brown's 1932 poem "Old King Cotton" as an epigraph. Brown's poem draws upon black work songs for its rhythms and for the collective voice of its narration. In the opening stanzas, cotton is personified as a relentless and diabolical landlord.

Ole King Cotton,
    Ole Man Cotton,
Keeps us slavin'
    Till we'se dead an' rotten.
Bosses us 'roun'
    In his ornery way,
"Cotton needs pickin'!"
    De Hell he say. . . . .[22]

Having challenged nostalgic depictions of the plantation past, Johnson hopes to have cleared space for close attention to the sharecropping present. One of the most striking aspects of *Shadow of the Plantation* is the interplay between Johnson's critical narrative and the voices of sharecroppers he interviewed. Johnson's critiques of the plantation system are trenchant, as when he claims, "The waste of the soil, the overproduction of cotton, the constant involvement of the credit system, have brought on an inevitable stagnation, both for planters and for the Negroes whose lives are linked with its ever declining fortunes." But such a conclusion is neither as poignant nor as telling as a sharecropper's story of exploitation and of a defiant assertion of dignity: "I stayed in that little house over there and paid $60 and never got nothing last year, I worked and dug and never got a thing, and when I told him I wasn't making nothing he said, 'Well you are making money for me, ain't you?' And I said, 'Well, I can quit.' I moved from there, and he didn't know it. Folks went up there looking for Dick Richards and Dick Richards done moved." Reflecting on how he has been cheated in his crop settlement, another cropper reflects that "white folks take it when they git ready and you looking right at them." In describing poor tenant housing, one woman explains, "My house is so rotten you kin jest take up the boards in your hand and cromple 'em up. Everything done swunk about it." None of the selections offer exchanges between Johnson and the croppers. They are presented as monologues. Johnson thus treats his subjects as central actors with their own volition, personalities, and ideas. As Patrick Gilpin and Marybeth Gasman argue, "the outstanding feature" of *Shadow of the Plantation* is that "black people were subject instead of object. Johnson went beyond white attitudes and opinions to determine what blacks felt and thought. His insistence that all interviews be in the first person and that they follow the 'own story' method gave [*Shadow*] a kind of authenticity and spontaneity that is rare in books on race relations."[23]

These sharecropper voices also trouble some of the literary and cultural stereotypes identified by Brown in "Negro Character as Seen by White Authors," especially the stereotypes of the "contented slave" and the "wretched freeman." On the minstrel-show stage, actors in blackface often praised a romanticized plantation. Joel Chandler Harris and Thomas Nelson Page used similar ventriloquism in their fictions, when ex-slave storytellers such as Harris's Uncle Remus nostalgically recall the grandeur of the Old South plantation. The words of real sharecroppers in *Shadow of the Plantation* counter such literary ventriloquism. One woman says, "Don't you believe no nigger when he says he ruther be no slave. Things happen then too awful to talk about." Some of the sharecroppers in the volume are indeed nostalgic for past days. One claims, "I done had a harder time since I been free than when I was a slave. I never had such a hard time in my life as I'm having now." But Johnson situates these comments within the poverty of the collapsing sharecropping system. He finds that the croppers most likely to ameliorate the antebellum past are those most mired in poverty.[24]

*Shadow of the Plantation* also counters another of the stereotypes identified in Sterling Brown's essay—"the wretched freeman." Johnson compares the black population of Macon County, Alabama, with that of Gibson County, Tennessee. Gibson is a region of diversified farming with a smaller black population. Johnson finds there a "greater and longer-range migration, a more pronounced interest in education, more property ownership, and more clearly recognizable affectional ties within the families." The key difference, for him, is the absence of the exploitative plantation system, which negatively affects all aspects of its laborers' lives. In Gibson, "the lack of dependence upon a staple crop and the absence of a plantation economy may be pointed to as being, in part at least, responsible for the higher home-ownership proportions."[25] Proprietorship and diversification lead to a better standard of living, especially in terms of housing conditions.[26] They lead to more circulating money and greater independence on the part of the black community. And they lead to healthier familial and communal relationships. He claims that in such regions, "the frequency of active affectional relations between parents and children creates a distinctly different picture [than in plantation areas] of the dominant pattern of family life."[27] Against the stereotype of the "wretched freeman," Johnson finds that independence, self-determination, and land ownership lead to thriving communities. He ties wretchedness to the sharecropping in the shadow of the plantation, not to independence.

Sterling Brown makes similar juxtapositions in his poetry. His 1938 poem "The Young Ones," for instance, focuses on a large, impoverished sharecropping family on a plantation devoted to cotton monoculture: "With cotton to the doorstep / No place to play; / No time: what with chopping cotton / All the day." The mother of this family is in the farm's "two-roomed shack," where she has just given birth to another young son. She is "crying," not so much because of the pains of childbirth, but because of the poor prospects for this new baby and the family: "Another mouth to feed / Another body to bed, / Another to grow up / Underfed." Yet while the mother is wracked by worry about her children, "their pappy's happy." He sees in this new child more help with the cotton crop. He says, "It's two more hands / For to carry a row; / Praise God from whom all blessings flow."[28]

Brown's poem thus offers contrasting perspectives from mother and father. The mother's perspective on the new birth illustrates the despair of the sharecropping system. There is no prospect for a better future. The birth of a new child, rather than being the iconic moment of hope, is an instance of hopelessness. It represents the family's further slide into poverty and their increased dependency on cotton and its labor system, a dependency that promises little succor in return. The father's perspective, on the other hand, suggests that the instrumentalization of labor and land in the sharecropping system has extended into the familial relationships. The "happy" father sees his new son as "two hands" to help pick the crop. The child becomes an instrumentalized means to working the cotton crop, which has enframed the family and its prospects. The family's limited horizon is suggested by its trips to town: "In the broken down car / They jounce up and down / Pretend to be steering / On the way to town."[29] They only "pretend to be steering." Their agency is largely illusory.

"The Young Ones" can be profitably contrasted with the 1932 poem "After Winter." This poem focuses on a father who owns—or at least has control over—his own "ten acres." He is thus free from the sharecropping system and its enthrallment to cotton: "He snuggles his fingers / In the black loam / The lean months are done with, / The fat to come."[30] This farmer plans to plant a variety of crops, raising primarily food for his family rather than cash crops for market. He eagerly looks beyond spring planting to the harvest to come, singing a hopeful song in his head.

> Butter beans fo' Clara
> Sugar corn fo' Grace
> An fo de little feller
> Runnin' space.
> Radishes and lettuce
> Eggplants and beets
> Turnips fo' de winter
> An' candied sweets.
> Homespun tobacco
> Apples in de bin
> Fo' smokin' an' fo' cider
> When de folks draps in.[31]

Here children are an occasion for neither despairing grief nor exploitative satisfaction. The family members are themselves a source of joy, and the family is a site of loving gift exchange rather than instrumentalization. Rather than having cotton planted up to their doorstep or "pretending" to steer their fate, the members of this family have real "Runnin' space," agency, and choice. Their independence and control over the land allow for healthier familial relationship and for wider conviviality and sharing "When de folks draps in."

Brown's vision here is not as idealistic as it may first appear, though. It is carefully qualified. The family has just suffered through "lean months," and the father himself "stands ragged / An old scarecrow."[32] We are given harvest dreams in "After Winter," not realized crops in the fall. Still, in this poem, autonomy allows for hope—something often absent from Brown's dramatizations of sharecroppers.

Both Brown and Johnson use antipastoral critique of the plantation myth, then, at least in part to clear space for a constructive vision for the southern countryside. Both imply that the unfulfilled Reconstruction promise of "forty acres and a mule" has contributed to the problems of the 1930s South. Many black rural southerners remained dependent—farmers without land—allowing for the continued dominance of the plantation and cotton monocultures. Both, in turn, suggest that proprietorship and crop diversification should be Depression-era goals.[33] In the conclusion of *Shadow of the Plantation,* Johnson claims that "the [sharecropping] system suggests the need of a complete reorganization of agriculture, and particularly in the Cotton Belt, in respect to both production and distribution."[34] In his short 1935 book *The Collapse of Cotton Tenancy,* Johnson argues, "The pressing needs of the millions of tenants, whose lives have always been barren and precarious, and who now find themselves disposed from even the poor living they formerly had, can be met only by some new distribution of land ownership." During the 1930s, Johnson served on Franklin Delano Roosevelt's Technical Committee on Farm Tenancy. His work helped inform New Deal programs like the Farm Security Administration (FSA) and the Bankhead-Jones Tenancy Act.[35]

Still, a second reconstruction of the southern countryside never happened. Black farm ownership made marked gains in the early decades of the twentieth century. Historian Pete Daniel claims, "A combination of husbandry, diplomacy, and ambition allowed black farmers to secure land, and the fact that so many succeeded during some of the darkest years of racist violence testifies to their character and determination."[36] During the Civil Rights period, though, widespread discrimination in the Department of Agriculture prevented black farmers from obtaining credit. As Daniel makes clear, the number of black-owned farms thus plummeted during the third quarter of the twentieth century at a pace far outstripping white farm decline.

Daniel's study is a reminder that some of the problems plaguing the Depression-era South were not solved by the decline of sharecropping, the Great Migration to the industrial North, and the rise of mechanized agriculture. The consolidation of the land into fewer hands continued, as did the reliance on cash-crop monocultures. Asymmetrical, exploitative labor relations persisted in new forms. Southern meat-processing plants, for instance, have been scrutinized for their working conditions and treatment of migrant workers. Significant animal welfare and ecological concerns have been raised about conventional poultry and pork farming, and agribusiness has also been criticized for using corporate contracts that grant farmers a modest share of the profits while making them shoulder most of the risk.[37] Yet the packaging and supermarket advertisements for the commodities of agribusiness are often adorned by pastoral images of red barns, verdant fields, and happy farmers in overalls. The elision of labor thus continues, as well.[38] The work of Brown and Johnson provides insight into the Depression's turn against the plantation myth, but it also provides a model of critique and constructive reimagining of the southern countryside that remains valuable today.

## NOTES

1. Classic studies of the plantation myth include Lewis Simpson's *The Dispossessed Garden: Pastoral and History in Southern Literature* (Athens: University of Georgia Press, 1975), Lucinda MacKethan's *The Dream of Arcady: Place and Time in Southern Literature* (Baton Rouge: Louisiana State University Press, 1980), and Jan Bakker's *Pastoral in Antebellum Southern Romance* (Baton Rouge: Louisiana State University Press, 1989). Among recent studies, Karen Cox's *Dreaming of Dixie: How the South was Created in American Popular Culture* (Chapel Hill: University of North Carolina Press, 2011) focuses on the pervasiveness of the plantation myth in early twentieth-century popular culture. See also Scott Romine's *The Real South: Southern Narrative in the Age of Cultural Reproduction* (Baton Rouge: Louisiana State University Press, 2008) and Elizabeth Christine Russ's *The Plantation in the Postslavery Imagination* (New York: Oxford University Press, 2009).

2. George Tindall, "Mythology: A New Frontier in Southern History," in *Myth and Southern History*, vol. 2 of *The New South*, ed. Patrick Gerster and Nicholas Cords (Urbana: University of Illinois Press, 1989), 4.

3. Louise Clarke Pyrnelle, *Diddie, Dumps, and Tot; Or, Plantation Child-Life* (1882; New York: Harper and Brothers, 1899), vi.

4. Dorothy Scarborough, *In the Land of Cotton* (New York: Macmillan, 1923), x, ix.

5. Paul Whiteman's Rhythm Boys, "Mississippi Mud," Victor, 1927, LP.

6. Bing Crosby, "Cabin in the Cotton," Brunswick, 1932, LP.

7. *Gone with the Wind*, directed by Victor Fleming (1939; Burbank: Warner Home Video, 2009), DVD. My transcription.

8. John Crowe Ransom, "Reconstructed but Unregenerate," in *I'll Take My Stand: The South and the Agrarian Tradition*, by Twelve Southerners (New York: Harper and Brothers, 1930), 14.

9. Chris Rieger claims that the Southern renaissance is a time when "the ecological de-

struction wrought by the South's historical abuse of the land reaches a point where it can no longer be masked by moonlight and magnolias," in *Clear-Cutting Eden: Ecology and the Pastoral in Southern Literature* (Tuscaloosa: University of Alabama Press, 2009), 5.

10. Sterling Brown, "A Romantic Defense," in *A Son's Return: Selected Essays of Sterling A. Brown,* ed. Mark A. Sanders (Boston: Northeastern University Press, 1996), 281.

11. For a brief overview of Sterling Brown's life and work, see John Edgar Tidwell and Steven C. Tracy's introduction to *After Winter: The Art and Life of Sterling A. Brown* (New York: Oxford University Press, 2009), 3–18.

12. Sterling Brown, "Negro Character As Seen By White Authors," in *A Son's Return,* 150, 154, 151. Brown notes that a character may combine more than one of these stereotypes. For instance, in many plantation romances, the contented slave is also often intended to be comedic.

13. See the preface to Eric Foner, *Reconstruction: America's Unfinished Revolution* (New York: Harper and Row, 1988), xvii–xx. See also John David Smith, *An Old Creed for the New South: Proslavery Ideology and Historiography, 1865–1918* (Westport, CT: Greenwood, 1985).

14. Sterling Brown, "Old Lem," in *The Collected Poetry of Sterling A. Brown* (Chicago: TriQuarterly Books, 1989), 180–81.

15. Sterling Brown, "Master and Man," in *The Collected Poetry,* 183.

16. Ibid.

17. For more on Johnson's life and career, see Patrick Gilpin and Marybeth Gasman, *Charles S. Johnson: Leadership Beyond the Veil in the Age of Jim Crow* (Albany: State University of New York Press, 2003).

18. Charles Johnson, *Shadow of the Plantation* (Chicago: University of Chicago Press, 1934), 1, 2.

19. Ibid., 2–3. Johnson's juxtaposition of idealized leisure and hard labor in the opening pages is an example of a countertrope in works that critique the plantation myth. Consider, for instance, how Ab Snopes in William Faulkner's 1939 short story "Barn Burning" tracks manure across Major de Spain's white carpet and thus effectively besmears the plantation myth with the realities that it obscures.

20. Ibid., 209–10. Johnson's focus on the westward-moving plantation anticipates the work of more recent scholars like Gavin Wright and Steven Stoll. Wright claims, for instance, that planters "were not landlords, but 'laborlords,'" who moved their slaves when the soil was depleted; see *Old South, New South: Revolutions in the Southern Economy Since the Civil War* (Baton Rouge: Louisiana State University Press, 1986), 18. See also Stoll, *Larding the Lean Earth: Soil and Society in Nineteenth-Century America* (New Have: Yale University Press, 2002).

21. This contrasts markedly with the more conventional academic style of two of the most prominent southern sociologists of Johnson's day, Howard Odum and Rupert Vance.

22. This poem is also collected in Brown, *The Collected Poetry,* 64–65.

23. Johnson, *Shadow of the Plantation,* 104, 127, 120, 99. Gilpin and Gasman, *Charles S. Johnson,* 131. In its use of photographs and interviews, *Shadow of the Plantation* prefigures a number of later works on sharecropping. These include influential studies by fellow sociologists, such as Arthur Raper's *Preface to Peasantry* (1936), a study of black sharecroppers in Georgia's Macon and Greene Counties, and Margaret Jarman Hagood's *Mothers of the South*

(1939), a study of women on southern tenant farms. *Shadow of The Plantation* also prefigures better-known and more overtly literary sharecropping photo-documentaries, such as Erskine Caldwell and Margaret Bourke-White's *You Have Seen Their Faces* (1937), James Agee and Walker Evans's *Let Us Now Praise Famous Men* (1941), and Richard Wright and Edwin Rosskam's *12 Million Black Voices* (1941).

24. Brown critiques this ventriloquism in "Negro Character As Seen By White Authors," 156–59, 20, 19, 18–23.

25. Johnson, *Shadow of the Plantation,* 94–98, 211–12.

26. See the comparative figures and graphs for "scores on physical housing," ibid., 95–97. Johnson finds that "the median [score] in Gibson County was 46.6 as compared with 36.01 in Macon County." Also, the dwellings "of owners in both states had consistently higher ratings than those of tenants."

27. Ibid., 211–21. For a recent collection of scholarly essays on post-Reconstruction black landowners, see Debra A. Reid and Evan P. Bennett, eds., *Beyond Forty Acres and A Mule: African American Landowning Families Since Reconstruction* (Gainesville: University Press of Florida, 2014).

28. There is a difference between the diversified plantation of "Master and Man" and the plantation of "The Young Ones," which has "cotton to the doorstep." Brown, "The Young Ones," 179.

29. Ibid. In a 1936 review of *Shadow of the Plantation,* Brown noted that in sharecropping "more children mean more hands for picking cotton," *Journal of Negro History,* 21, no. 1 (1936): 71. This reductive synecdoche returns in "The Young Ones," published two years after the review.

30. Brown, "After Winter," in *The Collected Poetry,* 74.

31. Ibid.

32. Ibid.

33. Such proposals became increasingly common during the Depression. They were offered by the Regionalist sociologists Howard Odum, Rupert Vance, and Arthur Raper. See Jack Temple Kirby, *Mockingbird Song: Ecological Landscapes of the South* (Chapel Hill: University of North Carolina Press, 2006). The Agrarians, stung by the criticisms of *I'll Take My Stand,* offered their own plans, in some ways similar to those of the Regionalists, in the 1930s as they attempted to address the problems of sharecropping. See Emily S. Bingham and Thomas A. Underwood, eds., *The Southern Agrarians and the New Deal* (Charlottesville: University Press of Virginia, 2001). See, esp., John Crowe Ransom's perhaps surprisingly positive review of *Shadow of the Plantation* collected in this volume, 239–43.

34. Charles Johnson, *Shadow of the Plantation,* 212.

35. Charles Johnson, Edwin R. Embree, and W. W. Alexander, *The Collapse of Cotton Tenancy: Summary of Field Studies and Statistical Surveys, 1933–1935* (Chapel Hill: University of North Carolina Press, 1935), 65. Gilpin and Gasman, *Charles Johnson,* 112–13. Gilpin and Gasman claim, "To gain the ear of the president, Johnson used his personal contact with the first lady, Eleanor Roosevelt, who responded by placing a copy of *The Collapse of Cotton Tenancy* on President Roosevelt's nightstand and 'insisted that he read it'" (110).

36. Pete Daniel, *Dispossession: Discrimination Against African American Farmers in the Age of Civil Rights* (Chapel Hill: University of North Carolina Press, 2013), vii. Wendell Berry offered significant reflections on the dispossession of black farmers in *The Hidden Wound* (New York: Houghton Mifflin, 1970).

37. See, e.g., the documentary film *Food, Inc.*, directed by Robert Kenner (Dallas: Magnolia Pictures, 2009). See also Kirby, *Mockingbird Song*, 191–99.

38. See Steven Knepper, "Seeing the Countryside: Behind the Pastoral and Progressivist Veils," *Telos* 162 (Spring 2013): 131–49.

# Time Is the Longest Distance

## *Tennessee Williams, New Orleans Tourism, and the Long Shadow of the 1930s*

ANTHONY J. STANONIS

When Thomas Lanier Williams III stepped from a bus at Lee Circle on the morning of December 28, 1938, he was looking to reinvent himself. And he knew New Orleans, an emerging tourist center and haven for writers, was the ideal place to do so. On the eve of his arrival, he had even adopted a new name—"Tennessee" Williams. Like the playwright, New Orleans boosters of the interwar years were busily reinventing themselves and their city. Business leaders were transforming the commercial port into a tourism-based economy. Defining identity was thus vital to Williams and New Orleanians. From his arrival in 1938, Williams developed a symbiotic relationship with the city. Williams, as one scholar has written, "championed the lowly, disenfranchised flotsam of American society," often via characters set in the Crescent City. His extraordinarily successful writings also promoted New Orleans, and tourism boosters returned the favor by imprinting his work on the cityscape and perpetuating it in the popular imagination. The collaboration brought the art of marketing into high American theater. Whether onstage or on screen, an ephemeral New Orleans appeared wherever directors parted the curtain on a Williams play—a pioneering moment in the modern gimmick of product placement.[1]

During the 1920s and 1930s, local leaders developed the tourism industry that remains the bedrock of the New Orleans economy. The city anticipated the regional shift from an agricultural to a more service-oriented economy. Whereas fellow Mississippian William Faulkner briefly deviated from his Yoknapatawpha tales to examine New Orleans tourism in his novel *Pylon* (1935), Tennessee Williams found a career's worth of material in the Crescent City. Tourism meant packaging identity, gentrifying neighborhoods, and crafting façades. For a young playwright grappling with his homosexuality, the city's hedonistic tourism industry supplied a narrative of rewritten pasts and closeted truths, all designed to collect tourists' dollars. Williams returned to the city frequently throughout his life, but his first months there had a particularly profound effect on him. "Feelings are bound up in place, and in art, from time to time, place undoubtedly works upon genius," explained Eudora Welty, another Mississippian, whom Williams greatly admired from early in his career. Her claim certainly was true for Williams and his relationship to New Orleans.[2]

Williams felt an immediate affinity for the Crescent City. He spent his first day in a cheap hotel near Lee Circle, writing in his notebook, "Here surely is the place that I was *made* for if any place on this funny old world." The next day he ventured to another hotel located at 431 Royal Street in the famed French Quarter. Soon, he took an apartment nearby at 722 Toulouse Street, where he resided until he left the city in February 1939.[3]

He soon learned lifelong lessons from the literary artists residing in New Orleans. Roark Bradford was well acquainted with publishing, theater, and film. His tales of black religious life, thick in dialect and racial stereotypes, drew a wide readership. Bradford's most celebrated novel *Ol' Man Adam an' His Chillun* (1928) was adapted into the popular play, then film, *The Green Pastures* during the 1930s. Williams's landlady, Ella Anderson, inadvertently brought the two writers together. Anderson had opened a restaurant called the Eat Shop, for which the Mississippian coined the slogan "Meals in the Quarter for a Quarter." The restaurant lasted a week. Shortly afterward, Anderson, angry over a rowdy party in the ground-floor apartment, poured boiling water through cracks in her kitchen floor onto the celebrants below. A judge later fined her $15 for her actions. In a letter to his mother, Williams recounted how he had testified in defense of Anderson, who denied the attack: "[I] could not perjure myself—the best I could do was say I thought it highly improbable that any lady would do such a thing!" At court he met Bradford's wife, Rose, whose dress had been ruined by the dousing. Williams sought to damper any ill will from the Bradfords: "I went to see her afterwards to assure her my part in the affair was altogether unwilling—she was very nice and cordial and assured me there were no hard feelings at least toward me."

At the Bradfords' residence at 719 Toulouse, Williams also met Sam Bird, a New York producer. He wrote home, "As all my plays are in New York I had nothing to show him." But they clearly discussed the craft of writing and producing plays. The events inspired Williams: "I'm using my colorful experiences here as the background for a new play which is well under way." He would tinker with this work for the rest of his life, finally publishing *Vieux Carré* (1979), a semiautobiographical drama about his experiences at 722 Toulouse, before his death in 1983.[4]

Williams also met Lyle Saxon, a master of cultivating a national readership by tapping local history. Saxon was one of the most popular Louisiana writers of the interwar period, regularly appearing on national best-seller lists with his nonfictional accounts of New Orleans and Louisiana. These included *Father Mississippi* (1927), *Fabulous New Orleans* (1928), *Old Louisiana* (1929), and *Lafitte the Pirate* (1930)—the latter eventually adapted into Cecil B. DeMille's film *The Buccaneer* (1938). Saxon's works exploited tourists' interest in New Orleans while proliferating many of the images and stories business leaders used to develop the tourism industry. By 1937, Saxon had published his mildly successful novel *Children of Strangers,* about Creoles of color in the Cane River region of Louisiana. Saxon's ability to produce work quickly and with proven mass appeal led to his appointment as director of the Federal Writers' Project's American Guide Series in Louisiana. Williams applied to work for Saxon. Saxon seemed "very much concerned and sympathetic about my precarious situation," according to Williams. The young Mississippian continued, "He gave me a list of trade journals yesterday, that I might get temporary writing jobs from. I'm making a round of their offices." As with Bradford, Williams clearly admired Saxon's success as a writer—explicitly mentioning *Fabulous New Orleans* in a letter home.

Besides learning from literary role models, Williams's encounter with the New Orleans tourism industry taught him about cultivating popular appeal. About a radio station interested in performing one of his ghost stories, Williams commented that the "radio-stations here are in pretty bad shape, in fact everything is except the business which caters directly to the tourists." Williams was learning to use the New Orleans area to attract a mass audience. He was not only making connections but gathering ideas from proven masters of the writing trade: "I already know twice as many people here as I ever knew in St. Louis—some of them highly influential such as the Bradfords and Saxons."[5]

Biographers and literary scholars have neglected the centrality of the New Orleans tourism industry to Williams's plots and themes. Williams recognized the city as a familiar setting for his viewers and readers and incorporated different parts of it, referencing numerous popular sites. For instance, the Musée Mécanique at 528 Royal Street, with its advertised "assemblage of mechanical curiosities that delighted royalties of old," appears in *The Eccentricities of a Nightingale* (1964). In the play, Williams provides a fictionalized backstory and relocates the museum, but he retains the name and recounts the "mechanical marvels" held inside. These marvels include a "mechanical man that plays the flute," a "mechanical drummer," a "mechanical soldier" that waves a flag, and a "mechanical bird-girl . . . the biggest mechanical triumph since the Eiffel Tower."[6] The actual exhibit consisted of such automatons as the "Bird Man," "Smoking Monkey," and "famous Swiss village, century-old mechanical marvel built as a hobby for a Czech nobleman."[7]

Renowned restaurants also appear prominently in Williams's plays. *A Streetcar Named Desire* (1947) includes Galatoire's; *The Mutilated* (1965) comments upon Galatoire's, Commander's Palace, and Arnaud's.[8] As if reassuring viewers and tourists, Williams in *Vieux Carré* offers a parenthetical aside after one character lambasts a fictional French Quarter restaurant for sometimes including roaches on its menu: "There are a lot of great eating places in New Orleans, like Galatoire's, Antoine's, Arnaud's in the Vieux Carré and . . . Commander's Palace and Plantation House in the Garden District . . . lovely old mansions, you know, converted to restaurants with a gracious style . . . haunted by dead residents, of course, but with charm."[9] That most of these restaurants remain staples of the New Orleans culinary scene reinforces the bonds between Williams's plays and the city's tourism industry. When Mel Gussow chronicled the locations important to Williams's literature for the *New York Times* in 2001, he noted that the "plays and sites in the city are so intertwined that it is difficult to determine which came first." But he made a point of calling attention to Galatoire's, "one of Williams's personal favorites," which remained "as it was in his lifetime."[10]

Williams's use of actual locations tapped the familiarity of Americans—and even foreign globetrotters—with New Orleans. *Suddenly Last Summer* (1958) incorporates the famed Dueling Oaks in City Park.[11] Plays like *Sweet Bird of Youth* (1959) and *Small Craft Warnings* (1972) feature the Old Spanish Trail, a highway developed during the 1920s to foster tourist traffic between Florida and California.[12] Bourbon Street emerges in *Auto-Da-Fé* (1941) as a "lurid procession of bars and hot-spots."[13] Jackson Square in the heart of the French Quarter makes appearances in plays like *The Mutilated:* "Andrew Jackson is all wet, shiny green like he's rode up out of the sea."[14] Williams regularly referred to the French Quarter and its "richness of decay."[15] The weather-beaten, aged buildings of New Orleans, especially its French Quarter, supplied a realistic element of deterioration that complemented the moral wear suffered by Williams's characters.

Mardi Gras, the city's signature tourist event, appears in several plays. Blanche Dubois wears a "worn-out Mardi Gras outfit" during the scene in *A Streetcar Named Desire* in which Stanley rapes her.[16] A woman in *Suddenly Last Summer* declares, "At a Mardi Gras ball some—some boy that took me to it got too drunk to stand up!"[17] Chance, the protagonist in *Sweet Bird of Youth,* comments on how wealthy locals along the Mississippi Gulf Coast encouraged their boys to "belong to the Junior Chamber of Commerce and some of them, clubs in New Orleans such as Rex and Comus and ride on the Mardi Gras floats."[18]

Williams recognized New Orleans as a universal place—a tourism destination with a global reach from which plots could speak to the common condition of humanity while appealing to public curiosity about the Crescent City. Though set in an unnamed Latin American town, for instance, Williams's *Camino Real* (1953) recalled a "tropical seaport that bears a confusing, but somehow harmonious, resemblance to such widely scattered ports as Tangiers, Havana, Vera Cruz, Casablanca, Shanghai, New Orleans."[19] Even when focusing on hamlets on the Mississippi Gulf Coast or along the Old Spanish Trail, Williams noted the international character of the city. He frequently biked or hitchhiked to these surrounding areas during subsequent visits to New Orleans and appreciated the port's role in facilitating immigration.[20] Italians, who migrated to the Gulf South and New Orleans during the early twentieth century, receive attention in several dramas. *The Rose Tattoo* (1951) focuses on a "village populated mostly by Sicilians somewhere along the Gulf Coast between New Orleans and Mobile." Williams emphasizes their ties to New Orleans, demonstrating how the hedonistic tourist mecca challenged traditional Sicilian culture, much as it challenged the conservatism of southern society. At one point, several women speak of a city "full of excitement" because a convention of American Legionnaires dropped "paper sacks full of water" out of the French Quarter's Monteleone Hotel and even "tore the clothes off" a woman on Canal Street. Far from being repulsed, the women are enticed to see these antics for themselves. Famously, *A Streetcar Named Desire* includes a range of immigrant groups, from a Mexican street-crier to a Chinese restaurateur to the Polish Stanley Kowalski.[21]

Williams's use of New Orleans stretched into the more abstract as well. The theme of identity often underlying the playwright's compositions mirrors the conflict between the raw realities of life within the city and the potentialities that prominent citizens struggled to actualize. Molding New Orleans into a Valhalla for tourism required extensive revitalization efforts and a fairly thick coating of proverbial sugar. Williams, however, mined the city for the flaws hidden by the façades. He reveled in the contrasts manifested within the French Quarter, a place that served increasingly as a polished tourist attraction even as its inhabitants struggled to survive. To draw a line from *The Lady of Larkspur Lotion* (1942), Williams embraced the neighborhood occupied by "Quarter rats, half-breeds, drunkards, degenerates, who try to get by on promises, lies, delusions!"[22] Williams described the French Quarter in *Auto-Da-Fé* as a "fetid old swamp . . . Every imaginable kind of degeneracy springs up here, not at arm's length, even, but right in our presence!"[23]

Williams's work pivots upon his manipulation of New Orleans, especially its French Quarter, in which boosters packaged the district to mean more than its face value suggested. Just as Stanley Kowalski uncovers the secrets kept by Blanche DuBois, Williams erases the misleading charm of the district, a charm based on illusion, to reach the naked truth as he saw it. *Vieux Carré,* for instance, focuses on the inner turmoil of the inhabitants of 722 Toulouse in 1938 and 1939. Outside the dramatized boardinghouse, however, proper-mannered ladies examine the courtyard as part of an Azalea Festival—a thinly veiled reference to the Spring Fiesta, an open-house festival created in 1937—only to be shocked when a practically unclothed resident appears at an upstairs window. The refinement suggested by the real-life festival disguised the event's profit-driven motives. In preparation for the weeklong Spring Fiesta, for example, city workers planted flowers and cleaned streets, while storeowners, in the words of local writer Robert Tallant, "lick[ed] their chops."[24] Such disharmony between the pleasant façades and the harsh realities serves as a general theme in much of Williams's work.

Williams often compares the effect of tourism to the prostitution of talented individuals. The single-armed ex-boxing champion of his short story "One Arm" (1948) and the single-breasted harlot of the play *The Mutilated* reflect this focus on exploited bodies. Whether in short stories like "The Yellow Bird" (1948) or dramas like *A Streetcar Named Desire,* prostitution frequently appears as a key theme in Williams's works about New Orleans. As physically deformed or grotesque as these and other characters appear, they fit well into the city, which boasted during the late 1930s of the World's Fair Museum at 620 Canal Street and the similar World's Wonder Museum at 336 South Rampart Street. The Canal Street establishment advertised its headless girl "Sontain" and tiny man "Bozo."[25] The nearby museum on Rampart heralded its living mermaid "Sea Tiny," as well as "the strangest married couple in the world, Paul Harold, Military Giant, standing 8 feet, 1 inch, while his better half is Princess Buttons, only 3 feet, 6 inches."[26] The ample supply of material from which to write led Williams to declare New Orleans his "favorite city of America . . . of all the world, actually."[27]

Moreover, politeness, which was necessary to attract tourists to the city, stifled the raw quality of French Quarter life needed for artistry. Though "a first-rate talent" in painting, Irene from "In Memory of an Aristocrat" must literally sell herself to survive. In a loose reference to the Spring Fiesta, Irene submits her drawing to a local art pageant. Williams's snide description of the event suggests his personal sentiments: "It [the Annual Spring Display] was sponsored, of course, by a select private group of the more successful painters, the ones who if they lived in the Quarter lived there only because it had atmosphere and whose studios were sparsely furnished with beautiful things, great oval gilt-framed mirrors and inch-thick Oriental carpets." This "society crowd" rejects Irene's drawings in "a gracious bow to respectable art."[28] On the other hand, artist Nightingale, in the drama *Vieux Carré,* expresses frustration over his failure to achieve recognition. Instead, he produces cheap sketches of tourists for a living. Nightingale sarcastically sneers that he has "*no shame about it,* no guilt at all, since what I do there is a travesty of my talent, I mean a prostitution of it, I mean, painting these tourists."[29]

Williams's personal identity crisis over his homosexuality aided him in grasping the actual and artificial in and about New Orleans, a city that allowed him to explore his sexuality. As one scholar comments about Williams's first visit to New Orleans, "If Tom did not actually join the bisexual group, he observed them closely."[30] Biographer Lyle Leverich agrees, "There can be no question, though, that the impact of New Orleans upon Tom's puritan nature was profound and lasting, nor can there be any doubt that these initial events affected the character and content of his writings."[31] Of his own struggle, Williams once answered an interviewer: "In New Orleans, I found the kind of freedom I had always needed. And the shock of it against the puritanism of my nature has given me a subject, a theme, which I've probably never ceased exploiting."[32] Williams embraced the freedom allowed by the French Quarter, a tourist attraction that catered to carnality. Like the preacher's daughter Alma Tutwiler in "The Yellow Bird," the innocent Tom Williams was "gone for good" after his first encounter with the French Quarter. Whereas Alma informs her parents of her new residence with a "card from New Orleans," Williams announced his fascination with the Big Easy through his writing.[33]

Though the practically penniless Mississippian departed westward along the Old Spanish Trail to California early on February 20, 1939, the day before Mardi Gras, the playwright's remaining years consisted of regular physical and literary returns.[34]

Though critical of the tourism industry's exploitation of art and bodies, Williams's writings showed an enthusiasm for New Orleans nightlife—including its gay nightlife—that rivaled that of the most hedonistic tourist. The creator of *The Bachelor in New Orleans,* a 1940s guidebook, admitted, in a biased tone, the presence of a homosexual community: "Fluffy, painted, willowy men are to be seen here and there (though there are sections where his dilemmatic type is more plentiful) in the less reputable clubs."[35] Other than the Wonder Bar, a male strip club on the shores of Lake Pontchartrain, the French Quarter possessed the most prominent homosexual-oriented establishments in the New Orleans area, particularly Le Rendezvous on St. Peter Street and the St. James Bar on Royal Street, where "there's always an atmosphere of friendliness and refinement."[36] On a return to the city in 1941, Williams thrilled at gaining a room on Royal "right opposite *the* gay bar—The St. James, so I can hover like a bright angel over the troubled waters of homosociety."[37] His plays included a few of these haunts. A character in *Orpheus Descending* (1957) boasts of having experienced "The Club Rendezvous, the Starlite Lounge, the Music Bar, and all the night places."[38] Williams admitted the unreserved openness of the homosexual community in his *Memoirs:* "I did know some very obvious types in New Orleans . . . when I first 'came out.'"[39] He wrote of another visit to New Orleans in 1954: "Tonight the gay bars, Trade! The best I can get! And I promise myself I will get some."[40]

As Williams's plays—and film adaptations—gained international acclaim in the late 1940s, city boosters embraced the playwright and his New Orleans–related material. Since the late nineteenth century, works of fiction had been drawing tourists in growing numbers. These visitors often clutched their volumes, using them as guidebooks, and Williams's plays, especially *A Streetcar Named Desire,* were a literary bonanza for tourism promoters. Eleanor Nicholson, columnist for the *Times-Picayune,* recognized the significance of the play in December 1947: "It is The Play on Broadway. And it is The Talk in New Orleans because its author . . . set his hit in our Vieux Carre and, almost most important of all, it has quite suddenly made our Public Service's streetcar system famous." She prophesized that "we're betting that as soon as the sightseeing people catch on, our passionate trolley will be added to the list of New Orleans' famous sites."[41] The continued output of Williams's mind cemented a more prominent place in the nation's consciousness for New Orleans. And though scholars have explored his use of streetcars, vendors, and neighborhoods, and others have analyzed the playwright's visits to the city, few have appreciated how a lifetime of literary masterpieces created a symbiotic relationship with a tourism industry that gave international audiences experiences of the place utilized by Williams for dramatic effect.

Although Williams examined the brutal realities of life at the margins, New Orleanians generally celebrated his work. *A Streetcar Named Desire* proved most influential since it became the playwright's greatest success. Rather than harp on the harsh elements within the text, such as rape, New Orleans boosters emphasized the positive image presented by Williams, who described the setting with elegance: "The sky that shows around the dim white building is a peculiar tender blue, almost turquoise, which invests the scene with a kind of lyricism and gracefully attenuates the atmosphere of decay." The "perpetual 'blues piano' around the corner" also hinted at the city's romantic, leisurely qualities.[42] A 1948 review of *Streetcar* in the *Times-Picayune* declared, "It's a rough play about tough and rough people. Psychopathic cases and criminally maladjusted souls. They aren't the kind of people you want in your living room or your dreams, but they come alive for you and they are human." To assure readers, the newspaper reiterated, "it isn't a sordid story. It's human."[43] When the Broadway performers came to New Orleans to stage the play in November 1949, the city celebrated their arrival. The troupe stepped off the train at Union Station, where a "chartered bus called 'Desire' was waiting to take them to a streetcar named 'Desire' at the New Orleans Public Service Inc. carbarn on Canal near Broad." The streetcar then carried the cast to the prestigious Roosevelt Hotel.[44]

New Orleanians could not ignore how popular media repeatedly linked Williams—and especially *Streetcar*—with New Orleans. Reporting for *Jet* during the 1950s, Vincent Tubb wrote, "Actually, much of what is best known about historical New Orleans is no longer true. The Streetcar Named Desire is now a bus."[45] A journalist for *Life* in 1969 described the architecture of one New Orleans home as "looking like the stage set for *A Streetcar Named Desire*."[46] Allan Horing, writing in *New York Magazine* in 1990, noted the "dozens of romantic pensiones in the Vieux Carré itself, with courtyards and wrought-iron terraces right out of *A Streetcar Named Desire*."[47] In these instances, reality and fiction blurred in the popular imagination.

New Orleanians cashed in on Williams's *Streetcar.* In 1954, for instance, Jack Hyer advertised for sale his "black and white pen and ink sketch of the 'streetcar named Desire'" from its last run in 1949, when the city replaced the line with buses.[48] Hyer's claim to have the only sketch of the streetcar sparked a wide response. A bar owner claimed to have a drawing of the streetcar on his tavern's wall. Claire Wise offered an "ashtray with a 'streetcar named Desire' painted on it" and revealed that "these trays are in many local gift shops."[49] Such trinkets have remained a common feature of the tourist trade. During the mid-1970s, the D. H. Holmes department store stocked several items of gold jewelry marketed to tourists, including a "Streetcar Named Desire Charm," advertised as an "enchanting New Orleans memento." Louisiana-born jewelry designer Jose Balli currently sells high-end streetcar pendants, rings, and earrings labeled "Desire" in his French Quarter shop and two outlying stores. Local chef Scott Boswell opened Stella!, a fine-dining landmark during the 1990s and 2000s, and the diner Stanley, which continues to thrive on the crowded restaurant scene.[50]

Not surprisingly, the international popularity of *A Streetcar Named Desire* on stage and screen led boosters to give tourists a physical manifestation of the "Desire" streetcar. The removal of most streetcars from the city situated the play as a period piece. The physical transformation of New Orleans, already evident by the time the playwright completed *A Streetcar Named Desire,* meant that boosters too lived in the shadow of the past when they chose to embrace Williams and his most famous creation. The "Desire" streetcar became a romanticized symbol of a bygone New Orleans that simultaneously showed how far the city had progressed since the 1930s and 1940s. Such temporal distancing mitigated the most negative themes addressed by the Mississippian's works. New Orleans Public Service Incorporated (NOPSI) spent $30,000 during the early 1960s to refurbish one of twenty-five Brill semiconvertible streetcars purchased in 1906. Ironically, these cars—except for 435—were retired and scrapped in 1935 as NOPSI converted to later-model streetcars as well as buses. Car 435 was retained as a training vehicle. As more buses replaced streetcar lines, car 435 became expendable—and ideal as the "Desire" streetcar, even if Williams had never seen one of its like. John Carroll, director of the Louisiana Tourist Commission, proposed using funds to send the streetcar on a nationwide tour. Instead, in February 1967, NOPSI opted to place it on display in the French Quarter with signs marking it as the "Desire" streetcar.[51]

With its motor replaced by a wooden replica to lighten the load, NOPSI hauled car 435 to its place of honor on a flatbed truck, as the rail lines had long been replaced, except for the historic St. Charles line. The streetcar now named "Desire" came to rest on the 1100 block of Decatur Street near the famed French Market. Not until October 1970 did Tennessee Williams finally set his eyes on this streetcar—and pose at the controls for photographs.[52]

The streetcar sat prominently between the popular tourist sites of Jackson Square and the French Market in the French Quarter but failed to satisfy the city or its guests. When the French Market underwent renovation in the early 1970s, the streetcar was relocated from its sheltered pavilion to Barracks Street on the opposite end of the French Market. Exposed to the elements, tourists, and vandals, the "Desire" streetcar began showing considerable wear.[53] Though deteriorating, the vehicle remained important to the tourism industry. In 1976, Perry Como recorded a musical special for NBC that featured him visiting the streetcar before hopping on a carriage and riding past the French Market while aptly singing "Who Will Buy."[54] In 1978, the Louisiana State Museum accepted the streetcar from the Louisiana Tourist and Development Commission with the intention of restoring the vehicle and displaying it outside the old US Mint, across the street from where it had been rusting away.[55] But journalist Jeanie Blake in the late 1970s spoke for many locals and tourists when she declared the streetcar an "awkward monument." The "charm and worth" of the streetcar or Williams's drama was poorly represented by the "immobile mobile frozen in the French Market." Instead, she suggested visiting its "kinetic kinsmen that clang and clumpsily [*sic*] cruise up and down St. Charles." Pat Neisser concurred in a report for tourists attending the 1984 World's Fair: "The streetcar named Desire may be on blocks in the French Market, but the St. Charles Streetcar is ready for all comers."[56] During the early 1990s, the streetcar was placed in storage to undergo renovations that have yet to occur.[57]

Although Williams died in 1983, the playwright was far too important to the city to allow him and his work to fade into memory. New Orleanians organized the inaugural Tennessee Williams / New Orleans Literary Festival in 1987. The festival merged the efforts of directors at Le Petit Theatre du Vieux Carré, who sought to develop a Williams-related festival around its production of *Cat on a Hot Tin Roof* (1955), and local literature aficionados, who prepared to launch a literary festival in the city. Squeezing an event onto New Orleans's crowded tourism calendar was no easy task. The two groups settled on hosting the festival in early April in honor of Williams's March 26 birthday. Stretching the shoestring budget, Le Petit Theatre's executive director Don Marshall joked, "All we need is a Xerox machine." The celebration began with the dedication of a plaque at 632 St. Peter Street, where Williams completed *A Streetcar Named Desire*. The subsequent weekend of events included performances of Williams's plays, other theatrical presentations, panel discussions, walking tours of literary sites within the French Quarter, film screenings, readings, and a book and art fair. The festival culminated with a midnight jazz Mass at Our Lady of Guadalupe Chapel on the edge of the French Quarter. The *Times-Picayune* editors recognized the potential: "The Tennessee Williams-New Orleans Literary Festival might be the core around which could be built—and profitably marketed—an attractive annual event that could reflect well on the city."[58]

The festival grew rapidly. By the third year, attendance at the three-day event approached four thousand. Positive press reports accumulated and so did the number of sponsors, participants, and tourists. Over six thousand attendees, more than 40 percent from outside the New Orleans area, now annually attend the festival. It has developed into a five-day celebration, but the content has remained much the same—with one popular addition. To attract greater media exposure, the festival since the mid-1990s has concluded on Jackson Square with the Stella and Stanley Shouting Contest, reenacting the famous scene from *A Streetcar Named Desire* within the heart of the city's tourism center.[59]

Other cities have envied New Orleans's Williams-related tourism market. The Pennsylvania Trolley Museum near Pittsburgh has displayed its own Streetcar Named Desire since 1964, when curators paid New Orleans a dollar for the retired streetcar 832 "featured in Life Magazine in 1947 when the eponymous play opened on Broadway."[60] The National Streetcar Museum in Lowell, Massachusetts, promotes a former New Orleans streetcar as "one of the famed cars that rolled through the French Quarter and inspired Tennessee Williams' play 'A Streetcar Named Desire.'"[61] The Market Street Railway in San Francisco currently operates "two such icons" from New Orleans, boasting that the Desire line "lives on."[62]

Even when boosters elsewhere have tried to tap into Williams's popularity, they have been forced to contend with the prominence of New Orleans in his life. St. Louis boosters have considered promoting sites associated with Williams during the time he resided there in his youth—despite his biting criticism of the city. In 1989, the *St. Louis Post-Dispatch* contrasted the lack of local Williams-related tourism with a detailed, lengthy list of New Orleans sites associated with the writer. The newspaper by the late 1990s coveted how New Orleans was "cashing in on Williams' legacy," especially the ability of the literary festival to draw "more than 6,000 Williams fanatics." The Missouri city offered little more than a star for Williams on the St. Louis Walk of Fame.[63] By the early twenty-first century, three festivals dedicated to him competed against the event in New Orleans. Columbus, Mississippi, where the writer was born, offered the Tennessee Williams Tribute and Tour of Victorian Homes. Clarksdale, Mississippi, where he spent some of his boyhood, staged the Mississippi Delta Tennessee Williams Festival. And Provincetown, Massachusetts, where he enjoyed the freedom of the gay community, organized the Provincetown Tennessee Williams Festival. Yet whenever such festivals stage his plays—a standard feature of these events—they reinforce Williams's fixation with New Orleans by temporarily bringing the city to life. Williams's product placement of the Big Easy within his work is inescapable.[64]

Tennessee Williams and the New Orleans tourism industry lived in the shadow of the playwright's visit to the city in the late 1930s. Though Williams regularly returned there, even maintaining an apartment in the French Quarter during the latter part of his life, his first stay left an indelible impression. A safe harbor during the Great Depression, Williams recognized New Orleans as "the cheapest and most comfortable place in America for fugitives from economic struggle." This struggle between economic demands and artistic expression—a conflict clearly manifested within the New Orleans tourism industry—emerged as a driving force in his writing.[65]

Though he died in New York, Williams frequently expressed his desire to die in the French Quarter.[66] Whereas businessmen took liberties with reality when romanticizing New Orleans, the playwright utilized the city's antebellum mansions and colonial dwellings to celebrate age-old human struggles for expression and freedom. The quirky hedonism of New Orleans was ideal for Williams. He wrote in 1953: "For God's sake let's have a little more freakish behavior—not less."[67] The focus on hedonism within the tourism industry gave Williams's work credibility. Whether dealing with sexual exploitation, substance abuse, or the gritty nature of New Orleans, Williams continuously addressed issues true to the place he had cherished since 1938. The Crescent City provided him a fountainhead of material and a comfortable freedom to explore himself and others. Williams spoke for many tourists when he described the significance of New Orleans in "The Angel in the Alcove" (1948): "This lunar atmosphere of the city draws me back whenever the waves of energy which removed me to more vital towns have spent themselves and a time of recession is called for. Each time I have felt some rather profound psychic wound, a loss or a failure, I have returned to this city. At such periods I would seem to belong there and no place else in the country."[68] For a city that has been devoted to tourism since the interwar years, Tennessee Williams remains the kindest of strangers.

## NOTES

1. John Bak, *Tennessee Williams: A Literary Life* (New York: Palgrave Macmillan, 2013), 2. For background on Williams's experiences in New Orleans, see John Lahr, *Tennessee Williams: Mad Pilgrimage of the Flesh* (New York: Norton, 2014), 69–80, 99–104, 279–80; Lyle Leverich, *Tom: The Unknown Tennessee Williams* (New York: Crown 1995), 275–76, 280; W. Kenneth Holditch, "The Last Frontier of Bohemia: Tennessee Williams in New Orleans, 1938–1983," *Southern Quarterly* 23, no. 2 (Winter 1985): 6. For more biographical background on Williams, see Mark Cave, "Something Wild in the Country: The Fugitive Life of Tennessee Williams," *Southern Quarterly* 48, no. 4 (Summer 2011): 11–31; Pnina Rafailovich, "Tennessee Williams's South," *Southern Studies* 23, no. 2 (Summer 1984): 191–97. For insight on New Orleans's literary presence during the interwar years, see John Shelton Reed, *Dixie Bohemia: A French Quarter Circle in the 1920s* (Baton Rouge: Louisiana State University Press, 2012).

2. Eudora Welty, *The Eye of the Story* (New York: Vintage, 1990), 123. Williams wrote in 1941 that Welty, Carson McCullers, William Faulkner, and Katherine Anne Porter "have practically got a deep southern corner on the best imaginative writing in America." Tennessee Williams to Audrey Wood, Nov. 24, 1941, in *The Selected Letters of Tennessee Williams, 1920–1945*, ed. Albert Devlin and Nancy Tischler (New York: New Directions, 2000), 358. For background on the New Orleans tourism industry during the twentieth century, see Anthony Stanonis, *Creating the Big Easy: New Orleans and the Emergence of Modern Tourism, 1918–1945* (Athens: University of Georgia Press, 2006); Mark Souther, *Tourism and the Transformation of the Crescent City* (Baton Rouge: Louisiana State University Press, 2006); Mark Zelinsky, "Tennessee Williams and New Orleans: Rewriting the Playwright, Rewriting the City" (PhD diss., Louisiana State University, 1999).

3. Tennessee Williams, *Notebooks*, ed. Margaret Bradham Thornton (New Haven: Yale University Press, 2006), 131.

4. Tennessee Williams to Edwina Dakin Williams, c. early Feb. 1939, in *The Selected Letters*, 146–47.

5. Tennessee Williams to Edwina Dakin Williams, Jan. 2 and c. early Feb. 1939, in *The Selected Letters*, 140–41, 146–47. For more on the importance of Lyle Saxon, see James Thomas, *Lyle Saxon: A Critical Biography* (Birmingham, AL: Summa, 1991); Anthony Stanonis, "'Always

in Costume and Mask': Lyle Saxon and New Orleans Tourism," *Louisiana History* 42, no. 1 (Jan. 2001): 31–57.

6. Advertisement, *Item,* Jan. 7, 1939; Tennessee Williams, *Eccentricities of a Nightingale,* in *Tennessee Williams: Plays, 1957–1980* (New York: Library of America, 2000), 451.

7. Advertisement, *Item,* Jan. 12, 1939; advertisement, *Item,* Jan. 16, 1939.

8. Tennessee Williams, *A Streetcar Named Desire,* in *Tennessee Williams: Plays, 1937–1955* (New York: Library of America, 2000), 483; Tennessee Williams, *The Mutilated,* in *Plays, 1957–1980,* 592, 619.

9. Tennessee Williams, *Vieux Carré,* in *Plays, 1957–1980* 837. For a thorough analysis of food in Williams's works, see W. Kenneth Holditch, "Southern Comfort: Food and Drink in the Plays of Tennessee Williams," *Southern Quarterly* 44, no. 2 (Winter 2007): 53–73.

10. Mel Gussow, "Arts in America," *New York Times,* May 1, 2001.

11. Tennessee Williams, *Suddenly Last Summer,* in *Plays, 1957–1980,* 132.

12. Tennessee Williams, *Sweet Bird of Youth,* in *Plays, 1957–1980,* 168, 173; Tennessee Williams, *Small Craft Warnings,* in *Plays, 1957–1980,* 763.

13. Tennessee Williams, *Auto-Da-Fé,* in *Plays, 1937–1955,* 360.

14. Williams, *The Mutilated,* 600.

15. Williams, *Auto-Da-Fé,* 360.

16. Williams, *A Streetcar Named Desire,* 552.

17. Williams, *Suddenly Last Summer,* 131.

18. Williams, *Sweet Bird of Youth,* 181.

19. Tennessee Williams, *Camino Real,* in *Plays, 1937–1955,* 749.

20. Williams, *Notebooks,* 247.

21. Tennessee Williams, *Rose Tattoo,* in *Plays, 1937–1955,* 654, 477, 493, 547, 654, 677. For an insightful discussion of race and ethnicity in Williams's work, see Joanna Kurowska, "Colonialism in the French Quarter: Tennessee Williams and Joseph Conrad," *Southern Quarterly* 50, no. 2 (Winter 2013): 109–22; Robert Rea, "Tennessee Williams's The Rose Tattoo: Sicilian Migration and the Mississippi Gulf Coast," *Southern Literary Journal* 46, no. 2 (Spring 2014): 140–54.

22. Tennessee Williams, *The Lady of Larkspur Lotion,* in *Plays, 1937–1955,* 332.

23. Williams, *Auto-Da-Fé,* 362.

24. Robert Tallant, *The Romantic New Orleanians* (New York: E. P. Dutton, 1950), 330–32.

25. Advertisement, *Item,* Jan. 11, 1939.

26. Advertisement, *Louisiana Weekly,* Feb. 4, 1939.

27. Tennessee Williams interviewed by Louise Davis (1957), "That Baby Doll Man: Part I," in *Conversations with Tennessee Williams,* ed. Albert Devlin (Jackson: University Press of Mississippi, 1986), 48.

28. Tennessee Williams, "In Memory of an Aristocrat," *Collected Stories* (New York: New Directions, 1985), 84, 87, 88.

29. Williams, *Vieux Carré,* 837, emphasis in original. For more on the way Williams uses New Orleans to explore sexuality and human suffering, see Milly Barranger, "New Orleans as Theatrical Image in Plays by Tennessee Williams," *Southern Quarterly* 23, no. 2 (Winter 1985): 38–54.

30. Allean Hale, "Two on a Streetcar," *Tennessee Williams Literary Journal* 1, no. 1 (Spring 1989): 33–35.

31. Leverich, *Tom,* 288.

32. Tennessee Williams interviewed by Don Lee Keith (1970), "New Tennessee Williams Rises from 'Stoned Age,'" in Devlin, *Conversations with Tennessee Williams,* 151.

33. Tennessee Williams, "The Yellow Bird," *Stories of the Modern South* (New York: Penguin Books, 1986), 517.

34. Tennessee Williams to Edwina Dakin Williams, Feb. 21, 1939, in *The Selected Letters,* 148.

35. Robert Kinney, *The Bachelor in New Orleans* (New Orleans: Bob Riley Studios, 1942), 98.

36. Advertisement, *Times-Picayune,* Feb. 17, 1939; Hale, "Two on a Streetcar," 35.

37. Tennessee Williams to Paul Bigelow, Sept. 25, 1941, in *The Selected Letters,* 343.

38. Tennessee Williams, *Orpheus Descending,* in *Tennessee Williams: Plays, 1957–1980,* 52.

39. Tennessee Williams, *Memoirs* (Garden City: Doubleday, 1975), 50.

40. Williams, *Notebooks,* 659.

41. Eleanor Nicholson, "On the Square," *Times-Picayune,* Dec. 28, 1948. For the role of literature in tourism, see Lafcadio Hearn, *Inventing New Orleans: Writings of Lafcadio Hearn,* ed. S. Frederick Starr (Jackson: University Press of Mississippi, 2001) x–xxvi.

42. Williams, *A Streetcar Named Desire,* 469, 483.

43. Elise Beauchamp, "Literature and Less," *Times-Picayune,* Feb. 22, 1948.

44. Harry Heintzen, "Ranks of Educators Raided by 'Streetcar Named Desire,'" *Times-Picayune,* Nov. 28, 1949.

45. Vincent Tubbs, *Jet,* Apr. 7, 1955, 14.

46. "Revival of the Southern Showpiece," *Life,* Aug. 1, 1969, 40.

47. Allan Horing, "New Orleans," *New York Magazine,* Mar. 5, 1990, 8A.

48. "Up and Down the Street," *Times-Picayune,* Mar. 25, 1954.

49. "Up and Down the Street," *Times-Picayune,* Apr. 9, 1954.

50. "Holmes," *Times-Picayune,* Dec. 31, 1976; Jose Balli Jewelry, www.joseballi.com (accessed Aug. 8, 2015); Stanley, *www.stanleyrestaurant.com* (accessed Aug. 30, 2015).

51. C. M. Hargroder, "Will Spend Funds as He Sees Fit, Says Carroll," *Times-Picayune,* Dec. 1, 1965; Earl Hampton and H. George Friedman, "New Orleans Car 453: A Streetcar (Mis) Named Desire," http://web.engr.illinois.edu/~friedman/car453/Car453.htm (accessed Aug. 8, 2015).

52. "Streetcar Named Desire Travels through City," *Times-Picayune,* Feb. 6, 1967; "New Tennessee Williams Rises from 'Stoned Age,' "*Times-Picayune,* Oct. 18, 1970.

53. "A New Home," *Times-Picayune,* Jan. 16, 1974; "Desire Streetcar: No Room," *Times-Picayune,* Oct. 26, 1975.

54. Jill Jackson, "Perry Como Special in N.O.," *Times-Picayune,* Feb. 9, 1976.

55. "Desire Streetcar to Get New Home," *Times-Picayune,* May 26, 1976.

56. Jeanie Blake, "Streetcars Are Coming Back," *Times-Picayune,* Feb. 11, 1979; Pat Neisser, "New Orleans," *Orange Coast Magazine,* June 1984, 216.

57. Hampton and Friedman, "New Orleans Car 453."

58. Richard Dodds, "Williams Fest Declared a Success," *Times-Picayune,* Apr. 9, 1987; "Tennessee Williams Festival," *Times-Picayune,* Apr. 3, 1987. Also see Mabel Simmons, "Raising a Toast to Tennessee," *Times-Picayune,* Mar. 29, 1987; Richard Dodds, "Tennessee Williams Honored at April Festival," *Times-Picayune,* Feb. 5, 1987.

59. Thomas Harrison, "A Tour of Tennessee," *St. Petersburg Times,* Mar. 21, 1989; Janet McConnaughey, "The Nation's Oldest Tennessee Williams Fest Is Full Blast," *Associated Press State and Local Wire,* Mar. 29, 2008; Emilie Bahr, "New Orleans' Tennessee Williams Festival Partners with Southeastern Louisiana University to Tap North Shore Audiences," *City Business North Shore Report,* Mar. 1, 2009; Tennessee Williams / New Orleans Literary Festival program, 2015.

60. Pennsylvania Trolley Museum, http://pa-trolley.org/ptm-quick-history/the-1960s/ (accessed Aug. 30, 2015).

61. National Streetcar Museum, www.trolleymuseum.org/lowell/streetcars.php (accessed Aug. 30, 2015).

62. Market Street Railway, www.streetcar.org/streetcars/952–952-new-orleans-desire/ (accessed Aug. 30, 2015).

63. Holly Hildebrand, "Tennessee Williams' New Orleans," *St. Louis Post-Dispatch,* May 14, 1989; Diane Toroian, "Troubled Tennessee," *St. Louis Post-Dispatch,* Mar. 13, 1997.

64. Beth Greenfield, "Blanche, Big Daddy and Menagerie," *New York Times,* Sept. 1, 2006.

65. Williams, "In Memory of an Aristocrat," 80.

66. Leverich, *Tom,* 1.

67. Tennessee Williams, "Something Wild . . . ," in *Tennessee Williams: Plays, 1937–1955,* 850.

68. Tennessee Williams, "The Angel in the Alcove," *Collected Stories,* 92.

# E. P. O'Donnell

## *A Life in a Handful of Leaves*

BRYAN A. GIEMZA

This essay, reworked as a straight-ahead, chronological narrative, became the introduction for LSU Press's 2015 reissue of E. P. O'Donnell's *The Great Big Doorstep*. Yet there are arguably virtues endemic to this sketch that are lost to the just-the-facts rendering. Good writers always point to the importance of subject emphasis in developing perspective, and here the emphasis is as much on the atmosphere of time and place as on the writer.

This version describes a little more fully the 1936 *New York Times* National Book Fair, in which we can recognize the familiar trappings of the book festival as we now know it, replete with signing booths and author talks. There, the rising visibility of the South's regional contingent presaged the publication (September 1942) of "The Deep South Issue" of the *Saturday Review,* an issue now recognized by scholars such as Sarah Gardner as a watershed moment in the marketing of a distinctive modern southern literary culture, with spokespeople like Cleanth Brooks as its interpreters.

Indeed, it might be said that issue helped to consolidate a southern aesthetic. The steamboat so memorably depicted on the cover, a stern-wheeler belching black smoke, was in some sense the right symbol to denature—a symbol, simultaneously, of cultural mixing, mass transportation, enslaved labor, and high times. The steamboat was the real engine of plantation commerce, of course, so it requires a little distance to see how it could be rendered into something quaint. In the classrooms of my childhood, the fall line was described as an accident of geography. Only much later would I learn that geography is destiny, and that the presence of so many southern cities along fall lines was because of their part in the reach of plantation economies, the fall line being as far as the steamboat could easily go. The fall line, our Fall line . . .

The steamboat of imagination, it might be said, chuffed off the cover of the Deep South Issue as a loaded signifier, to be reprised in every sort of format: fifteen years later with Paul Newman loafing on the bow in the Faulkner mash-up of *The Long, Hot Summer* and some seventy years later in the troubled wake behind the steamboat of *Twelve Years a Slave.* From the pages of the *Saturday Review* it was a short hop to what would be deemed, generically, Americana of a kind—steamboats, eagles, saloons, fife drums, all that sort of thing—folded into the bicentennial celebration and 1970s theme parks, and remembered in the charmingly roughhewn illustrations of children's books such as Bill Martin Jr.'s *Tatty Mae and Catty Mae* (1969). In the *California Delta,* an aged but serviceable fleet of pleasure steamboats, including the *Delta King,* could be called upon to do service in westerns and films with southern settings. The way was prepared for Mike Fink without the meanness, William Clark Falkner's *The White Rose of Memphis* without bloodshed, Mark Twain without race.

And the paintings scattered across the pages of the Deep South Issue captured the atmosphere of Bohemian provincialism—in the French register of the word—so evocatively described in John Shelton Reed's *Dixie Bohemia.* The issue channeled the spirit of the times so attractively that it imbued it with the legitimacy of reality.

In its first annunciation, then, a southern literary culture ripe for commodification seemed likely to be marketed by local color, a compromise that its participants seemed willing to live with for the time being. In the 1930s they inhabited a South that was making an economic transition but that could not sever its roots in colonialism. Into this setting came O'Donnell, the unlikely artist whom Brooks would hold up to Faulkner in the Deep South issue. The entanglement of class and race gave him passage across the color line and offered a measure of street-level credibility to literary critics. In his early years he knew working steamships, from loggers to retrofitted banana boats, and later he knew, too, the diesel luggers that announced the age of Gulf Coast petrochem.

Biographical survivals concerning O'Donnell have floated down the time stream like so many tumbled leaves; by discerning the means of their transmission, we find lessons in the making and unmaking of literary culture. In compiling the permissions for the reissue, I would come to know the generosity of O'Donnell's grandchildren, scattered to the two coasts, and to see how narratives emerge from the churn of American experience and economic scrabbling. To outside eyes, perhaps, O'Donnell's story is a cheerful narrative of a scrappy Irish American without so much as a high-school education, a self-taught stylist who wrote a well-selling novel against the odds and captured the attention of Broadway and Hollywood. But then there is a competing narrative, of a feckless man in the grips of addiction, whose family endured in spite of, not because of, him, and whose prosperity schemes were hastily assembled driftwood forming the raft of an unspoken desperation.

## I.

It's a water-stained photo born of the Delta. It's in the sort of place that Lafcadio Hearn, an Irish-born Louisiana writer of an earlier generation, liked to call *lacustrine,* situated on a margin, a world being neither entirely land nor liquid. It is a place of "lenient dusk," as O'Donnell wrote in his poem "Lines to Jules Petit," an edge where the land subsides. A place suitable to low thickets of shrubby inkberry and red bay, forming an ecotone that E. P. "Pat" O'Donnell called the *bay-gall.*

Today the place is a suburb called Kenner. Sixty-five years prior to the making of the photograph, before logging and rail, Kenner was little more than a notion.

In this portrait, perhaps the only one of the couple that survives, they stand, windswept, facing the photographer and squinting toward the sun. The idiosyncratic couple chose, capriciously, to be photographed while standing atop a massive log. The bark would feel like sodden cork underfoot, its heavy-as-lead body from an ancient gum tree of the sort favored by the fast-disappearing ivory-billed woodpecker.

Rail and river, the tides of broken family, economic hardship, and forced migration have conspired to carry E. P. O'Donnell to this southern port. His mother, Alice O'Brien, was a native Louisianan whose parents were born in Ireland. His father, born in Indiana and later orphaned, was a locomotive engineer in an industry that opened those swamps to human hands. The elder Edward's father was an Irish American contractor whose career busted on the Brooklyn Bridge shortly before he vanished—where? Into American anonymity, leaving his offspring first to the goodwill of relatives and then, finally, to strangers.

Now it's their turn to make something of an American life and each other. So they stand on doll feet, toes forward, E. P. O'Donnell and bride Gertrude, dressed in Sunday walking clothes but with the odd delicacy of two logrollers, near the interlaced skeins of whitecaps hissing off of Lake Pontchartrain. No levee is visible where the waves spill on the estuary's grassy shore, and there are none of the low-slung suburban ranch houses that would come with the land-filling development of the 1950s.

If you know those places, then you can smell the tang of the water, and the sulfur from the mud, and feel a bit of the spume on your face, too. You can imagine a string of level-necked cormorants flying by between water and the skies, and you can see a place where O'Donnell, in his own words, might "Stand on blue sands / watching a pelican / spurn the clouds."[1]

This is O'Donnell's world. In a time before environmentalists and ecologists, his writing shows that he was both. And if you read O'Donnell's fiction, you will be transported to these places by a level of detail that can come only from someone who loves them.

* * *

Something about Gertrude's pose implies deep affection for her husband. Today they would be counted a young couple, but at the time of the photo, E. P.'s walk through life was halfway finished. Born when pneumonia, flu, and tuberculosis were the leading causes of death, the young couple had survived the 1918 flu pandemic. Or were surviving it when the shutter clicked. O'Donnell would claim to have driven an ambulance for the Red Cross during this period, which is entirely possible, if very reminiscent of Ernest Hemingway, his literary hero.[2] The New Orleans of 1918 was as rough as it was decadent. Soon Prohibition would be the law of the land. Faulkner would claim to have been a rum runner, but in his work as a barman on board the *Cartago,* shipping to Panama in the 1920s, it's more likely that O'Donnell had some experience in that area.[3] In 1918, Jelly Roll Morton was singing his "Murder Ballad" in the brothels of Storyville.

It was a moment when you might hear someone on the river road singing "The Tale of the Bumble Bee," as Mrs. Crochet does, in Cajun accent, in *The Great Big Doorstep.* The song, about a faithless bee and his cl/lover, was popularized by Gertrude Quinlan, an American actress whose father was born in Ireland.[4] Music *is* time, and there is indeed lost music in *The Great Big Doorstep,* as, for example, in the snatch of song recited by Louisiana children playing the Victorian parlor game of forfeits.

Life expectancy in 1895, O'Donnell's birth-year, was forty-seven. E.P. would squeak out forty-eight. Gertrude would live to be ninety-seven.

So the moment in the picture is the meridian of Pat O'Donnell's life.

For the moment, they were forward-looking, and the future was bright. He had perhaps a middle-school education, yet O'Donnell had made his way through trades and into the solidity of employment as the advertising manager at the Ford Plant. The couple had found a footing in the middle class, and the Great Depression had not yet descended. Pat O'Donnell was one of those rare men equally at ease with the working poor as with the leisured class of New Orleans's moneyed arts boosters. For him, it was a short step to becoming a writer, a profession with white-collar respectability.

For Gertrude, who was about to begin her own family, this photo might have been captioned "Hope Springs." The photo was the only one that would be passed down to her grandchildren, and it might have been one of the few that she could bear keeping. In retrospect, it must have evoked all the emotions of a promising harbor that life washed out and away, one wave at a time. Even the perch on the log seems to suggest that the stability of the moment won't last long. Within a few years, E. P. O'Donnell would be rambling on the Gulf waters aboard American banana boats.

E. P. was almost entirely an absentee father to his two sons as he became more involved with far-flung schemes and an art scene that never could provide a sustained income. The Kenner photo was taken before he had met the woman who would become his second wife, the usurper whom Gertrude would for the rest of her days regard as illegitimate and remember only as "that other woman." The homewrecker.

For the moment, as a woman of her time, Gertrude stands by her man, and slightly behind him. And E. P. stands as a man of his time: forward, almost as if alone, jaunty, perhaps not altogether pleased to suffer the intrusion of photography on life. We're reminded of his contemporary Hemingway, who also walked log-strewn shores, as ecological frontiers closed suddenly all the way from the deep swamps of Louisiana to the lakes of Michigan. Like Hemingway and Thomas Wolfe, O'Donnell benefitted from the literary patronage of Sherwood Anderson, who in correspondence referred to him as "the immortal Pat."[5] Though he would be eulogized by the *Times-Picayune* as a "quiet and reticent man," other accounts paint O'Donnell as gregarious and brash. The image of the photo, with his crossed arms and chest-forward posture, is one of confidence.

On the other hand, it's also possible that O'Donnell, who had once given boxing lessons, crossed his arms to conceal the three fingers missing from his left hand. The loss of those fingers might well have spared him from frontline action in the century's first great war.[6]

Like the dead in all photos, these two seem to want to know something from us; we squint back across time and suppress the urge to shield *our* eyes. *You've seen this before, perhaps lived some bit of it yourself,* they say to us. *And what will be your judgment, and what, your part? And where will you stand when the living look back on you one day?*

## II.

Here is the former shoeshine, having his shoes shined. A *Times-Picayune* profile of 1928 called E. P. O'Donnell a "ferryboat bootblack turned writer."[7] A later profile confirmed that one of his first jobs was shining shoes on the ferry from New Orleans to Algiers.

In the *Saturday Review* article where the photograph appears, Robert Disraeli still refers to the place by its older name, Longacre Square, which had been superseded for thirty years.[8] Even now you can see that his shoes are shined on Times Square. Or so we call it now.

To my eye, at least, the picture of O'Donnell says a great deal. He looks aged well beyond his years, uncomfortable, haunted, out of place, almost out of time.

The Depression had taken its toll on him. There are echoes in *The Great Big Doorstep:* a girl learns that coffee is an ineffective remedy for hunger. A mother offers a prayer for contraception. Call it the period of the Chilblain Stomp.[9] Writing to Bennett Augustin sometime in 1936, O'Donnell looked back on this period of lean living as a time of "depending on my people for tobacco and carfare."[10]

For the moment he might hope that hard times would come again no more. "In this country I have sufficient following to insure a good living," he wrote in the same letter. Now he had arrived at New York City on the crest of fame gathered from his recently published first novel, *Green Margins.* The occasion was the inaugural *New York Times* National Book Fair, which O'Donnell's friend Carl Carmer would say portended the end of the age of the "book snob."[11] Carmer was featured, along with Pearl S. Buck, on a day that showcased first-time novelists.

What did O'Donnell, as a first-time novelist himself, make of this heady company? Perhaps it strengthened his resolve to style himself as Pat O'Donnell, Novelist.

Yet even here it's not clear if O'Donnell was officially on the marquis, as the *Saturday Review* photo would suggest, or if he was merely on the scene as a coattail-rider. The latter seems more likely, since O'Donnell's name does not appear on the author schedules published in the *New York Times*. Too late, perhaps, for his own party.

* * *

The fair was hosted in the Rockefeller Center and designed to showcase the complete life cycle of a book to the public. In a recognizable forerunner to the convention center setups of today, but still a novelty at the time, booths of "striking and original design" provided positions for all the major publishers of the day.[12] Mayor Fiorello La Guardia was there to cut the "symbolic ribbon of book-binder's tape" that stretched across the main aisle.[13] Attendees who paid their thirty-five cents could marvel at the original manuscript of *Gone with the Wind,* the year's best seller. (*Green Margins* sold almost half as many copies in its first year.) A miniature paper machine burped out pulp and made paper before spectators' eyes; the fifty-two-inch-wide device had just barely cleared the fifty-three-inch windows.[14]

Sixty authors read from their work, including three Pulitzer Prize winners. James Weldon Johnson, Norman Rockwell, Archibald MacLeish, and James Farrell all made speeches over the course of a two-week exposition that drew more than eighty thousand attendees.[15] A cage of lizards, on loan to accompany a book on the subject, watched with unblinking eyes over a reading given by seven poets, including Edgar Lee Masters and Carl Sandburg; "Lizards Find It Dull," the *Times* byline reported.[16] There were ongoing children's exhibits, and in the "the second speech I've made in my life," Pamela Travers, who wrote *Mary Poppins,* would explain that she tried to capture the "essential magic which lies in reality."[17] To read about it gives the impression that magic hung over it all; the whole thing was suffused in a festival atmosphere, according to the coverage, with overflow crowds singing and making jokes while they waited in line.

Perhaps O'Donnell passed the time signing his books, but if there was one session that he almost certainly attended, it was "Regional Literature," where the speakers included his friends Carmer and Anderson, as well as George

Jean Nathan, editor of *The Smart Set* and longtime paramour of Lillian Gish, whose sister Dorothy would star in the adaptation of *The Great Big Doorstep*. "One goes abroad, surely, when one crosses State lines," Carmer told his audience, pointing to the exoticism associated with local-color writing.[18]

Now local color connotes artlessness, in every register of that word; *local color* is synonymous with *dated*. Erskine Caldwell, who also spoke at the book fair, would cede his critical ground to Faulkner after being deemed a colorist. It was said that his books were too melodramatic, that they made caricatures of southerners. These criticisms might be levelled at O'Donnell, too. Indeed, the Broadway adaptation of *The Great Big Doorstep* would be likened by some critics to an unfunny version of Caldwell's *Tobacco Road*.[19] On the other hand, Arthur Murdock, reviewing *The Great Big Doorstep,* maintained that the novel established O'Donnell "in the tradition of the American humorists of another era, the era of Ward, Twain, Harte, and Billings."[20] One is reminded of the various Louisiana sketches of Kate Chopin, too. Of course, O'Donnell belonged to his own time as well, at his worst resembling Roark Bradford and, at his best, favoring Faulkner and other heirs to the southwestern humor tradition.

But see the photograph. The person of color who shines the former shoeshine's shoes is undifferentiated, invisible, a blot in the black-and-white. In the period of local color, there is no color, and yet color is king. The palette clashes with our time. Even the names can get under our skin; in the opening pages of the *Great Big Doorstep,* a slingshot is referred to as a "nigger shooter." Caught stealing books in a hapless attempt to write a letter of recrimination, a feckless bluesman nicknamed Shoepick is coerced into retrieving puppies from under a porch. The comic payout, culminating to his injury, is about as subtle as an Amos 'n' Andy sketch. The scene evokes long traditions of minstrelsy, and the conventions of Shoepick's day in court, with a locutor/interlocutor setup, can be traced to the nineteenth-century stage. In using Shoepick as the butt of the joke, O'Donnell novel is a reminder that the pie-in-the-face traditions of southwest humor are based in physical and racial cruelty.

Without exonerating O'Donnell, we might say that there's more here. "If a book is any good," intoned Roger Burlingame, one week into the book fair, "it will leave a great deal for the reader to do."[21] We are not permitted to forget that Commodo Crochet (his name riffing both on the grandiose "Commodore" and the musical notation meaning "at a relaxed speed") is scheming for property rightfully belonging to Shoepick and his half-sister, the scions of a family that has endured unimaginable losses. O'Donnell likely had in mind the hurricane of 1918, which killed thirty-four Louisianans, as the prototype for the storm that killed Shoepick's father. He "had worked like a slave to make a fine house for his big family," only to find his life washed away with his efforts.

Shoepick is a precursor to *A Confederacy of Dunces*'s LeRoy Jones, and like LeRoy, he talks back. Haled before the justice of the peace for the theft of schoolbooks, Shoepick says, in a quick aside, "Dishya ain no cote." When a well-intentioned librarian imposes her charity, even Evvie, still a child, notices that "the librarian used the same tone . . . [she used] when speaking to children." But Shoepick knows how to play more than his guitar, and he manages to subsist without any obvious income.

Eudora Welty notes that the only dated feature of the novel is in its expression of a prevailing attitude of the time, that the poor are passive victims. Of course, this is an attitude that O'Donnell enjoys skewering. Welty was too polite to say, directly, that O'Donnell wrote from within about a dignified underclass, impecunious but rarely poor. Ultimately, the documentary nature of *The Great Big Doorstep* might offer its best claim to posterity, for O'Donnell wrote about the lives of ordinary people struggling at the end of the road with less condescension and more familiarity than many of his contemporaries.

As Antonio Benítez-Rojo imagines the plantation, it is an "extraordinary machine . . . [that] repeats itself ceaselessly."[22] So little has changed from the time of plantation culture that Shoepick's ravishing half-sister Juarelle must either submit to the concubinage of designing townsmen or else find a way to ward them off. The problem of *The Great Big Doorstep* is the problem of the plantation after the Civil War: who will occupy the Big House, so referred? In Faulknerian terms, will it be a come-lately Snopes? Or a latter-day Sutpen? Juarelle's eventual employment as a domestic by the Crochets provides the final proof that the family are heirs to the plantation, legitimate or not. That Arthur, one of the Crochet's sons, joins her in the garden should not be overlooked.

In a 1941 column, the *Times-Picayune* editors refer to the territory of O'Donnell's novels as the "Teche country" of Lafourche and Barataria, an area peopled by "Slaves, Filipinos, Negroes, Indians, and native whites."[23] It should have said "Slavs," not "Slaves," but given the real-life condition of blacks in the Delta at the time, the typo seems a kind of Freudian slip. Barataria is a community in Louisiana, and it also happens to be the name of the imaginary island (from *barato,* "cheap") awarded by noblemen as a practical joke to Don Quixote's Sancho Panza. O'Donnell's joke is naming it "Grass Margin" in *The Great Big Doorstep.*

So here is soft-shoe O'Donnell, the man from Barataria, and his shoeshine, at the gates of the literary giants.

## III.

The jacket is an American original. It's a homespun article from the Delta cane, done up in red, white, and blue. The patriotic colors are a reminder that the Second World War is underway. The blue strands are braided through the red field, and shading enhances the optical illusion that the novel has a wicker bottom. That's how it was floated, in fact: "It took the Mississippi draining half the continent to produce the richness of this book," writer Sterling North says in his jacket blurb.

You might say that it's a trickle-down economy, without much trickling. O'Donnell lived as far down the Mississippi River as one could possibly live without actually being over water, in a place where the gift of good land was appreciated. Consider the scene where Evvie goes along on a midnight visit to her mother's illegally planted lily patch, the waist-high stalks "stately, bristling wet" in the moonlight: "Evvie smelled a pinch of the earth. The harsh black soil had been laid down here in the Delta by the river. The river had brought it from the states of the North, laid it here like a present for those who would come."[24] Indeed, the Crochet family lives on the *batture,* a squatter's zone where alluvial soil builds up between the waterline and the levee, contested ground where precarious shantytowns had formed even before the Depression, land for anyone who was willing to brave its inevitable loss.

The era of resource extraction is in full gear. It's a time of bizarre proximity, the rural poor living alongside the soaring derricks of petrochemical industry, the time of the strange tableau of the classic documentary film, *Louisiana Story.* (Like the boy of the film, the Crochet family keeps a pet raccoon.) Dave Tobin, the lanky Texan heartthrob who saunters into the novel, arrives on transfer from the Freeport Sulphur Company to Port Sulphur, reeking of the infernal stuff. He more than likely works at the Lake Grande Ecaille mine, where the Frasch Process—injecting superheated water to liquefy sulfur—is being employed. The largest sulfur dome known to the world lies ten miles to the west of the port along the Mississippi, under a tidal estuary at land's end. The mosquitoes are so bad that the company uses airplane propellers, powered by Model T motors, to keep them away from workers. At the outset, the mine earns a reputation for being unbuildable.

Yet they built it. With her mother's help, Evvie's school report on the resources of Louisiana drums up a proud list of state commodities: molasses, oil, sulphur, salt, Easter lilies, oranges, seafood, rice, cotton, perique tobacco, fur. Cypress, orangewood, pine, magnolia, cottonwood, oak, ash, elder, rosewood, duckwood, poisonball tree, myrtle, cedar, sycamore. Oyster shells, too: "They mash them up for chickens up north to eat, them shells," Mrs. Crochet says.[25]

In her words there is an awareness of what it means to be economically colonized in a place where a president would visit only on a hunting trip. (The spot where Teddy Roosevelt's horse was hitched is dutifully remembered in the text.)[26] The Crochets are small links in a supply chain that provides out-of-season produce to markets as far away as Chicago. The folks at the end of the road who "have no ills that a dollar won't cure" are part of an American tapestry, too: Indian, Filipino, Caribbean, Cajun, and Croatian. Each a reed in the basket of a cast-off culture. Each of them the effervescence, the flotsam of empires that have broken apart on land and water.

The global economy is not new. It already lives on these pages, where the locals know the sound of every visiting motorboat plying the waters and scavenge goods from ships calling in from every corner of the globe. Thus the paradox of the novel, which is at once intensely local and global: there are many blessings of place. And many reasons to escape them.

The obvious place to go, to get away from land's end, is to the cities, as Topal intends, or onto the water. By his mid-twenties, the author was launched on those waters, on the crew of the steamship *Cartago,* which, in its heyday, was used to ferry workers from the West Indies to the banana colonies. The banana boat was owned by United Fruit Company, which presides over various banana republics and controls almost two-thirds of the global market.[27] O'Donnell started as a shipboard checker and eventually became barman. He would have heard the patter of many languages, since the crew typically required about ninety-five souls, of which around a third were Americans, and the rest, foreign-born.[28] From offshore he might have glimpsed the repeated pattern of banana workers' longhouses, set about soccer fields and elevated on stilts. Calling in at Cristobal, O'Donnell would have seen the conjoining of American industrial might and the banana empire in the Canal Zone—not terribly different, in its way, from certain cane fields and orange groves of home.

O'Donnell's world lies on the broad expanse of this echoing, deeper South, stretching across the Gulf, and to the Caribbean. In the story of human migrations and the exploitation of workers, you could say that he's a citizen of the global South, of the plantation South, broadly conceived. Call it the

Meridional South of the Republic of New Orleans. Or the Maritime Zone of the Southern Wilds.

Its participants don't necessarily see themselves as actors on the field of history or as pawns of American imperialism. They see connections, relationships, action, the hard facts of geography. "Evvie liked geography," O'Donnell writes: "Unlike history, geography had a shape and a color that could be seen from the window. . . . The Delta winds and vapors belonged to geography; the big dunes of oyster shells; the clotheslines leaping like colored puppies; the bearded waterspouts; the naked willows heavy with birds; the rumbling truckloads of oil-pipe; the foggy sun bare as a skull. Geography made strangers strangers, such as the ones from Texas, or the passengers leaning on the rail of a white ship in the river."[29]

Soon, U-boats. Soon, another global war at the Gulf's doorstep. Another war to end regionalisms. Another war pitting the local and indigenous against the global. Geography is destiny, yes.

## IV.

In the newspaper he is pictured, above moonlight and Spanish moss, naturally, and beside an ad with a bantam rooster, and another for a "great head of hair" like his own. Befitting a former boxer, he has a crooked nose and a bantamweight's watchfulness. The singularly inauspicious timing of what should have been O'Donnell's breakout book meant that it was lost to the tides of war. Even as Cleanth Brooks held forth on the relative virtues of O'Donnell's prose on the pages of the *Saturday Review* (Sept 19, 1942), a splashy callout from Bell Telephone exhorted readers to hang up: twelve thousand consultative calls were needed in the construction of a single bomber, it said, and "copper, nickel and rubber are shooting, not talking, materials, right now."[30]

Having once served as "the adjutant general's department during the [first] World War," O'Donnell finds himself once again at the home front, this time taking up the pen for the *Times-Picayune*. By the end of the month he will cover the LSU-Tulane match (a 19–0 washout). Though O'Donnell wryly notes that "the game was full of things that almost happened," he was interested in what did happen at the end, especially the donnybrook that culminated in the tearing down of the goalposts.

But it is another series of reports that will make his war contribution. The connections between petrochemical agriculture and war industries are made explicit in his series titled, "Plowshares Are Swords." "No traveler studying America fails to call us the most wasteful people on earth," he observes in an article showing how a seventy-year-old cotton gin might be transformed into an antiaircraft gun. Over the span of eight articles he would demonstrate the importance of canning, poultry, milk, and every sort of thrift to the "government"—for so he refers to the federal administration.[31]

O'Donnell holds himself out here as a champion of the southern poor white. Only a few years prior he had been quoted on the pages of the *Times-Picayune,* speaking up for orange farmers in the Louisiana Farmers Union in a dispute with the French Market over "speculators" and other issues.[32] Meanwhile, O'Donnell's prolabor, legendary agent, Maxim Lieber, whose clients included Erskine Caldwell, John Cheever, Langston Hughes, Carson McCullers, and Thomas Wolfe, was promoting O'Donnell's work abroad.

It was Lieber who arranged for *Green Margins* to be published in German under the title *Das große Delta: Roman* (*The Big Delta, A Novel*) by Bermann-Fischer Verlag. With the Jewish publishing house caught in the Nazi regime, O'Donnell never received any royalties. These small losses mattered; the 1940 census taker would note that O'Donnell's marital status was uncertain, that he was a writer, and yet that he had no income to declare from his trade. Meanwhile, Lieber's alleged connections to the likes of Richard Wright, James Farrell, and Leon Trotsky, and his implication in the Alger Hiss affair, result in his exile from the United States by the end of the decade.

For its part, the newspaper was quick to assuage any worries that O'Donnell might be "red" or writing in a Studs Lonigan vein. It walked back O'Donnell's ties to labor and union: "For Pat is labor, and there is not an ounce of self-pity in him," the newspaper claimed.

There might have been reasons for self-pity in a man increasingly estranged from his wife and children. He had lost Elma Godchaux and Sherwood Anderson, whose literary patronage he once enjoyed. He had suffered an early heart attack, leaving him prostrated and writing, alone, in what all visitors described as a "shack." The shack must have been stuffed with books, so many, in fact, that used-book vendors still routinely encounter O'Donnell volumes *ex libris,* inevitably spotted from the hot damp of southernmost Louisiana.[33]

Here was a man who had already reached the point in life where he must come to terms with his addictions, one who had yet to settle his course, and who found the clock running against him.

## V.

O'Donnell told the papers there was talk of a movie. And why not? Dashiell Hammett invested in the play.[34] Dorothy Gish and Louis Calhern were screen stars, in their time, and they were on the marquis for the Broadway version of *The Great Big Doorstep.* Some reviews had been favorable, and although Calhern was reputedly drunk for every show, his performance won effusive praise.[35] As for the novel, one of O'Donnell's reviewers pointed out that second novels are notoriously difficult, but this one, it was universally agreed, was better than the first, which caught the favorable attention of reviewers as far flung as Julian Huxley, brother to Aldous.

The stakes were high now. O'Donnell was trying to spark a second courtship, a second life, really, with Mary King, who had moved to New Orleans and, like him, received a Houghton Mifflin Literary Fellowship. By June 1941 she was writing postscripts on the bottom of his letters, referring to them with a wifely "we."[36] As usual, he needed money. If he had seemed haunted and uneasy during his 1936 visit to New York City, he was more so now.

Here, another bit of flotsam surfaces from the stream of ephemera. In December 1942, Charles B. Driscoll published a portrait of O'Donnell in his nationally syndicated "New York by Day" column.[37] Driscoll interviewed O'Donnell approximately "three weeks" after *The Great Big Doorstep* opened on Broadway. The "dark, black-haired, nervous Louisianan" was passing the time attending the play and riding the buses, making conversation with strangers. "Despite every attempt to be natural and to take part in the general conversation," Driscoll wrote, "O'Donnell was strained, tense, absent-minded. He was thinking about the boxoffice. Authors are that way."

O'Donnell needed a second act. The play closed on December 19, and as the theater lights darkened, no doubt visions of cinema lights dimmed, too. The war hung over everything. "Christmas Eve tomorrow!," Driscoll wrote.

Then, morosely: "Undoubtedly the darkest Christmas Eve in the lives of any of us now living."

## VI.

It was the last call, a phrase that applies alike to stage, drink, and port. "The river was a place where you could not stay still," O'Donnell writes in *The Great*

*Big Doorstep,* a place where "dabs of paint" were brushed on "by hands that liked a splash of color." He had traveled from New Orleans to Chicago, from Los Angeles to New York. Now the rivers of his life were running together, from the Hudson to the Ohio to the Mississippi. For a century they've borne artists to New Orleans in a kind of human confluence of painters, writers, musicians, and free spirits. Modernism had come to Louisiana art on those ripples.[38] In the headline of February 5, 1928, the *Item-Tribune* might fairly deem "New Orleans As Artist's Mecca—Nearly All Reside in Quarter."[39] O'Donnell had the singular good fortune to be alive and working and footloose in New Orleans at a time when it could claim to be the seat of Dixie Bohemia, as John Shelton Reed terms it.[40] With Irish insouciance, O'Donnell found himself drifting among a remarkable company of aesthetic innovators.

One of them was a radical artist named Douglas Edwin Brown, who accompanied O'Donnell on a legendary three-week stroll in mid-November of 1928. Cashing in his accumulated vacation time at the Ford plant, O'Donnell and his new friend walked the levees all the way from New Orleans to land's end, some seventy miles away. Brown would later travel to Haiti and come to know Diego Rivera in Mexico before teaching art at Dillard University in New Orleans.[41]

In February 1929, O'Donnell joined with Brown and other organizers to establish the Provincial Gallery on Jackson Square, a place intended to showcase the work of local artists. It opened its doors with an exhibition of watercolors by Brown and Myron Lechay. Perhaps Ohio-born Alberta Kinney knew the Provincial crowd, as it was one of her paintings, "Bayou Country," that the *Saturday Review* chose to accompany O'Donnell's poetry. And if O'Donnell knew Kinney, he likely came to know her friend Clarence Millet, whose painting of the Treme Market appeared in the same issue and who loved to paint the grass margins of precarious communities dotting the river going south. Perhaps it was one of these artist-friends who cast the bust of O'Donnell that appeared on the jacket of his first book.

Other artists arrived in his life, too. Among the late arrivals to this southern Bohemia were Ohioans Jon Edgar Webb and his wife Louise, who came to New Orleans in the summer of 1940. They were shown hospitality by a circle of Sherwood Anderson's friends, including Marc Antony, O'Donnell, and Mary King. The Webbs, who are credited with helping to "discover" Charles Bukowski, later founded Loujon Press (a portmanteau of their names) and established their beatnik magazine, *Outsider.*

Jon Webb would remember Pat O'Donnell for his "giant smile with the deep grooves lining his face." Those grooves had been etched by tobacco, strong drink, light reflected from water, and assorted hard lessons. There were moments of transient jollity, as when, for Mardi Gras in 1941, O'Donnell was granted the honor of taking the lead as the head of a 120-foot long dragon. (He had the ill-advised idea of shooting real fire from its nostrils.)

Now attic memories were getting mixed up, fading, as the body failed. For O'Donnell, at least, time at the artists' party was running out. How many of his artist-friends were among those standing by to offer "transfusions" as he lay dying in New Orleans Charity Hospital, a couple of years later? According to *Times-Picayune* coverage, his death came at the end of a "long illness," on April 19, 1943.[42] He and Mary King had gotten their marriage license in New Orleans not two months earlier. O'Donnell died during Holy Week on the day after Palm Sunday.

Not long before his death, O'Donnell would pause to remember his years on the artist's wandering path. Accompanying Kinney's painting of the bayou country were O'Donnell's "Lines to Jules Petit," the ubi sunt in which he reminisces,

> Let us remember we were younger . . .
> Together we gambled money, Jules, and it was noon everywhere,
> And afterwards our debts were forgotten like schoolbooks.
>
> Who would not remember that plentiful bayou, and warm as a heart?
>
> I can close my eyes and remember that often we fought, two friends
>     embracing in the mire.
> It was always without knives, but with good hatred, for the wine was stern.
> But the lightning no longer strikes in the day
> And the rushes are not heard.[43]

So this is E. P. O'Donnell remembering the good fight. He had a habit of seeking, or perhaps being driven to, the end of land. Such is the flotsam of a life. The cliché for it, *washed up,* doesn't really do it justice. But it is indeed about things lost and found. As Thomas Wolfe once wrote, "Remembering speechlessly we seek the great forgotten language, the lost lane-end into heaven, a stone, a leaf, an unfound door. Where? When? O lost, and by the wind grieved, ghost, come back again."[44]

We might listen for those grieved by the wind, even when the rushes are no longer heard. O'Donnell never realized his ambition to start a "model farm" somewhere around Boothville. With his death came an end to an unfinished novel, envisioned as the third work in his Grass Margins trilogy, concerning "the building of a big, white highway through the marshes and sleepy river villages," and depicting "the impact of the automobile and electrical technics on the Delta people."[45] The highway has come, but the book is a lost lane end.

In the end, like some of his ancestors, O'Donnell was lost even to his family in a restless country. His son Daniel settled on the West Coast, and there a branch of the family remains. The other son, Patrick, married a New Orleans bride and settled near Baltimore, another port town with southern roots and a Catholic history. Gertrude did her best, but the sons inevitably endured a childhood clouded by unhappiness. One son would remember, during one of E. P.'s infrequent visits, finding twenty dollars in his father's coat pocket at a time when his mother was struggling to make ends meet.[46] One son seemed overtaken by E. P.'s baggage and would become an absentee father, too. Both would take to the water—Patrick to the Navy, Daniel to the Merchant Marine—as if the voice of a lost father might be found there. E. P. O'Donnell's name would become a subject to be avoided by family, so much so that his grandchildren would come to know little about him. Eudora Welty, in her afterword to his book, regrets never knowing him or anyone who did. It was the beginning of anonymity.

"I've the great fault of the Irish," O'Donnell said in one *Times-Picayune New Orleans States* profile. "I can't stand a slide rule existence." Flannery O'Connor once described the "slide-rule mentality" that prevailed among American Irish when it came to sins and sinning. "I think that the reason such Catholics are so repulsive is that they don't really have faith but a kind of false certainty," she wrote in a letter to Cecil Dawkins on July 16, 1957. "They operate by the slide rule," she said, "and the Church for them is not the body of Christ but the poor man's insurance system."[47]

One appreciates the situation of a former altar boy from a slide-rule culture who cannot lead a slide-rule life. *The Great Big Doorstep* offers a portrait of a family struggling with the same irreconcilabilities. If O'Donnell ran out of insurance over the years, his real-life family might find buried in the verses of these pages a better, or at least more shaded, man: a man who dedicated the book to his estranged wife, and who loved his sisters well enough to model characters on them. A man with a deeply spiritual bent, hidden in bygone novenas and devotionals and in the secret awe of nature. A man who would use pig Latin to slip a banned word past censors in *Great Big Doorstep*. (The Hacketts groused about Catholic-school censors, who liked the play but wanted the language cleaned up.) A man who gathered friends from every walk of life for the sake of feasting on *fruits de mer* and sharing a joyful story. A man, ultimately, who could not resist a joke, least of all the larger jokes that life plays on us.

"Who touches a book, touches a man," the *New York Times* coverage of the book fair reminded readers in the year that O'Donnell attended. It is possible to take his measure not by slide rule but by these printed leaves from the Delta. We look for grace, and we find some of it in the humanity of the texts he left behind, especially *The Great Big Doorstep*.

## NOTES

1. K. T. Knoblock, "Painter and Poet Discover Vivid Hues of Lower Coast, *Times-Picayune*, Dec. 9, 1928.

2. Lou Van Sicklen, "'I was Robbed by Hitler,' Mutters Pat O'Donnell," *Times-Picayune New Orleans States*, Nov. 8, 1941.

3. Joseph Blotner explains the origins of Faulkner's claim, and its likely falsehood, in *Faulkner: A Biography* (New York: Vintage, 1991), 143. For O'Donnell's career on the water, see Crew Lists of Vessels Arriving at New Orleans, Louisiana, 1910–1945, National Archives and Records Administration, series T939, roll 58. Within those records, see *Cartago* entries of Dec. 5, 1921 and Jan. 16 and 26, Feb. 6, Mar. 20 and 27, 1922, and *Coppename* entries of Jul. 10 and Aug. 21, 1916.

4. Julia W. Howe et al., *Sketches of Representative Women of New England* (Boston: New England Historical, 1904), 489; Ethan Mordden, *Anything Goes: A History of American Musical Theatre* (New York: Oxford University Press, 2013), 64–65.

5. Sherwood Anderson to Gordon Lewis, June 26, 1939, Albert and Shirley Small Special Collections Library, University of Virginia, Charlottesville.

6. World War I Selective Service System Draft Registration Cards, 1917–1918, National Archives and Records Administration, Orleans Parish, roll 1684920. In the 1930 census he would claim to be a veteran, which remains to be corroborated by military records. In the Van Sicklen interview he mentions that he served "the adjutant general's department during the [first] World War."

7. Knoblock, "Painter and Poet."

8. Robert Disraeli, "Fair Days in New York," *Saturday Review* 25, no. 3 (Nov. 14, 1936): 12.

9. The following year, Thomas Wolfe would find Pat O'Donnell and his wife in the Roosevelt Hotel Bar, the closest thing to the Algonquin in New Orleans. "Young, phony, fast," Wolfe dismissed them. Thomas Wolfe, *Notebooks of Thomas Wolfe*, ed. Richard S. Kennedy and Paschal Reeves (Chapel Hill: University of North Carolina Press), 2:862.

10. Undated letter, E. P. O'Donnell to Augustin, Bennett M. Augustin Collection, MSS 15, Louisiana and Special Collections Department, University of New Orleans.

11. "Peril to Writers Seen in Book Flood," *New York Times*, Nov. 13, 1936.

12. Eugene Reynal, "The Forthcoming New York Times National Book Fair," *New York Times*, Nov. 1, 1936.

13. "Mayor to Open Book Fair At Preview on Wednesday," *New York Times*, Nov. 1, 1936.

14. "Paper Machine Put in Place at Exhibit," *New York Times*, Oct. 30, 1936.

15. "Authors' Programs for Book Fair Set," *New York Times*, Oct. 25, 1936; "Book Fair Closes," *New York Times*, Nov. 20, 1936.

16. "Book Fair Throng Hears Seven Poets," *New York Times*, Nov. 9, 1936.

17. "Book Fair Visitors Pass 50000 Mark," *New York Times*, Nov. 15, 1936.

18. "Throngs View Book Fair Exhibits," *New York Times*, Nov. 6, 1936.

19. See "New Plays in Manhattan," *Time* 40, no. 23 (1942): 57.

20. Arthur Murdock, "The Delta," *New Masses*, Mar. 17, 1942, 24–25.

21. "Peril to Writers Seen in Book Flood," *New York Times*, Nov. 13, 1936.

22. Antonio Benítez-Rojo, *The Repeating Island: The Caribbean and the Postmodern Perspective* (Durham: Duke University Press, 1992), 11.

23. Van Sicklen, "'I Was Robbed."

24. E. P. O'Donnell, *The Great Big Doorstep*, with an introduction by Bryan Giemza and an afterword by Eudora Welty (Baton Rouge: Louisiana State University Press, 2015), 76.

25. Ibid., 63.

26. Roosevelt's well-publicized 1907 bear hunt took place in northeastern Louisiana.

27. Jason M. Colby, *The Business of Empire: United Fruit, Race, and U.S. Expansion in Central America* (Ithaca: Cornell University Press, 2011), 126.

28. See the *Cartago* crew manifest of Dec. 5, 1921, for a typical tally.

29. O'Donnell, *The Great Big Doorstep*, 63.

30. Brooks, *Saturday Review* 25, no. 38, "The Deep South Issue" (Sept. 19, 1942), 26–29; the Bell Telephone ad appeared on p. 21.

31. The *Plowshares* series ran in the *Times-Picayune New Orleans States* weekly from February 15 until April 19, 1942.

32. "Orange Growers Protest Actions of Speculators," *Times Picayune*, Nov. 9, 1938, 11.

33. This fact was confirmed by Terry Halladay, the literature manager of William Reese Company-Rare Books and Manuscripts.

34. Dashiell Hammett, *Selected Letters of Dashiell Hammett, 1921–1960* (Washington, DC: Counterpoint), 194.

35. David L. Goodrich, *The Real Nick and Nora: Frances Goodrich and Albert Hackett, Writers of Stage and Screen Classics* (Carbondale: Southern Illinois University Press, 2004) 147.

36. E. P. O'Donnell to Gordon Lewis from Boothville, with postscript from Mary King, May 29, 1941, Albert and Shirley Small Special Collections Library, University of Virginia, Charlottesville.

37. The text of Driscoll's column was retrieved from *The Palm Beach Post,* morning edition, Dec. 23, 1942.

38. For an examination of modernist painting in Louisiana, see chapter 8 of Estill Pennington, *Downriver: Currents of Style in Louisiana Painting, 1800–1950* (Gretna, LA: Pelican, 1991).

39. Susan Saward, "Clarence Millet," in *KnowLa Encyclopedia of Louisiana,* ed. David Johnson (Louisiana Endowment for the Humanities, 2010), www.knowla.org/entry/1127/.

40. John Shelton Reed, *Dixie Bohemia: A French Quarter Circle in the 1920s* (Baton Rouge: Louisiana State University Press, 2012).

41. Askart.com, citing Clark Marlor, *The Salons of America* (Madison, CT: Sound View, 1991); Peter H. Falk, *Who Was Who in American Art* (Madison, CT: Sound View, 1985), and Derek Coursen, the artist's great-nephew.

42. "Records of the Day," *Times-Picayune New Orleans States,* Feb. 28, 1943, 22.

43. *Saturday Review,* Sept. 19, 1942, 26–29.

44. Thomas Wolfe, *Look Homeward, Angel* (New York: Scribner, 1997), 3.

45. Albert Goldstein, "Literature and Less," *Times-Picayune New Orleans States,* Dec. 25, 1942, 7. O'Donnell provides a verbatim description of his intended third novel to Bennett Augustin in an undated letter. Bennett M. Augustin Collection.

46. Maureen Selby, phone interview with the author, Jan. 27, 2014.

47. Flannery O'Connor, *The Habit of Being: Letters of Flannery O'Connor,* ed. Sally Fitzgerald (New York: Farrar, Straus, and Giroux, 1988), 231.

# II

# ART AND THEATER

# From Farm to Factory

*New Deal Murals Celebrating the Tennessee Valley Authority*

LISA DORRILL

In 1938, Minna Citron, a painter and printmaker from New York City, traveled to Newport, Tennessee, population 2,989. Citron had won a commission from the US Treasury Department's Section of Painting and Sculpture—a New Deal arts program—to paint a mural for the post office in Newport, and she had come in search of a subject. As a recipient of Treasury Section funding, Citron understood the importance of her subject matter, as artists were encouraged to appeal to their viewers through positive scenes of local interest. After visiting Newport and interviewing residents, Citron determined her topic: the Tennessee Valley Authority (TVA), a massive New Deal program designed to improve life in the impoverished and environmentally damaged Tennessee Valley, in which Newport is located. She titled her mural *TVA Power.*

Citron was, in fact, just one of many New Deal muralists to explore this subject. Like Citron, the vast majority of them had no direct connection to the Tennessee Valley, with most residing in northeastern states. Nevertheless, artists were drawn to this topic and considered it a fitting choice for federal buildings from Huntsville, Alabama, to New York City.[1] Although artists differed in their focus—with some exploring the TVA's contributions to agriculture and the environment, and others emphasizing the TVA's role in generating and distributing electricity—they were united in their resoundingly positive view of the TVA. By analyzing what these artists portrayed, as well as what they omitted, we gain new insights into contemporary attitudes toward agriculture and the environment, the rural South, and the role of the federal government in each during the 1930s and early 1940s.

## THE TENNESSEE VALLEY AUTHORITY

In 1933, during his first one hundred days in office, President Franklin Roosevelt created one of the most ambitious and controversial New Deal programs.

The TVA was founded in response to alarming environmental and socioeconomic conditions in the Tennessee Valley, a seven-state region including portions of Tennessee, North Carolina, Virginia, Kentucky, Georgia, Alabama, and Mississippi. For decades, the region had suffered from rampant poverty, high unemployment, frequent flooding, and severe and disastrous soil erosion—the result of decades of improper farming practices. Largely due to such devastating environmental conditions, most rural families in the Tennessee Valley were poverty stricken and lacked basic amenities, including access to electricity.

Roosevelt, in fact, considered southern poverty to be the biggest economic crisis he faced when taking office in 1933. Regarding the typical resident of the region, the president explained, "We . . . come to a shack on the side of the mountain where there is a white man of about as fine stock as we have in this country, who, with his family of children, is completely uneducated—never had a chance, never sees twenty-five or fifty dollars in cash a year. . . . He certainly has been forgotten, not by the Administration, but by the American people." With this mountain man in mind, Roosevelt described the purpose of the Tennessee Valley Authority: "We are going to give him a chance on better land. If he should use it, we are going to try to bring him some of the things he needs, like schools, electric lights, and so on. We are going to try to prevent soil erosion, and grow trees, and try to bring in industries. It is a tremendous effort with a very great objective."[2]

Roosevelt's TVA responded to the crisis in the Tennessee Valley through a sweeping, multipronged approach that involved building massive hydroelectric dams to create cheap electricity and control flooding, manufacturing powerful fertilizers to revitalize the soil, working with the Civilian Conservation Corp (CCC) to plant millions of seedlings, and establishing fifteen thousand demonstration farms designed to educate local farmers. In addition, the Authority offered classes in childcare, weaving, pottery making, and the use of electricity for domestic work.

With its broad and radical mission, crossing state lines and bringing together a range of regional and federal organizations, the TVA served as a model for later New Deal programs. Stuart Chase, an economist and engineer who was among Roosevelt's inner circle of advisors, described the Authority as "The New Deal's Best Asset," and President Roosevelt himself considered the TVA "a social experiment that is the first of its kind in the world, as far I know."[3]

The TVA was not without critics, however. Private utility companies were alarmed by the government's intrusion into energy management, accusing the agency of unfair advantage. Many residents of the Tennessee Valley were equally outraged when the government forced them from their homes as a result of dam and reservoir construction. Indeed, some 125,000 people were displaced, more than twenty thousand graves were dug up and relocated to new cemeteries, and countless churches, schools, and businesses were destroyed.[4] In addition, many proud southerners, such as the poet Donald Davidson, resented what they saw as the meddling of patronizing northerners in southern affairs, and they warned that TVA dam construction would destroy the rich agrarian culture of the South.[5]

Critics of the Tennessee Valley Authority were so committed, in fact, that they attempted to shut the program down through countless lawsuits challenging its constitutionality. In spite of such criticism, however, the Roosevelt administration managed to persuade a majority of Americans to rally behind the TVA mission. The Authority launched an aggressive publicity campaign involving pro-TVA press releases, documentary photographs, short films, and even a theatrical production. In the end, for most Americans—and notably artists—the TVA came to symbolize the great hope for the New Deal during this difficult decade.

## THE TVA IN MURALS: FROM AGRICULTURE TO ELECTRICITY

In their courthouse and post-office murals, artists demonstrated strong support for the TVA's ambitious goal of shaping environmental, agricultural, and economic conditions in the South. The New York painter Dahlov Ipcar, for example, celebrated the TVA's dramatic transformation of the eastern Tennessee landscape, in her mural for the LaFollette, Tennessee, post office. More specifically, Ipcar examined the environmental impact of the TVA's Norris Hydroelectric Dam, located along the Clinch River some twenty miles from LaFollette.

Norris Dam was the first major project completed by the TVA, for the enormous sum of $34 million. Its primary functions included controlling flooding and producing affordable electricity. In addition, when completed in 1936, the dam project established the extensive Norris Dam State Park, with hiking trails, beaches, and boat docks, and eight hundred miles of shoreline surrounding the pristine Norris Lake. In her mural, titled *On the Shores of the Lake,* Ipcar portrayed the Arcadian landscape produced through the TVA project. Rather than illustrating the dam itself, Ipcar painted the lush, wooded seashore surrounding the lake, with a sportsman proudly displaying his catch of the day, a large-mouthed bass. In the background, floating mist rises above the water while verdant mountains recede into the distance. Using vibrant shades of blue and green, Ipcar emphasized the TVA's important role in restoring healthy environmental conditions in the Tennessee Valley.

William Zorach, the New York sculptor and father of Dahlov Ipcar, also celebrated the TVA's Norris Dam in a pair of teak panels carved for the federal courthouse in Greeneville, Tennessee. While the first panel portrays a voluptuous woman holding a small child, the second panel presents a muscular male figure grasping a shovel. Whereas the female figure is positioned in front of a natural waterfall, the male figure stands before a man-made waterfall: Norris Hydroelectric Dam.

Though located in a remote area of Tennessee, Norris Dam was recognizable to most Americans in this period for its strikingly modern design of smooth surfaces and simplified lines. Indeed, architects working for the Authority intentionally developed a modernist aesthetic for all of their buildings to advertise the TVA's modern efficiency.[6] As David Lilienthal, codirector of the TVA, explained, "We wanted these dams to have the honest beauty of a fine tool, for TVA was a tool to do a job for men in a democracy."[7] Norris Dam in particular received widespread attention in newspapers, government pamphlets, New Deal documentaries (for example, *The River,* 1938), and countless souvenirs. Tourist books, such as the WPA guide to Tennessee (1939), promoted the dam as a "powerhouse of modern design . . . in a primitive forest" and equated it with the architecture of ancient Egypt, stating, "In simplicity, directness and power of design as well as in the immense scale of the undertaking, Norris Dam may justly be compared with the most impressive works of the Egyptians."[8]

With its sleek structure and audacious engineering, Norris Dam became a recognized symbol for the extraordinary accomplishments of the TVA—indeed for the entire New Deal. Stuart Chase proclaimed, "A new architecture, bold as the engineering from which it springs, is rising in the valley. Nothing like it has ever been seen before. Look at it, and be proud that you are an American."[9] Tourists who flocked to the dam clearly understood its magnitude, with one commenting in 1938, "That sight . . . somehow fills me with conviction that the United States is at last beginning to hit her stride."[10]

Echoing the words of this tourist, Zorach described the TVA dam in his Greenville panel as a symbol for "man's effort and his development of the possibilities of this country and the tremendous projects which his brain conceives and his labor rings into being."[11] Using the title *Man Power,* Zorach juxtaposed Man, in the guise of a bare-chested male laborer in the foreground, with Power, symbolized by the majestic Norris Hydroelectric Dam in the background. By linking the two visually, Zorach celebrated the power of man—through bold government action—to control nature for the betterment of mankind.

In Crossville, Tennessee, Marion Greenwood portrayed the Norris Dam with a more specific message celebrating the TVA's impact on American agriculture. Indeed, at first glance, Greenwood's mural resembles a typical Regionalist scene of the 1930s (much like those of Grant Wood) with a large plow and undulating fields to the right, and a healthy farm family gathered beneath an abundant apple tree in the center. Directly to the left of this quaint farm scene, however, we find the source of such abundance—the Tennessee Valley Authority, as represented by Norris Dam. By placing the dam's massive, modernist structure into an otherwise natural landscape, Greenwood stressed the necessity for government involvement—indeed intervention—into agricultural affairs in order to restore farming conditions in the South.

Like Greenwood, Xavier Gonzalez included Norris Dam in his tribute to the TVA's agricultural and environmental work. In the lower right corner of his mural for the federal courthouse in Huntsville, Alabama, titled simply *Tennessee Valley Authority* (1937), Gonzalez painted the dark fissures of severe soil erosion common in the valley due to decades of improper farming practices. Yet he also illustrated the new "scientific" methods promoted by the TVA to combat erosion, such as strip-cropping and contour plowing, as seen in the neat rows of alternating and curving crops at the upper right. In addition, Gonzalez addressed the role of TVA dams in controlling severe flooding. He portrayed Wilson Dam in Alabama, as well as Norris Dam, along with the serene, blue waters of Norris Lake.

Such images of monumental dams, pristine lakes, and scientifically plowed fields in the works of Gonzalez, Greenwood, Zorach, and Ipcar demonstrate a clear understanding of the TVA's environmental and agricultural work in the South during the 1930s and early 1940s. Notably, however, none of these artists actually hailed from the valley, and none had experience in agriculture or the environment.[12] Instead, artists most likely relied on New Deal publicity—or what might be better termed propaganda—for their informed and celebratory views. Indeed, reports on the TVA, which were often shaped by such publicity, appeared regularly in mainstream publications, from *Fortune, Life,* and *Time* magazines to the *New York Times*.

Artists would have been familiar with photographs produced by the Resettlement / Farm Security Administration (RA/FSA) and distributed widely in the popular press.[13] Such photographs presented the broad range of TVA accomplishments, including demonstration farms exhibiting the effects of new TVA fertilizers, construction workers dredging rivers and building imposing TVA dams, and sunbathers enjoying newly built TVA state parks. New Deal agencies also produced several short films explaining the environmental work of the TVA, including a *March of Time* film of 1933, *The TVA at Work* (1935), and, most notably, *The River* (1938). Pare Lorentz's award-winning film served as a wake-up call for Americans, confronting them with the devastating effects of improper land management in the South and the need for government intervention. Such widely disseminated New Deal propaganda helped to rally the nation—and notably artists—behind the TVA's important environmental and agricultural initiatives.

In addition to its work in land management, the TVA was charged with an equally critical mission: to produce and distribute affordable electricity in the Tennessee Valley, a subject addressed by several muralists. Before the creation of the TVA, private electric companies in the South manipulated the market for electricity, keeping rates high and often refusing to develop electrical infrastructure in rural areas they deemed unprofitable. As a result, businesses refused to invest in the region, unemployment remained high, and residents lived in impoverished, and often primitive, conditions. With the creation of the TVA in 1933, the Roosevelt administration took control of energy management in the region, constructing sixteen hydroelectric dams to generate power and making that power available across the region through an extensive electric grid.

Because private utility companies put up strong resistance to the TVA, the Roosevelt administration carefully shaped its publicity to emphasize the need for affordable electricity. For example, RA/FSA photographers produced gripping views of impoverished families living in primitive shacks that lacked electricity, as well as, conversely, images of smiling housewives enjoying the benefits of new, electric appliances. Filmmakers such as Lorentz celebrated the TVA's role in modernizing the South. In *The River,* Lorentz shows striking views of majestic hydroelectric dams and electrical towers, against which the narrator chants,

> But where there is water there is power.
> Where there's water for flood control and water for navigation,
>     there's water for power—
> Power for the farmers of the Valley.
> Power for the villages and cities and factories of the Valley.
> West Virginia, North Carolina, Tennessee,
> Mississippi, Georgia, and Alabama.
> Power to give a new Tennessee Valley to a new generation.
> Power enough to make the river work![14]

Even the Federal Theatre Project (FTP) rallied to the cause. Sponsored by the Works Progress Administration (WPA), the FTP produced a theatrical production entitled *Power* (1937), which addressed the TVA's valiant efforts to provide affordable electricity despite resistance from private utility companies. Staged across the country (with ninety-nine performances in New York City alone),[15] *Power* was unabashedly pro-TVA in its viewpoint, with Harry Hopkins, head of the WPA, explaining to the actors, "People will say it's propaganda. Well, I say what of it? If it's propaganda to educate the consumer who's paying for power, it's about time someone had some propaganda for him." As Hopkins noted, "The big power companies have spent millions in propaganda for the utilities. It's about time that the consumer had a mouthpiece. I say more plays like *Power* and more power to you."[16]

Such ubiquitous and blatant propaganda undoubtedly shaped artists' views of the TVA's energy initiatives. For example, Grace Greenwood, the sister of Marion Greenwood, titled her Lexington, Tennessee, mural *The Power of Progress* (1940) and described its message as "modern industrial development through the generation of power through natural resources." She contrasted the central figure, symbolizing "the evolution of power in this part of the country," with a horse and broken wheel representing "the old order, which is being gradually eliminated." To the right, a male figure stands before an imposing turbine while grasping a lever, anticipating the moment in which electrical current will be unleashed. Underscoring her overall message, a row of disc insulators, used on electrical transmission poles, symbolizes the transmission of this power throughout the region.[17]

New Deal muralists frequently illustrated the source of TVA power: hydroelectric dams, including Wilson Dam. Begun during World War I, Wilson Dam was initially designed to power government munitions factories in nearby Muscle Shoals, Alabama. However, in 1933, with strong backing from President Roosevelt, the newly formed TVA took control of the dam, both to combat severe flooding and to provide cheap electricity in the impoverished region. With its series of graceful arches, Wilson Dam would inspire future TVA dam projects—as well as many New Deal artists.

In Chattanooga, Tennessee, for example, Hilton Leech placed Wilson Dam in the background of his complex mural honoring the history and future of the city, entitled *Allegory of Chattanooga* (1937). Although Wilson Dam is located in northwest Alabama, more than 150 miles away, Leech used its familiar arches as a symbol for the TVA, whose national headquarters were located in Chattanooga. Similarly, Gonzalez, in his Huntsville mural, portrayed Wilson Dam (in addition to Norris Dam) connected to a series of transmission towers and electrical wires. By linking the TVA dam in the background to distant farmland in the foreground, Gonzalez emphasized the TVA's role in spreading access to electricity across the rural South.

Ben Shahn, the noted leftist artist, also highlighted Wilson Dam in a 1939 mural for the central post office in the Bronx, the only TVA mural *not* located in the Tennessee Valley. During the mid-1930s, Shahn had traveled extensively in the South as a photographer for the RA/FSA and had gained an appreciation for the TVA. In his painting for the Bronx post office—one of thirteen murals there celebrating American labor—Shahn portrayed a muscular worker installing rows of insulator discs in front of Wilson Dam. The awe-inspiring structure, with its monumental row of arches stretching across the composition, serves as the perfect backdrop to honor American labor and to celebrate the TVA's important work in providing affordable electricity.

Of course, not all muralists focused on TVA dams. David Martin, for example, addressed the TVA's role in spreading access to electricity through power lines.[18] In his Lenoir City, Tennessee, post-office mural, titled *Electrification,* Martin portrayed burly workers assembling insulator discs and directing utility poles into place with ropes and winches. Martin's subject matter was appropriate for the region at this time: the TVA had recently announced plans to build the Fort Loudon Hydroelectric Dam along the Tennessee River just north of Lenoir City.[19] Electricity would be transmitted from the dam to Lenoir City customers along giant, wooden utility poles like those envisioned in Martin's mural.

In Columbia, Tennessee, Henry Billings portrayed yet another manifestation of TVA power: a gleaming electrical substation. Though a resident of New York, Billings was well versed in TVA accomplishments as the illustrator for the book *Rich Land, Poor Land: A Study of Waste in the Natural Resources of America,* by Stuart Chase. Billings clearly shared Chase's admiration for the TVA and was eager to explore this subject in his mural. Writing to Edward Rowan, the administrator in charge of the Section mural program, Billings said, "I made a trip some years ago to Norris Dam and have always been very keen about the whole T.V.A. idea."[20] In fact, Billings considered the subject matter so appropriate for a Tennessee mural that he feared his painting would duplicate the works of other artists: "Undoubtedly you have had murals painted in this region before and I imagine they have used T.V.A subject matter before. Is there any way of your sending me a list, particularly in regard to subject matter, so as to avoid any possibility of duplication of theme."[21] In the end, Billings produced a unique view of the TVA's role in modernizing southern industry through electricity.

In the left foreground of his painting *Maury County Landscape* (1942), Billings portrayed a sleek, electrical substation with polished transformers and gleaming metal trusses. Notably, he created a row of transmission towers leading directly from the TVA station in the foreground to a smoke-spewing factory located in the background. During the 1930s, Maury County experienced an explosion of growth, with the establishment of four major phosphate-mining companies, including the now infamous Monsanto Chemical Company, on which Billings appears to have based his factory. Monsanto—the much-maligned producer of Agent Orange, Roundup, and genetically modified foods—was once the pride of Columbia, Tennessee, and its largest employer.

Private Tennessee phosphate-mining companies like Monsanto shared an important relationship with the TVA during the 1930s and 1940s. Using vast quantities of Tennessee phosphate, the TVA, through its National Fertilizer Development Center in Muscle Shoals, produced highly potent fertilizers with impressive names like Triple Superphosphate and Calcium Metaphosphate. Agricultural researchers working for the Authority, in turn, promoted the use of such potent fertilizers on their TVA demonstration farms. As a result, demand for Tennessee phosphate increased dramatically, with one reporter commenting, “Farmers are beginning to demand these new combinations [of fertilizers] from their dealers and already demand exceeds supply.”[22]

To increase factory productivity, phosphate-mining companies required greater sources of electricity. In 1936, the TVA constructed a major electrical substation just outside of Columbia to serve Monsanto’s growing needs; within the year, the Authority needed to upgrade the Columbia transformer, and further expansions to the Maury County substation would take place in 1940, the year before Billings received his commission.[23] In *Maury County Landscape,* Billings emphasized this symbiotic relationship between the local phosphate industry and the TVA, as a series of transformer towers visually link the factory in the background to the sleek substation looming in the foreground. In short, Billings emphasized the TVA’s significant role in spurring industrial and economic growth.

Like Billings, Minna Citron addressed the importance of TVA electricity in her Newport, Tennessee, post-office mural titled *TVA Power* (1940). Citron went well beyond Billings’s narrow focus on electricity, however, and instead created the most comprehensive and instructive mural addressing the work of the TVA. For example, she portrayed *both* Norris and Wilson Dams situated beside their respective lakes, showcasing the TVA’s success in controlling flooding in the region. Citron also addressed the Authority’s important contributions to agriculture. In the background, for example, she portrayed a series of low buildings representing the National Fertilizer Development Center, while in the foreground she painted farmers plowing their fields according to the modern, scientific methods advocated by the TVA.[24] Notably, Citron did not portray such farming techniques in her original design; however, when she shared her preparatory drawings with David Lilienthal, the director of the TVA, Citron soon realized her error. As the artist recalled, Lilienthal complained, “Look—all wrong. You are making nice, neat little rows and for two years now we have been trying an entirely different method—you’ll have to do those drawings over.”[25] In response to Lilienthal’s directives, Citron painted undulating strips of green and gold crops that hug the contours of the landscape, demonstrating the proper methods of contour plowing, strip-cropping, and terracing. In the foreground, she even included modern equipment used to implement such techniques, including a mechanical cultivator and a terracing tractor used to carve terraces on hilly ground.

Though Citron addressed the TVA's work in agriculture and the environment, she was most impressed by the Authority's role in producing affordable electricity, as summed up in her title *TVA Power.* While conducting research for her mural design, she spent several weeks touring Tennessee, "observing the effects of cheap electricity and all of the other benefits of T.V.A."[26] Citron was especially interested in the effects of electricity on industry and agriculture in the Newport region. Through an extensive row of electric transmission towers crisscrossing the landscape, she linked the Wilson and Norris Hydroelectric Dams in the background with Newport businesses in the foreground, including Newport's most successful venture: the Stokely Brothers Canning Company (Stokely Van Camp). Founded in Newport in 1905, the company quickly became a leader in the market for canned vegetables. In *TVA Power,* Citron provided a cutaway view of a canning plant, with elaborate tubes attached to machines and workers carting and stacking rows of cans. A tall electric transmission tower hovers over the building with several wires connecting to it, a reminder of the role TVA power played in Stokely's success.

In addition to industry, Citron also linked TVA power with Newport dairy production. Indeed, one of the most curious aspects of her mural involves a revolutionary milking machine located in a barn in the immediate foreground. Cows are arranged on a rotating platform powered by electricity, again suggested by the wires connecting the building to a tall transmission tower.

Citron appears to have modeled the machine after the famous Rotolactor mechanical milking machine invented in New Jersey in the 1930s and highlighted at the New York World's Fair of 1939, the year in which she painted her Newport mural while living in New York. Tourists flocked to the Borden Dairy Company's "Dairy World of Tomorrow" building, where a Rotolactor was on display. There, viewers could watch cows being milked three times a day at an astonishing rate of fifty cows in just twelve minutes. In promoting the display, Borden also created a bovine celebrity, Elsie the Cow, who could be seen in a special exhibit of her own, "Elsie in her Boudoir." As a resident of New York City, Citron would undoubtedly have been aware of the Rotolactor display, which appeared in souvenir booklets and was covered extensively in the press.[27] Indeed, according to the *New York Times,* by November of 1939, an estimated 3 million fairgoers had already visited the Borden building.[28] By portraying the futuristic Rotolactor machine in her Newport mural, Citron presented an optimistic, yet ultimately fictitious, vision of agriculture in the Tennessee Valley. The Rotolactor—representing Borden's "Dairy World of Tomorrow"—served as the perfect symbol for the TVA's role in modernizing the South through access to electricity.

Citron expressed this same, pro-TVA sentiment in a 1940 article for *Friday* magazine, a weekly paper with a progressive outlook. In her essay, "Here Comes Old Tennessee: TVA Brings Power to the Proud Hill Folk of the Smokies," Citron described the dire living conditions of Tennessee Valley residents and the great need for TVA assistance. Photographs accompanying the article juxtaposed "the old way" of completing domestic chores versus "the new way," made possible with electricity. One photograph of a woman carrying buckets of water has this caption: "Toting water has been the hill woman's chore since the eighteenth century. Now TVA brings electric power to the people and water is pumped direct to kitchen sinks." Another photograph shows a woman standing before a brand-new electrical box attached to her ramshackle cabin: "'The magic box.' That's what they call the electric meter in the hill country where man's new power is harnessed for work inside ancient mountain cabins. Hill people, proud, reserved, take the new power in their stride, build a different kind of community life around it, and ease their work-burdened lives."[29]

Thus in both her photo-essay and mural, Citron celebrated the TVA's significant role in modernizing the rural South through the spread of affordable electricity.

## THE TVA AND THE RURAL SOUTH

In examining these murals, certain similarities become evident. On the one hand, they all present positive views of the TVA. Although they focused on different aspects of the TVA's work, from agriculture to electricity, the artists were united in their enthusiasm for this New Deal program. Significantly, however, absent from these optimistic murals are the very people for whom the TVA was created: the rural "hill folk" described by Citron and many others.

Such hardscrabble residents of the valley received widespread attention in the national press, often serving as justification for TVA intervention. Although President Roosevelt praised the mountain dweller as "a white man of about as fine stock as we have in this country," most writers were less complimentary. In her *Friday* article, for example, Citron provided a condescending description of "the real mountaineers of Tennessee and Kentucky" as "separated from all contact with the outer world, incredibly poor, superstitious, illiterate, talking a pidgin-Elizabethan, steeped in fierce religious convictions, following old-fashioned ways, wild, stubborn, proud."[30] Russell Porter expressed a more prejudiced outlook in a lengthy 1938 *New York Times* photo-essay on the TVA. According to Porter, the valley contained numerous residents "who can neither read nor write, who get all their ideas out of an ultra-fundamentalist interpretation of the Bible without any other source of knowledge, who know little or nothing of the modern world, and who seem content to remain entirely cut off from the stream of its activity." In fact, he continued, "they appear satisfied with their meager cash incomes of $100 or $200 a year, their one or two room unpainted shacks, their lack of modern sanitation and medical attention, their diet of pork and corn meal and their faded, patched and tattered clothing." With a tone of disbelief, he concluded, "Some are so ignorant that they have been unable to understand the explanations of how the construction of the TVA dams would flood their land."[31]

Yet in spite of the ubiquitous (and often derogatory) descriptions of rural hill folk in the popular press, such individuals—those who were most directly affected by the TVA—remain glaringly absent from New Deal murals, which contain no images of impoverished mountain families or their run-down shacks. This contradiction can best be seen in the works of Ben Shahn. In his RA/FSA photographs of the Tennessee Valley, Shahn frequently presented emaciated tenant farmers and dilapidated lean-tos, but in his post-office mural, he portrayed a brawny laborer before a gleaming TVA dam. In other TVA-themed murals where human figures are portrayed (as in the works of Zorach, Gonzalez, and Grace and Marion Greenwood), they appear as idealized, allegorical figures with no true connection to the mountaineers of the Tennessee Valley. In short, muralists largely overlooked the effects of the TVA on the rural residents for whom the organization was created and instead focused on its impressive engineering and agricultural accomplishments.

At its core, though, the TVA was designed to create economic, ecological, *and* social improvements in the rural South. As the writer James Agee explained in *Fortune,* "the mountaineer is a part of TVA's plans."[32] Indeed, Arthur Morgan, first chairman of the TVA, characterized the Authority's goal as to "build up the permanent social and economic prosperity of the Tennessee Valley," and President Roosevelt labeled the TVA a "social experiment" intended to transform residents of the region, those he termed the "forgotten man at the bottom of the economic pyramid."[33] Roosevelt believed the TVA would produce a "social revolution," particularly through its distribution of affordable electricity. Yet "[Electric] Power is really a secondary matter," he clarified. "What we are doing here is taking a watershed with about three and a half million people in it, almost all of them rural, and we are trying to make *a different type of citizen* [italics added] out of them."[34] In short, through a multipronged approach involving energy production and distribution, agriculture, and the environment, the TVA was designed to spur social uplift in the impoverished Tennessee Valley, transforming the "backward hillbilly" into a modern, productive American citizen.

In their post-office and courthouse murals, New Deal artists most likely ignored the TVA's social agenda for several reasons. First, by the time the muralists had received their commissions in the late 1930s, the organization's mission had shifted. Arthur Morgan, one of the founding members who championed the TVA's broad environmental *and* social engineering goals, had been fired. In his place, Lilienthal pushed the Authority to focus solely on power, rather than social planning.[35]

In addition, the artists were likely shaped by the constraints of their employment with the Section of Painting and Sculpture. As a fine art rather than relief program, the Section selected artists through an anonymous competition based on the merits of their design—not by their financial status. Artists working for the Section were required to present positive images appealing to local viewers, thereby avoiding subjects that might appear controversial or offensive, such as depictions of mountain folk as uncivilized. In contrast, artists working for New Deal *relief* agencies, such as the WPA's Federal Art Project (WPA/FAP), were selected according to financial need. Partly because of that, they enjoyed greater artistic freedom. Indeed, while muralists working for the Section often received heavy-handed coaching from administrators and were sometimes asked to alter their images,[36] artists funded through the WPA/FAP were free to explore subjects and styles as they wished. Lucienne Bloch, for example, presented a more nuanced view of the New Deal's accomplishments—and failures—in her WPA/FAP woodcut *Land of Plenty* (1935). While the background shows the positive effects of TVA modernization, with tall stalks of corn beneath impressive electric transmission towers, the foreground presents a darker reality: a destitute family separated from this abundance by a barbed wire fence. In other words, unlike Section muralists, Bloch was free to acknowledge that not all Americans had benefited from TVA initiatives.

It is impossible to surmise exactly why muralists overlooked the TVA's goals for social modernization in the valley. Perhaps the artists did not fully understand the Authority's larger mission, or perhaps they found the subject of rural hill folk visually unappealing or potentially controversial. In the end, New Deal muralists presented a resoundingly positive, though clearly limited, view of the TVA's accomplishments, one that overlooked social issues and instead focused on engineering, agriculture, and the environment.

## CONCLUSION

During the 1930s and 1940s, New Deal muralists celebrated the ambitious work of the Tennessee Valley Authority in post offices and courthouses from Alabama to New York, and they presented a range of TVA accomplishments, from monumental hydroelectric dams to bountiful crops. Though the muralists had little direct experience with the TVA and generally lived outside of the region, their informative and overwhelmingly positive views demonstrate widespread support for this radical New Deal program. However, in highlighting the TVA's success in environmental, agricultural, and energy initiatives, artists largely overlooked the "social revolution" at the heart of this New Deal program: the transformation of impoverished, southern "hillbillies" into successful members of modern society. Such an omission suggests either ignorance of the TVA's broader original mission or a disregard for the much-maligned, "backward" local population.

Turning away from the Tennessee Valley's ignoble past, New Deal artists embraced the region's noble future, made possible thanks to the TVA. Through images of gleaming hydroelectric dams and transformer towers, revolutionary milking machines, and scientifically plowed fields, the artists—themselves recipients of government funding—illustrated the great potential of this radical government program. Such celebratory views demonstrate a clear awareness of pro-TVA sentiment, as perhaps best expressed by Stuart Chase: "To see the [Tennessee Valley] authority in operation is a spiritually refreshing experience. To look at the clean, strong walls of Norris Dam between the hills of pine; to feel the will of achievement. . . . to know that, over this whole great valley from the Smokies to the Ohio, men's faces turn to a common purpose and a common goal—intoxicates the imagination. Here, struggling in embryo, is perhaps the promise of what all America will some day be."[37] In short, through striking and informative images of the TVA, New Deal muralists promoted the benefits of government intervention in ecological, agricultural—and ultimately social—conditions in the South during the 1930s.

## NOTES

1. Between 1935 and 1942, artists produced TVA-themed murals for at least seven post offices and three federal courthouses in three states.

2. Franklin Roosevelt, Meeting of the National Emergency Council, no. 19 (Dec. 11, 1934), quoted in Carroll Van West, *Tennessee's New Deal Landscape: A Guidebook* (Knoxville: University of Tennessee Press, 2001), 212.

3. In June 1936, *Stuart Chase* published a series of articles for the *Nation* using this title. Roosevelt, quoted in Van West, *Tennessee's New Deal Landscape,* 212.

4. David Ekbladh, *The Great American Mission: Modernization and Construction of an American World Order* (Princeton: Princeton University Press, 2010), 57. "Cemeteries Relocated by TVA," Tennessee Valley Authority, www.tva.gov/river/landandshore/culturalresources/cemeteries.htm (accessed Sept. 19, 2014).

5. See Edward S. Shapiro, "Donald Davidson and the Tennessee Valley Authority: The Response of a Southern Conservative," *Tennessee Historical Quarterly* 33, no. 4 (Winter 1974).

6. TVA architects and designers were even honored by the Museum of Modern Art, which launched an exhibit of TVA design in 1941.

7. David Lilienthal, "Remarks Made at the Members Preview of the Exhibition of TVA Architecture and Design," MOMA, Apr. 29, 1941, www.moma.org.

8. Federal Writer's Project, *The WPA Guide to Tennessee* (1939; reprint, Knoxville: University of Tennessee Press, 1986), 344–45.

9. Chase's words appeared at the entrance of MOMA's April 1941 exhibition and are quoted in Lewis Mumford, "The Architecture of Power," *New Yorker,* June 7, 1941, 58.

10. Quoted in Marshall Sprague, "Big Power Area Now A Resort," *New York Times,* Sept. 25, 1938.

11. William Zorach to Edward Rowan, Mar. 20, 1940, Brooklyn, NY, Record Group 121, series 133, National Archives at College Park, College Park, MD (henceforth NACP, 121/133).

12. Greenwood, Zorach, and Ipcar were from New York; Gonzalez was born in Spain and had lived in Chicago, Paris, and New Orleans before creating his Huntsville mural.

13. Regarding the dissemination of FSA photographs in the popular press, see Cara A. Finnegan, *Picturing Poverty: Print Culture and FSA Photographs* (Washington, DC: Smithsonian Books, 2003).

14. *The River,* directed by Pare Lorentz, 1938, US Department of Agriculture.

15. Barbara Melosh, *Engendering Culture: Manhood and Womanhood in New Deal Public Art and Theater* (Washington: Smithsonian Institution Press, 1991), 279.

16. Quoted in Hallie Flanagan, *Arena* (New York: Duell, Sloan, and Pearce, 1940), 185.

17. Grace Greenwood to Edward Rowan, Nov. 26, 1938, New York, NY, NACP, 121/133.

18. Unlike the other artists discussed here, Martin was personally familiar with the TVA as an illustrator and assistant exhibits artist for the Authority in Knoxville. Because of dual-compensation rules regarding federal employees, Martin had to temporarily resign from his TVA position in order to paint his Lenoir City mural. George Slover to Edward Bruce, July 28, 1941, Knoxville, TN, NACP, 121/133.

19. See www.lcub.com/about/SitePages/history.aspx. The TVA worked with the Rural Electrification Administration (REA), a separate New Deal agency founded in 1935, to build much of the infrastructure that connected TVA power to American homes.

20. Henry Billings to Edward Rowan, Sept. 18, 1941, Rhinebeck, NY, NACP, 121/133.

21. Indeed, in Tennessee alone, artists created TVA-themed murals for six post offices and two federal courthouses built during the late 1930s and early 1940s.

22. George C. Stoney, "A Valley to Hold To," *Survey Graphic* 29, no. 7 (July 1, 1940): 391.

23. Nancy Proctor, TVA librarian, e-mail message to author, Aug. 22, 2012.

24. *Two Murals of "T.V.A." for the Post Office, Newport, Tennessee, by Minna Citron* (New York: Art Students League, 1940), 2.

25. Minna Citron, quoted in "Ten Crucial Years: The Development of United States Government Sponsored Artists Programs, 1933–1943, A Panel Discussion by Six WPA Artists," *Journal of Decorative and Propaganda Arts* 1 (Spring 1986): 40–61.

26. Minna Citron to Edward Rowan, July 10, 1940, New York, NY, NACP, 121/133.

27. Anna Thompson Hajdik, "A 'Bovine Glamour Girl': Borden Milk, Elsie the Cow, and the Convergence of Technology, Animals, and Gender at the 1939 New York World's Fair," *Agricultural History* 88, no. 4 (Fall 2014): 475.

28. "3,000,000 Visit Rotolactor." *New York Times,* July 30, 1939.

29. Minna Citron, "Here Comes Old Tennessee," *Friday Magazine,* Sept. 13, 1940.

30. Ibid.

31. Russell B. Porter, "TVA's Domain: A Land Of Individualists," *New York Times,* July 10, 1938. For recent scholarship examining the responses of southern whites to widespread criticism of the South in the first half of the twentieth century, see Angie Maxwell, *The Indicted South: Public Criticism, Southern Inferiority, and the Politics of Whiteness* (Chapel Hill: University of North Carolina Press, 2014).

32. James Agee, "Where Did the Tennessee Valley Authority Come From?," *Fortune,* October 1933.

33. Arthur Morgan, quoted in Aaron Purcell, *Arthur Morgan: A Progressive Vision for American Reform* (Knoxville: University of Tennessee Press, 2014), 159. Franklin Roosevelt, "The 'Forgotten Man' Speech," reprinted in *The Public Papers and Addresses of Franklin D. Roosevelt,* vol. 1, *1928–32* (New York: Random House, 1938), 624.

34. Quoted in Ronald C. Tobey, *Technology as Freedom: The New Deal and the Electrical Modernization of the American Home* (Berkeley: University of California Press, 1996), 97.

35. William Bruce Wheeler and Michael J. McDonald, *TVA and the Tellico Dam, 1936–1979* (Knoxville: University of Tennessee Press, 1986), 6–9.

36. Ed Rowan, administrator for the Treasury Section, insisted Minna Citron, Marion Greenwood, Xavier Gonzalez, and Grace Greenwood change their original mural designs.

37. Stuart Chase, *Rich Land, Poor Land: A Study of Waste in the Natural Resources of America* (New York: Whittlesey House, 1936), 286.

# Three Dramatic Southerners in Depression New York

## *Stark Young, Tennessee Williams, and Horton Foote*

ROBERT W. HAYNES

Many rural southerners born before World War II believed that the Great Depression was, though a disaster, not as devastating for them as it was for those living in the city. In the country, the land produced food, and it was possible across the South to hunt and fish, and, after all, the region's farmers had, generally speaking, never had comfortable finances. Yet the urban world governed the public imagination, and the poverty existing in urban areas was accompanied by reports of a vigorous culture, which, though affected by economic conditions, generated an artistic productivity that defied the challenges of a stumbling economy. Ernest Hemingway turned thirty in 1929, William Faulkner was two years older, and Wallace Stevens was already a hoary fifty that year. Southerners interested in establishing themselves as artists naturally continued to turn to New York as the national center of culture in the 1930s, and their engagement in their vocation often brought forth concerns associated with their origins.

Although writers from the South contributed significantly to American fiction, their region is not widely thought of as having similarly influenced the theater. While the audience of Tennessee Williams, the most famous southern playwright, found his plays engaging more for his psychological effects than for his regional connections, readers of Faulkner's fiction entered a world in which cultural differences were central. In Faulkner, issues generally associated with the culture of the South—especially those issues arising from a social system derived from agriculture based on slavery—generated conflicts evidently connected to the political idiosyncrasies of the region, including its investment in slavery, its attitude toward the Civil War and the North, and its more-or-less official resistance to civil rights for black citizens. Yet the white southerners who devoted themselves to writing for or about the theater during the years preceding the war knew the same social reality that William Faulkner did. Reconsidering the artistic perspectives of some of these writers will provide a basis for better appreciating their contributions and the aesthetic decisions they made as they sought to serve their muses during a time of national anxiety and sweeping change.

This essay considers three writers from the South who were active in New York during the Depression. Stark Young, born in Como, Mississippi, in 1881, had long been established as a man of letters and as a brilliant theater critic before the 1930s began. Tennessee Williams, born in 1911 in Columbus, Mississippi, and Horton Foote, born in 1916 in Wharton, Texas, on the other hand, struggled during the decade to achieve recognition. Each of these writers managed to establish a reputation in the theater, though for Foote the quest was longer than it was for Young and Williams. As time passed, much was forgotten or disregarded about the attitudes and activities of these men, each of whom respected and appreciated the others' gifts. The primary focus of this discussion is Foote, whose political perspective became in the late twentieth century a source of some embarrassment for conservatives who mistakenly believed Foote shared their views. Foote's dear friend Young actually did endorse Agrarian attitudes, while Williams, who was in his early years something of an activist in human rights matters, gradually moved away from political affairs to focus on his own form of psychological drama. Thus this essay is intended to serve as a review of specific aspects of these writers' lives and careers and as a corrective to critical and historical misapprehensions.

In the autumn of 1930, as Stark Young worked to complete the chapter he was to contribute to the collection to be titled *I'll Take My Stand,* he wrote Allen Tate. He began by alluding to a review by Ellen Glasgow of his own story collection *The Street of the Islands* (1930): "Her review is kindness itself." He went on, "I've seen no others, but that leaves me free to remark how this New York life makes for thin, hasty criticism, and how little worthwhile comes out of this town—less all the time, I think. I think you so wise to be out of it. My job keeps me here and the fact that I have no place to go where I could get any peace, in my own country, either from others or from myself."[1] In fairness, it should be noted that Young was sick in bed when he wrote this letter and that any self-pity detected in his tone is understandable, but his engagement with writing about his home region and his disenchantment with New York's intellectual culture do invite the sympathy of the promising Tate as well as his promising wife, Caroline Gordon.

Allen Tate had already published a book of poetry as well as biographies of Jefferson Davis and Confederate general Thomas Jonathan "Stonewall" Jackson. Caroline Gordon, like her husband born in Kentucky, was working on her first novel *Penhally* at the time of Young's letter, and her proficiency in classical studies would continue to impress those around her. The Tates had recently returned from Europe, bringing into their concern with southern culture an international quality that the cosmopolitan Young liked very much. In so far as the antebellum culture of Dixie could be linked to a European tradition descending from the classical world, so it seemed to these artists, the detractors of the southern states could be chastened, and the tendency of even some southern writers to highlight the undeniable poverty and ignorance conspicuous in their region could be answered with dignity. Tate's admiration for T. S. Eliot associated the southern self-assertion in literature with a distinguished critical perspective, and Gordon's friendship with Ford Madox Ford gave evidence as well of an intellectual sophistication that boded well for the reputation of southern letters.

Young hoped to show that his native region's culture had developed on a highly respectable plane, its tradition embodying the wisdom and experience of civilized Europe. His inclination was strengthened by prejudice against the South, an attitude encouraged by some authors for comic purposes and by others because of the southern states' history of slavery and social inequality. Like the other writers who contributed to *I'll Take My Stand,* Young hoped to vindicate the former Confederacy and point out that the industrial mentality and commercial preoccupations of the victors of the Civil War fostered a degraded set of values in which the quantitative trumped the qualitative. His essay in the collection was titled "Not in Memoriam but in Defense," which might seem a declaration of reactionary belligerence, except that Young is actually more distressed by northern boorishness than by the political consequences of Appomattox. None of the other contributors who shared this aversion to the industrial, quantitative, meretricious aspects of northern culture had the cosmopolitan intellect or erudition of Stark Young, and, looking back nearly a century later, it at first seems strange that this man—a poet, a playwright, a painter (later in life), a translator of Chekhov and of Machiavelli, and one of the most astute theater critics of all time—would devote his energy to an intellectual defense of a society that had devastated itself in a ferocious defense of slavery. Yet, upon reflection, it is possible to see Young's regional loyalty as characteristic of a certain kind of personality, and not necessarily a deficient one. It is worth recalling the divided emotions of U. S. Army colonel Robert E. Lee, who wrote to a friend on January 22, 1861:

> God alone can save us from our folly, selfishness and short sightedness. The last accounts seem to shew that we have barely escaped anarchy to be plunged into civil war. What will be the result I cannot conjecture. I only see that a fearful calamity is upon us, and fear that the country will have to pass through for its sins a fiery ordeal. I am unable to realize that our people will destroy a government inaugurated [*sic*] by the blood and wisdom of our patriot fathers, that has given us peace and prosperity at home, power and security abroad, and under which we have acquired a colossal strength unequalled in the history of mankind. I wish to live under no other government, and there is no sacrifice I am not ready to make for the preservation of the Union save that of honour. If a disruption takes place, I shall go back in sorrow to my people and share the misery of my native state, and save in her defense there will be one soldier less in the world than now. I wish for no other flag than the 'Star spangled banner' and no other air than 'Hail Columbia.'[2]

Key words in Lee's letter are "my people," referring to his fellow Virginians, and "honour," a consideration Lee saw as requiring his primary loyalty and overriding conflicting claims upon him. Young, who was, like Douglas S. Freeman, the son of a Confederate soldier, would have been sympathetic to this attitude. His own family connections across the South were numerous and well documented, and the concept of honor, though it often invites one or another kind of grim or tragic outcome, does look attractive compared to the motives of ignorant fanaticism or stupid materialism. The complexity of Young's own perception of such a dilemma as Lee's and, less tragically, perhaps, his own, becomes clear in his fictional treatment in his novel *So Red the Rose* (1934) of the usually demonized Yankee general William Tecumseh Sherman.[3] Young carefully humanizes this character and even makes Sherman an oddly sympathetic figure, as though the burning of Atlanta and the March to the Sea were merely forgivable misdemeanors. Thus Young's reader must seek to appreciate a complexity of perspective that involves paradox and irresolution, both a reverence for history and a keen interrogation of it. Young's own accounts of his youth and his family history cast a theatrical glow upon his subject, but, from the point of view of southerners in the first half of the twentieth century, his background was quite impressive. According to Young, his father had joined Nathan Bedford Forrest's cavalry at sixteen.[4] Forrest, of course, is now notorious as a former slave trader and Ku Klux Klan leader, but in the century after the Civil War his bold exploits made him a legend in the South, and this legend was promulgated by such works as Andrew Lytle's *Bedford Forrest and His Critter Company* (1931) and Caroline Gordon's novel *None Shall Look Back* (1937).[5] Forrest's remarkable military career was a comfort to many southerners in the sad sequence of defeats that ended the Confederacy, and this audience paid little attention to reports of racial atrocities attributed to the cavalry leader. General Lee is, in fact, said to have called Forrest his best general.[6]

So, in terms of his personal connections to the southern Lost Cause, Young could claim an aristocratic status. His literary training and aesthetic perception, combined with a love of friendship and a natural generosity, gave him another kind of status, and his critical insights, arising as they did from a deep understanding of the history of literature, set him apart from less-erudite, more whimsical or arbitrary critics. His sympathy for the Nashville Fugitives was strengthened by his sense that their effort to capture the moral and aesthetic high ground for southern culture was in accord with tradition. Of Young's aesthetic perspective, John Pilkington has observed, "The more he understood the fine arts, the more convinced he became that the artist pointed out for society the ways to right living."[7]

Young's own family's status and history provided a dimension of his identity that enabled him to synthesize learning with high regard for a social system that honored privilege and tended to disdain abstract ideas of democratic equality. Aesthetic sophistication has often found itself in conflict with egalitarian perspectives, and, as kind a man as Young was, he did cherish a sympathy for the social order of the old agricultural South. At the same time, however, he was capable of recognizing his own bias as bias, for in a note to Tate in 1931 he observed, "it's curious how appallingly strong family and South can be in the blood."[8] His adverbial qualification of "strong" suggests an ambivalence that echoes Lee's resolution to return to Virginia in case of secession and "share the misery of my native state."

A writer much less concerned with the values and qualities of the Old South was Tennessee Williams. Born in Mississippi, Williams devoted his artistic energies to explorations of neurosis and the conflicts arising from false illusions. He sought to get his work produced in New York in the late 1930s during a period of itinerant creative effort, enjoying only limited success in those early days. After completing three years of college work at the University of Missouri at Columbia, he enrolled at Washington University. Never very mindful of grades, he applied himself to writing and soon decided to complete his studies at the University of Iowa, where it was possible to focus on writing drama. When he graduated with a degree in English, the education he had acquired was a substantial one. He did not by any means become as learned as Young, but there was nothing provincial or narrow about his learning, as he had worked through the texts of Chekhov, Rilke, Strindberg, and Ibsen.[9]

Although he wrote poetry and short fiction as well as drama, Williams emerged from his academic training focused on writing plays. He had had a number of short works staged before he graduated, but later he struggled, rambling to California and to New Orleans before being awarded in 1939 a one-hundred-dollar special prize in a playwriting competition sponsored by New York's Group Theatre.[10] The plays submitted by Williams were also sent to agent Audrey Wood, who offered the impoverished playwright a contract and subsequently assisted him in securing further opportunities and connections in New York. In July 1939, Williams wrote to Wood.

> I'm also considering the possibility of spending some time in New York this Fall as I've never been really exposed to the professional theatre. I think I'd learn some craftsmanship—(badly needed)—by attending a lot of Broadway plays. Perhaps I could find some employment in New York that would make this possible. I probably would have gravitated that way sooner except that I don't like the crumby sort of Bohemian studio life that an impecunious writer is subjected to in a large city—I got too much of that in the "Vieux Carre" and it's taken five months of California sunlight to fumigate my soul.[11]

Williams's chief concerns as a dramatist at this time derived from what he would call in 1974 his "anguished familial situation" in childhood and especially in the years immediately preceding his arrival in New York.[12] His mother, an Ohio-born woman who had convincingly adopted the mannerisms of a southern belle, had married a genuine southerner who was something of a rogue and a bully. Their daughter, Williams's beloved sister Rose, had developed such radical neurotic symptoms that her parents had, in 1937, allowed physicians to perform a lobotomy on her.[13] Williams's own lack of conventional masculinity had alienated him from his alcoholic, macho father, and many severe emotional conflicts bore upon the aspiring writer.

Due to the efforts of Audrey Wood, Group Theatre administrator Molly Day Thacher, and theater critic John Gassner, Thomas Lanier Williams, now calling himself Tennessee Williams, saw his one-act play "The Long Goodbye" (set in an unnamed Midwestern city) produced at the New School in February 1940.[14] Though his struggle for recognition would continue until the success of *The Glass Menagerie* in 1944 and 1945, the connections he established in New York would serve him well in the long run, as would the failure in Boston of his play *Battle of Angels* in 1940. Without becoming more than a temporary New Yorker, Williams brought his anxious southern dreams to the city and was soon enabled to share them with a sophisticated if often fickle audience that promised to bring him fame.

In the same year that Williams's first New York production was staged, another first dramatic production was performed in the city, this one written by a young actor from Texas who had been struggling for roles in New York for several years. Horton Foote, five years younger than Williams, was working on dramatic exercises with fellow members of the theatrical ensemble the American Actors Company. He was asked to work up an improvisation based on his own home region of Texas. When he presented his efforts to the group, Agnes DeMille suggested that he try writing a play. He quickly wrote a one-act drama based on his own experiences in his Texas high school, titled it "Wharton Dance" after the small town he came from, and found it so well received by his colleagues that the company included it with other one-acts in a public performance. Drama critic Arthur Pollock happened to see the program, which included pieces by Thornton Wilder, and wrote approvingly of it in the *Brooklyn Daily Eagle*. Other critics appear to have noticed Foote's first play as well.[15] The possibility of becoming a playwright took young Foote by surprise, as he still devoutly wished to succeed as an actor, but he soon realized that in writing he was able to fulfill his artistic aspirations in ways he could not upon the stage. He proceeded to write a three-act play, also set in his hometown, and this time it was leading critic Brooks Atkinson of the *New York Times* who wrote encouragingly of the 1941 production.[16] This recognition of talents he had not suspected he had galvanized Foote into energetic dramatic writing that would only end with his death in 2009 at the age of ninety-two.

Unlike Tennessee Williams, whose restlessness kept him moving more or less randomly from place to place, Foote developed a lifelong habit of gravitating between New York, his professional base, and Wharton, Texas, the small town an hour southwest of Houston, where his large family had a long history. Horton's great-great-grandfather Albert Clinton Horton was born in Georgia but had become a pioneer Texan, serving on the party sent by the state to identify a new location for a capital, choosing what is now Austin. He narrowly missed becoming a victim of the Goliad massacre of Texas supporters by Santa Anna, and he later became the first elected lieutenant governor of Texas, actually serving as governor in the prolonged absence of the man elected to that post. He was, in the prewar years, a planter with extensive properties, and he died late in the Civil War as the Confederate reverses brought about the loss of most of his wealth.[17] His granddaughter Corella Horton married Albert Harrison Foote, who was descended at a distance from a northern family of some distinction. One Pennsylvania ancestor was a friend of Benjamin Franklin, and, through another connection, Foote was related to Roxana Foote Beecher and her children Henry Ward Beecher and Harriet Beecher Stowe.[18] Albert Harrison Foote and his wife Corella were the parents of Albert Horton Foote Sr., father of the Texas playwright. Though connections to northern abolitionists would not have been a social asset in early twentieth-century Texas, Horton Foote's descent from an early pioneer and lieutenant governor did carry weight locally, despite the hard times on which the family had fallen after the Civil War. When Foote was named Playwright in Residence at Baylor University early in the twenty-first century, he noted with pride that it was his great-great-grandfather Albert C. Horton who had made a key donation for the Texas university's founding.

In Depression-era New York, as young Foote pondered new dramatic possibilities, he recognized that his memories of home and family opened for him an imaginative resource harmonious with the ancient idea that memory is the mother of the Muses. However, Foote wished to engage with issues of the kind taken on by his contemporaries who were writing for the stage, and, in a world at war or on the brink of it, a world still laboring in economic depression, he must at times have wondered whether the reality of rural Texas and his cotton-town experiences would be a sufficient vehicle for inspiration. Foote was a decent student in high school, but he had no further formal education except drama training. He read widely and loved literature, but if one compared his understanding of literary history to that of a Stark Young or a Thornton Wilder he would seem relatively deficient in learning. Foote's self-education prepared him differently for a literary life, and perhaps that aspect of his training became one of his strengths as a writer. Williams, who had navigated through academia to the point of graduating as an English major, was widely read and possessed academic training, but Foote, though he loved literature, especially modernist literature, learned over time that his own muse called him to a vision of the human situation that does not require infusions of academic wisdom. As it turned out, one of his most beneficial artistic resources was his independence of the sophistry, affectation, and cynical opportunism fostered by academia, a strength reinforced by a conviction that commercialism was the enemy of art. While in his career Foote had to take on paying projects of many kinds, from writing for the Gabby Hayes television show to laboring on screenplays intended strictly as box office attractions, his central focus as an artist was an honest engagement with his inspiration. Not only did he ground his major work *The Orphans' Home Cycle* on the lives of his beloved parents, but his rejection of Hollywood's profit-driven film-making process took him in the direction of independent film, where he hoped the writer's vision would be appropriately honored.

Foote completed the second year of a two-year program at the Pasadena Playhouse in the spring of 1935, and he accepted an offer to work that summer with two of his instructors, who regularly taught at the Phidelah Rice Institute on Martha's Vineyard. In Massachusetts, Foote assisted at the school, where his main achievement onstage was playing the lead in a production of Paul Green's 1925 one-act play "The No 'Count Boy."[19] That fall, he moved to New York City to look for work as an actor, and there he struggled for several years, playing what parts he could secure and working odd jobs to survive. Sociable and gregarious, he made interesting friends, and he was able to arrange to take acting classes from the Russian expatriates Tamara Daykarhanova and Andrius Jilinsky, who had been members of the Moscow Art Theater and now operated a school in the city. The Russians, devoted to the techniques of Konstantin Stanislavsky, liked Foote but deplored the training he had received in Pasadena, and he proved a receptive student. It was through his attendance of this school that he met the group that banded together in 1937 to form the American Actors Company. By 1939, he had established a number of friendships with gifted associates, including aspiring dancer and actress Lucy Rosengardt Land, later Lucy Kroll, who would eventually become his agent for nearly fifty years, and he had acquired a certain level of lean and hungry comfort in New York theatrical circles, at least on the lower levels. Unlike Williams, Foote regarded living in New York as essential to his desire for success in the theater, and, when he realized that his home and family in

Texas provided a necessary natural resource for his dramaturgic inspiration, the pattern of his life, generally speaking, would be set, with a regular migration between Wharton and New York governing his movements and his imagination.[20]

In his early years in the city, Foote yielded somewhat to the sympathies of some of his radically minded associates, whose leftist inclinations were fed by the economic rigors of the Depression, and, later, during World War II, by the collaboration of Stalin's armies with American troops against the Nazi machine. The popularity of Clifford Odets's plays reflected something of this anti-capitalist fashion, and indeed Odets would attend at least one of Foote's early plays. But there was a growing awareness during the war that major changes were coming in the theater, and a letter from Williams to Foote, dated April 24, 1943, sets forth that apprehension.

> We must remember that a new theater is coming after the war with a completely new criticism, thank God. The singular figures always stand a good chance when there are sweeping changes.
>
> Keep your ear to the ground and concentrate on honesty till you know what else is coming!
>
> All these people are going, going,—GONE![21]

Williams's suggestion that being "singular" is advisable indicates something of his own plan, but the phrase "concentrate on honesty" must, in the long run, have made more sense to his fellow playwright. Foote's fitful experiment with political drama in *Out of My House* (1942) had demonstrated some anxious skill but not much artistic coherence; however, the play he titled *Mamie Borden,* later changing the title to *Only the Heart,* returned to the narrative already begun in his first two plays "Wharton Dance" and *Texas Town,* laying out a predicament drawn from his knowledge of the world of his hometown. Naturally craving a box-office success and still being young and subject to being led astray by the apparent wisdom of established figures in the industry, Foote reluctantly agreed to recommended revisions of *Only the Heart* that weakened it significantly and eventually made him fiercely resistant to such compromises. As he realized that concentrating on honesty was essential to his artistic labor, Foote made a major advance in his apprenticeship as playwright. Even in his naïve first effort "Wharton Dance," in which he had thoughtlessly retained the actual names of the characters on whom the parts were based, it was the honesty of the situation and the dialogue that had provided charm.

Foote's freedom from intellectual indoctrination somehow resisted the ephemeral temptations of various social or political enthusiasms, and he retained a perspective over time that was fundamentally congruent with the politics of his father, a devout follower of Franklin Delano Roosevelt. Later in life, Foote's admiration for President Bill Clinton would distress some of his more conservative admirers, but he never backed away from supporting a political tradition he believed was humane. In the early days in New York, Foote sometimes flirted with radicalism and no doubt had been greatly stirred by such theatrical moments as the conclusion of Odets's play *Waiting for Lefty*, in which the audience joined the actors in chanting for a strike. Even so, however, he remained more profoundly aware of the particular shapes of inequality he knew from childhood in the world of hard labor that constituted the business of cotton farming in Texas. If abstract intellectual concepts floated around him in New York, it was the reality of memory and experience that would gain control of the playwright, a man whose great-great-grandfather was a major slave owner and planter and whose father had in childhood been saved from isolation by the friendship of working black people on a plantation run according to principles that would have pleased Simon Legree. This background did much to shape Foote's writing life, and he would plunge into it in his greatest dramatic work *The Orphans' Home Cycle*.

As Foote educated himself by reading and by living a theatrical life, one key moment occurred in 1933 during his Pasadena schooling when his grandmother took him to Los Angeles to see three of Henrik Ibsen's plays produced by Eva Le Gallienne's company. Foote recalled these plays as showing him the power of the theater in a new way, and clearly in some of his early work he drew on Ibsenian moments.[22] After his marriage in 1945 to Lillian Vallish, Foote would benefit from the academic training and insight of his wife, whose critical perception had developed in her literary studies at Radcliffe College. He always shared his father's regret, however, for the circumstances that had denied the senior Foote the education for which he had longed, and Foote himself must at times have felt himself relatively deprived as he noted the erudition of such southerners as the Agrarians. Yet it is one thing to know the Western literary tradition and another to understand the South, and, though Foote's life would be engaged with urban life in the North from 1935 onward, his mind and imagination lived in the world of small-town Texas.

Faulkner never vomited on Foote as he did on Caroline Gordon Tate at the Southern Writers Conference in 1931, but no such baptism was necessary for the young Texan.[23] The Mississippian, who in his younger years had slept on Stark Young's couch in New York, respected Foote's version of his own story *Tomorrow,* and Foote would write two other screenplays for Faulkner works.[24] Foote's Academy Award screenplay for Harper Lee's *To Kill a Mockingbird* was itself a work with affinities to Faulkner's 1948 novel *Intruder in the Dust,* which was made into a 1949 film shortly before the novelist received the Nobel Prize for Literature. Thus it is clear that Horton Foote's creative vision participated to some extent in a kind of dialogue with Faulkner, as indeed had been the case with many writers, not all from the South.

Cleanth Brooks has stipulated that "the two most brilliant manifestations of the great upsurge of letters in the twentieth-century South were the advent of William Faulkner, of Oxford, Mississippi, and of the Fugitive poets of Nashville, Tennessee."[25] Brooks goes on to record various acknowledgments by the Nashville authors, some of them slightly reluctant, of Faulkner's artistic skill, as he strives to support a thesis that Faulkner admired the Fugitives. However, while analyzing the relations between these southern writers, Brooks does perceptively outline Faulkner's situation. He explains:

> Of course, to have the association of a group of friendly critics who know you well and share your literary interests does confer great benefits. In some comments published in *The Harvard Advocate* (1951) Ransom draws upon his experience with his fellow Fugitives as he comments on Faulkner. He observes that Faulkner had "not had the advantage of the society of his literary peers" nor that of "intellectuals with their formidable dialectic." . . . Yet in the same passage Ransom sets out some of the advantages of Faulkner's relative isolation—which was, of course, never absolute. . . . Ransom remarks that for Faulkner there was no acquaintance with the literary "academy [to] adulterate the natural directness of his style." . . . In short, the leader of the Fugitives could see certain advantages that Faulkner had in not being a member of any literary group.[26]

Like Faulkner, Horton Foote brought to his work a unique background, and he developed his own kind of theatrical art to convey his vision. He had numerous friends, but few of them shared his southern background. His wife was from Pennsylvania, and his agent was from New York. Some of his early friendships in the city had been formed in Pasadena, and most of his personal connections, aside from family and hometown friendships, originated in the world of the theater or its connected realm of dance. Tennessee Williams was a poet and fiction writer as well as a playwright when Foote met him in New York, but Williams, who felt Foote to be a professional competitor in the years preceding *The Glass Menagerie,* was not himself an enthusiast of the pro-South faction.[27] At one point in college, as he prepared for an improbable fraternity wrestling match in 1931, Williams had posted a sign begging for alcoholic sustenance and reading, in part, "MUST HAVE LIQUOR TO FORTIFY MYSELF AGAINST THE AGGRESSIVE AGRARIANS!"[28] This was the year after the publication of *I'll Take My Stand,* so Williams is probably alluding to the "Twelve Southerners" listed as contributors to that volume. Foote, however, who regarded himself as a southern writer with somewhat more justification than Williams might have, was inclined to sympathize with certain values—courtesy, for example—associated with the southern past, and, when he met Stark Young, whose essay concludes the collection in *I'll Take My Stand,* a strong friendship grew at once. Young's fondness for old connections and theatrical ones as well met an admiration approaching reverence from the younger playwright, who knew Young's superlative theater criticism as well as the critic's connections in Texas.

Young's 1934 novel *So Red the Rose* had described a cultured South, combining factual elements with a measure of romantic nostalgia. It was quite a popular book and was adapted as a 1935 film starring Randolph Scott and Margaret Sullavan. The film drew a generally negative critical response, but Young's book appeared to be *the* Civil War novel until the success of Margaret Mitchell's *Gone with the Wind* pushed it into relative oblivion in 1936. Young's own Confederate connection was his father, and his childhood of association with plantation families in Mississippi gave him authentic material with which Foote could identify, although Foote's view of the plantation was far less sympathetic, as he would eventually show in his play *Convicts,* written in the mid-1970s. As a drama critic, Young no doubt knew of the young Texan's first productions in New York, but the friendship between the two men did not begin until much later, although Foote certainly knew of Young's critical work by 1935.[29] Young would write a striking review praising Tennessee Williams's *The Glass Menagerie* in 1945, in which he noted a belief that Williams was of aristocratic descent, an understandable mistake, as Williams sometimes liked to ameliorate his pedigree. Young's admiration for Williams shows an independence from the kind of attitude often associated with the Agrarians and may suggest that the ideological connection between the members of this group was in some cases not very substantial. It does not seem likely that Williams could have idolized Nathan B. Forrest, for example. The Agrarians did not, generally speaking, turn to the theater as a favorite mode of expression, although Andrew Lytle had studied drama at Yale and even played a part on Broadway in the 1928–1929 season. The theater is essentially an urban institution, which naturally reduces its rural potential, and the Agrarian endorsement of life in the country suggests that formal theater is less essential than the noncollaborative arts of poetry and fiction.

In 1945, when Young wrote his review of Williams's very successful play, Horton Foote managed a triumph of his own in securing the hand of Lillian Vallish. In the theater, though, things were not going so well for him. Foote was never an envious man, but his friend Williams was suddenly being greatly celebrated as playwright. Another friend, Jerome Robbins, had been launched to sudden fame in 1944 with his show *Fancy Free*. Foote, however, had seen his own play, *Only the Heart*—produced in a revised version on Broadway after a first production at the Provincetown Playhouse—deprecated by the critics and shut down after forty-seven performances. Facing a discouraging prospect in New York, and simultaneously having to reorganize his life as head of a family, Foote accepted a position teaching theater at the King-Smith School in Washington, DC, a kind of finishing school for girls from southern aristocratic families.[30] He would spend four years at King-Smith, developing plays and working with young actors, before returning to New York where his dramaturgic skills quickly made him a leading writer for the fast-developing medium of television.[31]

Foote's own connection to the Agrarians was primarily with Stark Young, who was not entirely in accord with the aesthetic principles of all members of the group. Young liked Tate very much and was fond of Gordon. His correspondence with Tate and with Donald Davidson is full of mutual encouragement and contemporary literary gossip. Foote, however, who had as a boy been alert to the critical importance of the always-chancy cotton harvest in his hometown, had little use for the celebration of the yeoman farmer favored by the Agrarians. As in Faulkner's Yoknapatawpha world, small cotton farmers in Texas hovered in or near that fatal category of "white trash," and planters, whether working their fields with slaves or, after emancipation, with convicts, tended to be inhumane and predatory. The most conspicuous plantation owner in Foote's work is Soll Gautier of *Convicts*, a primitive, brutal, and ignorant alcoholic whose abuse of black women on his place and whose exploitation of the boy Horace Robedaux are antithetical to ideas of a cultivated southern aristocracy. In Foote's treatment of a later period, oil replaces cotton as the primary instigator of avarice, but wealth remains a threat to morality. Though poverty degrades and humiliates, it is often the poor who see most clearly and show the most generosity of spirit. Wealth, or obsession with getting it, dehumanizes in a particularly reprehensible way, for greed is a selfishness grounded in competitive ill will.

Unlike Williams, Horton Foote had a long struggle to achieve recognition as an artist of major significance. Within theatrical circles, he had earned respect by the 1950s, but it would be more than a decade before his first Academy Award for the *To Kill a Mockingbird* screenplay, a work whose social importance is still not fully appreciated. Twenty years after *Mockingbird,* his original *Tender Mercies* earned a second Oscar, and Foote was nominated for another in 1985 for *The Trip to Bountiful.* A decade later, his play *The Young Man from Atlanta* was awarded a Pulitzer Prize, and Foote's dramaturgic career would still continue fourteen years until, still close to a work being produced, Foote died at ninety-two. As his work continues to appear onstage and onscreen, his reputation slowly develops before a wider audience, and the power of this quiet writer's drama reaches more people. He is recalled as a man of generosity and grace and as a writer whose compassion and vision have a value that will not be diminished by time. His early friend Tennessee Williams remains generally regarded as the South's leading playwright, but Foote's plays and screenplays are proving to have a lasting power. If time seems to have diminished the achievements of Stark Young, whose spirit even during Foote's early apprenticeship was that of an earlier generation, it must still be said that Young's penetrating theater criticism has a definitive quality that compares most favorably with much of the ideological criticism foisted upon the public in more recent times. His kindness and encouragement meant much to aspiring writers, particularly to Foote, and its benevolence was made more powerful by his learning and his perception.

## NOTES

This essay was made possible by a University Research Development Award granted by Texas A&M International University. My thanks go to Dr. Jeffrey Brown, Dean of Graduate Studies and Research, and to the University Research Council. I am grateful also for the kind assistance of the following persons: director Russell Martin and librarian Cynthia Franco of the DeGolyer Library at Southern Methodist University, Elizabeth Garver and Cristina Meisner of the Harry Ransom Center at the University of Texas, and Lewis Wyman and the Manuscript Reading Room staff at the Library of Congress. Matthew J. Boylan of the New York Public Library kindly located and provided some essential archival information.

1. John Pilkington, *Stark Young: A Life in the Arts: Letters, 1900–1962,* 2 vols. (Baton Rouge: Louisiana State University Press, 1975), 350.

2. Douglas Southall Freeman, *R. E. Lee,* 4 vols. (New York: Charles Scribner's Sons, 1934), 1:421–22.

3. Stark Young, *So Red the Rose* (New York: Charles Scribner's Sons, 1934), 297–316.

4. Stark Young, *The Pavilion* (New York: Charles Scribner's Sons, 1951), 11.

5. Andrew Nelson Lytle, *Bedford Forrest and His Critter Company* (New York: Minton, Balch, 1931) and Caroline Gordon, *None Shall Look Back* (New York: Charles Scribner's Sons, 1937).

6. See, e.g., James Dickens, "What General Lee Said," *Confederate Veteran,* Oct. 1930, 372, www.oldmagazinearticles.com.

7. Pilkington, *Stark Young,* xix.

8. Ibid., 366.

9. Donald Spoto, *The Kindness of Strangers: The Life of Tennessee Williams* (Boston: Little, Brown, 1985), 37–39, 45–50.

10. Ibid., 73.

11. Tennessee Williams, *The Selected Letters of Tennessee Williams,* vol. 1: *1920–1945,* ed. Albert J. Devlin and Nancy M. Tischler (New York: New Directions, 2000), 79.

12. Albert J. Devlin, ed., *Conversations with Tennessee Williams* (Jackson: University Press of Mississippi, 1986), 260.

13. Spoto, *The Kindness of Strangers,* 59.

14. Ibid., 78.

15. Arthur Pollock, "Actors at Work over a Garage: Plays by Paul Green, Thornton Wilder Done by the American Actors Company," *Brooklyn Daily Eagle,* Apr. 16, 1940, 15. http://bklyn.newspapers.com/image/52777103. See also Horton Foote, *Beginnings* (New York: Scribner, 2001), 199.

16. Brooks Atkinson, "American Actors Company Produces Horton Foote's 'Texas Town' in Sixteenth Street," *New York Times,* Apr. 30, 1941.

17. Matthew Ellenberger, "Illuminating the Lesser Lights: Notes on the Life of Albert Clinton Horton," *Southwestern Historical Quarterly* 88, no. 4 (Apr. 1985): 363–86.

18. Abram William Foote, *Foote Family, Comprising the Genealogy and History of Nathaniel Foote, of Wethersfield, Conn., and His Descendants* (Rutland, VT: Marble City Press, The Tuttle Co., 1917–1932).

19. Horton Foote, *Beginnings,* 139.

20. The best source for Foote biography is Marion Castleberry, *Blessed Assurance: The Life and Art of Horton Foote* (Macon, GA: Mercer University Press, 2014).

21. Horton Foote, *Beginnings,* 251.

22. Ibid., 66–71.

23. Veronica A. Makowsky, *Caroline Gordon: A Biography* (New York: Oxford University Press, 1989), 105.

24. Castleberry, *Blessed Assurance,* 204.

25. Cleanth Brooks, "Faulkner and the Fugitive-Agrarians," in *Faulkner and the Southern Renaissance,* ed. Doreen Fowler and Ann J. Abadie (Oxford: University Press of Mississippi, 1982), 22.

26. Ibid., 32–33.

27. Williams, *Selected Letters,* 1:467.

28. Spoto, *The Kindness of Strangers,* 37.

29. Foote, *Beginnings*, 130.

30. Castleberry, *Blessed Assurance,* 130.

31. Ibid., 151–55.

# III

# TOURISM AND MODERNIZATION

# Driving Southerners through the Great Depression

DOUGLAS E. THOMPSON

At the depot in Thomson, Georgia, in late September 1922, a cavalcade of automobiles met Thomas E. Watson's funeral train. The populist politician had died suddenly in Washington, DC, in the second year of his first term as a US senator. The photographs of the day show cars lining the dirt roads around the depot, which sits on the south end of Thomson's downtown area. Only twenty years into the new century and less than three decades from its introduction into American culture, the automobile had become a ubiquitous part of southern life.

Watson had for some time championed the automobile and to a greater extent the Good Roads movement.[1] From his vantage point in rural Thomson, surrounded by vast farming interests, Watson had argued from his newspaper, the *Jeffersonian,* as early as 1909 that the "motor car was here to stay." His disposition in the newspaper to appear reactionary on racial issues or demagogic in politics did not carry over to a Luddite outlook on technology. For all the weeping and gnashing of teeth over progress in the South in printed pages, technological innovation often met with success. Cars, telephones, tractors, and radios found their ways into southern life. Watson did caution readers to the potential health and social dangers of the automobile "to those who travel in it, as well as those who do not." He, however, felt strongly that the automobile's greatest threat came from its bringing outsiders into a community: "It is usually the non-resident who does devilment with the automobile." Confident that locals could put pressure on other locals to behave, the "stranger" became the concern for laws and enforcement. A nonlocal driver, Watson wrote, "doesn't care whose team [of horses] he frightens into a runaway, whose vehicle he smashes, and whose wife or child he hurts and kills."[2]

This tactic served other forms of paternalistic rhetoric that he would use to stir fear against outsiders of many stripes. Even as Watson appeared to see the threat that vehicles could create in a community, he also saw mechanized movement's value to economic progress. His position in Thomson and his paternalistic tendencies gave him a unique vantage from which to encourage the automobile's adoption while at the same time demanding that its use be controlled. Nearly two decades later, car usage dominated rural southern life, often in ways communities could not control.

Automobiles often reinforced social norms of the region, but the technology also created avenues to overcome those norms. Histories of mobility generally focus on roads or technological advances in vehicles. When they explore automobiles, these histories often see the car in an adversarial light.[3] Cars mattered to people, and by the 1930s they became an indicator of economic recovery. An example of this process occurred when the Federal Writers' Project (FWP) produced state guides as part of the Works Progress Administration (WPA). The stories the writers captured tell us a great deal about automobiles at the time, but the inclusion of a "Tour" section at the end of every state guide highlighted a critical assumption about the automobile and its importance in the economic system for folks with free time and money.

Because of the economic devastation of the Great Depression on the South and the region's tendency to reactionary politics, the rest of the nation has for almost one hundred years seen the South's backwardness as due to a built-in repulsion to innovation. Southerners' affinity for automobiles, regardless of racial or gender categories, suggests that we have misunderstood the process of adaptation. Southerners may have worried over the automobile's disruptive nature, but it fit their understanding of themselves as possessing independence, self-reliance, and freedom. With the automobile marketed to them in this way, southerners believed they could control the process of adapting it to southern norms. In the 1930s, however, we can already see how this adaptation was working against social norms.

An example of this kind of intrusion in southern life can be found in WPA narratives. Interviewing an elderly couple, Ella and Robert Gooding, in Winnsboro, South Carolina, W. W. Dixon recorded Ella Gooding's racial sympathies with the Ku Klux Klan and her concern over the use of automobiles in courting relationships. It appeared to her that young men had begun to show a "lack of respect and consideration" toward parents. "Boys and men," she noted, "do not exercise the same courtly manner toward girls and women as they formerly did." The automobile was both the example and, according to Gooding, the cause of the disrespect. "Young men," she added, "drive up to a young lady's home in an automobile, honk the horn, and sit until the young lady comes down to the automobile door." The slight to parents occurred in the first instance, but what frustrated Gooding more was "men do not even observe the courtesy to get out of the car and help the girl inside."[4] Good manners mattered, too.

It was clear that Ella Gooding held contempt for the way young men carried themselves with regard to young women in the 1930s—she was in her eighties when the interview occurred. The automobile, however, carried a specific form of disruption to proper manners: impatience. In her day, a young man would have to spend time courting a young woman, and that process would have let her family know whether he was worthy of the daughter's attention. The car, creating an ease of convenience, had affected all types of behavior. Not only did the young men no longer send notes requesting an afternoon outing, they simply sat in their automobiles and made a nuisance with the horn as they waited for the young woman to come out.

Johnny Haselton, an elderly farmer in South Carolina expressed a similar mistrust of cars. Recalling his attempt at "frolicking" when he was younger, and noting his failure to do much, he talked about weddings and the atmosphere built within the community around such activities, which could last for days. "In the old days," Haselton noted, "a boy asked a girl's father for her, then they had a big wedding to which the whole countryside were invited." "But now," he lamented, "a boy tells a girl, 'Let's try marriage and see if we like it.' Then they hop into an automobile, go to a preacher or more often a Justice of the Peace, and get married.'[5] Haselton, like Gooding, saw the automobile as an example of a larger problem with the way social norms were changing in the South. Marriage had lost some of its sacredness, they thought. Haselton lived in an isolated part of South Carolina, and many of the people in the area had moved on, largely abandoning the only life he had known, farming. Whether the car caused these problems or simply revealed that social relations were changing, it was unclear to Gooding and Haselton why young people failed to see value in community interactions as they used to be. In this way, the two interviews highlight how automobiles played a role in the changing dynamics of life in the South, but they also suggest that change had already occurred, and Gooding and Haselton were naming it. The stories assumed that the car had taken on a specific role in social relations and the interviewees were stating an obvious fact: people used automobiles for a variety of reasons, including courting, dating, and marriage.

In a region that emphasizes the importance of place, mobility threatened that sense of stability. Watson had pointed to this fact in the early part of the twentieth century. In cars, strangers could move freely from one place to another, passing through or stopping to put down roots. Strangers could even stop in to take away daughters. More importantly, automobiles became the means of escape from the constraints of small farming communities.

These WPA interviews reveal the nature of fear in rural communities in the early decades of the twentieth century. By 1927 more Americans lived in cities or metropolitan areas than in farming communities. The general mistrust of cities and the greater mobility of young people appears to have heightened the concern that change was coming and it was coming too fast. Both Gooding and Haselton focused on manners and how automobiles allowed younger folks to skirt their responsibilities. Hidden in their concerns, however, was the change in behavior that helped young people move freely without constraints. Mechanized movement sped up the pace of change, which would have ramifications on almost every part of rural, southern life. More important, automobiles placed that change in individuals' hands, tearing at a community's fabric. Watson thought it could be controlled in the early 1900s, but by the 1930s it was clear Gooding and Haselton knew that the change had occurred.

Fiction writers of the day used this transition period to explore how the life in the South had transformed under modernizing tendencies. Often railing against stifling traditions, writers like Erskine Caldwell and William Faulkner recognized the way change affected the South. The strange career of automobiles in the region found an odd outlet in twentieth-century southern fiction writers' repeated use of the car as a vehicle for tragedy. In these stories automobiles became symbols of "crisis" or destruction.[6] There does appear to be something of Gooding and Haselton's concern about the changing world in the stories.

Caldwell opens *Tobacco Road* with a scene of a dirt road, largely empty, and a broken-down automobile. In a twist that works in two different directions, one of the car tire's inner tubes has rotted, and the protagonist, Jeeter Lester, attempts to patch the tube but never manages to fix it. Through ingenuity Jeeter does get the car to run and thus helps bring some stability to the Lester family. Bemoaning the uselessness of mechanization, Jeeter sees his plight as a poor tenant farmer manifested in the car. These folks can see the mobility but have a hard time accessing it. The importance of who will inherit its benefits finds expression in a later scene. Children will access mobility in ways that destroy relationships to the land and each other.

Jeeter Lester's son, Dude, gets religion, a woman, and an automobile. (Really, he just gets a woman, Sister Bessie, but the other two parts of his new life come with her.) Caldwell makes a great deal of the "new" automobile that Bessie owns and Dude drives. A pivotal moment in the novel occurs when Bessie challenges Jeeter's right to the land, noting that the actual owner is someone else. When a fight breaks out between Jeeter, one of his daughters, and Bessie, Dude races to the automobile, backs it up to protect Bessie, and runs over his grandmother in the process.[7] The car vanquishes the matriarch. Interestingly, no one appears to care about Grandma Lester until much later, and even then no one seems saddened by her death. The threat is the automobile's ability to help folks leave the rural life they have been tied to. After Jeeter dies in a house fire, a farmer voices his concern: "It looks to me like his children ought to have stayed at home and helped him run a farm."[8]

William Faulkner has a similar vision of mechanized progress. In *The Reivers: A Reminiscence,* Faulkner has young Lucius Priest experience a car ride before a buggy ride, and an important component of the rural life is lost in the transition. Cynthia Dettelbach, reflecting on this scene, asserts that Faulkner's use of the car ride first meant that the young man could not go back and experience rural life the way it was. "Because the automobile experience comes first," she wrote, "the old world that Parsham represents can never be viewed by this young protagonist again with the same kind of complacency." Not letting the idea go, Dettelbach sermonizes Faulkner's intent: "Its foundations have been shaken by the intrusion of modernity, symbolized here, as it often is in Faulkner's words, by the car."[9]

Faulkner's older Lucius Priest, who tells the story from the perspective of an aged grandfather to his grandson, appears to be more gracious about the events than Dettelbach allows. I tend to see these theoretical frameworks as interesting and perhaps helpful to understanding the authors she examines, but I am less inclined to see them as more important than the historical patterns of automobile ownership and use. It was true that folks worried about the catastrophic nature of the cars but continued to use them. The WPA narratives suggest that whether Faulkner feared the automobile's presence in the South, southerners themselves adapted to it and saw the advantage to possessing one.

As Ella Gooding and Johnny Haselton attested, some folks, particularly older ones, saw the rise of automobile use as a problem, but most southerners who possessed cars either embraced them fully or, at worst, felt ambivalent to their effect on society.

The 1930s revealed the South's affinity for automobiles. Even as the Great Depression stripped families of their assets, automobiles became status symbols. In the WPA interviews, automobiles are evidence both of the status the car gave a family and the painful reminder it provided to some of their bleak financial circumstances. Interviewees would often go out of their way to show the interviewer a car in their possession, even if it was in a shed or on blocks. In *These Are Our Lives,* the first section revealed a variety of eleven farming family stories in the southeast, with most in Virginia and North Carolina. In almost every case, with both black and white families, the reference to an automobile suggested something important about its function in family life. John and Sarah Easton, who lived in Wilson County, North Carolina, and were tobacco farm laborers, mentioned their 1924 Dodge sedan, which they no longer used. "We made a good crop in 1924," Sarah remembered, "and that fall John bought the car. He was drunk when he bought it and he bent a fender before he got home." Sarah Easton's experience with the automobile resembled Jeeter's. Fiction expressed a truth about how the financial cost of owning an automobile runs up against other obligations in families. She said that they still had the vehicle but had little use for it or money to keep it going if they wanted to use it.[10] Caldwell's fear of the automobile is not present in Easton's life.

As with many of the interviewees, it appeared she had been prompted to talk about the car because she framed the example with remarks about not having a radio or using the electric wiring in the house they rented. Easton also noted that the house did not have any indoor plumbing. In a similar way, Gracie Turner, a sharecropper living with her husband, noted that they had asked their landlord to help them buy a car. The landlord forced the Turners to use their two mules as collateral. The Turners' boys wrecked the car, and the landlord took it and the mules from the family. "After [Mr. Anderson] had it fixed up," Turner said, "we tried to get him to sell it back to us. He wouldn't, but went and sold it to another man. So we was lackin' a car and mules too."[11] In both cases, the automobile had been part of the family story but no longer served any purpose. The attainment and loss of a car had little to do with one's racial category. The Eastons were white, labored hard, and found enough success to purchase a vehicle. While the Turners, who were black, needed the landlord's assistance to make the purchase, their success and assets meant that their proposition was feasible. The precarious nature of their livelihood and status as tenants / rent farmers, however, also showed that by the mid-

1930s the economic hardship of life on the farm reduced the opportunity to have such luxuries. Both black and white southerners saw the purchase of an automobile in a similar light and worked to be able to attain a standard of living that included a car. The Great Depression, however, stripped farm laborers and sharecroppers of any hope of overcoming their financial lot. Though the Turners lost their car and mules, they worked to regain the automobile. The Eastons appeared to have held on to their automobile but rarely used it. Clearly, the possession of a vehicle meant something different to these folks than it did to Ella Gooding or Johnny Haselton.

Both families appear to have been striving for what Thomas Doyle had. Doyle, a black cash rent farmer, had carved out a sufficient economic space for himself and his family through a series of smart management decisions. Though Doyle credited his success to clean living, there was nothing in the description of the Eastons or Turners that suggested they had made poor decisions. Their attachment to the land tied their assets to the landowner. Doyle had figured out how to work the system as a renter and learned the power of buying with cash. He walked the interviewer around the property he rented and complained that the property owners never supplied enough sheds for his possessions, including a V-8 and a Model A Ford. As the two walked through the sheds containing the vehicles (there were also sheds for his combine, which he owned, and a couple of other pieces of equipment that he rented), the interviewer noted that the Model A belonged to Doyle's son, who lived and worked the property with his father.

The narrative returns to the cars a little later during a discussion of politics and religion. Doyle, a Republican, had found Roosevelt's policies helpful to the farmer but felt little need to get excited by politics in general. Religion was a different matter. "If his interest in politics is little," the interviewer interjected, "Tom makes up for it by religious fervor. He is a deacon in the Missionary Baptist Church. Not only a deacon, but he is the treasurer of the church as well." The interviewer added an explanation for why Doyle owned a new car. "Every Sunday," the narration went, "he drives there with as many of his family as his '35 V-8 will hold. (In 1934 Tom had his most prosperous year and cleared one thousand dollars. Six hundred and fifty dollars of this he devoted to the V-8)."[12] Unlike the Eastons and Turners, whose ownership of their automobiles was tenuous, Doyle bought his car outright and used it to express his status in both the larger community in which he worked and lived as well as in his church community, where the car allowed him to show his independence from others. Not owning land worried the renter, and he hoped to correct that issue within a few years of the interview, but the stylish V-8, known for its power, gave this African American farmer an important part of the American dream. He could take his family to church on Sundays, and even though owning land escaped him at the moment, he was free to move and do as he pleased. The automobile, then, became a way of extending his freedom.

The buying power of a rent farmer in 1935 suggests that we have not fully understood the decade of the Great Depression in the South. The fact that an African American farmer built this kind of financial freedom means that some people in the downtrodden South had moments of uplift. Though the country in general and the South in particular spent most of the 1930s dealing with the effects of the Great Depression, automobile sales trended upward beginning in 1934, reaching their pre-Depression numbers even in the South in less than five years after the fall of Wall Street. By ignoring this trend and focusing instead on the WPA narratives for the problem South, a construction many fiction writers reinforced, we have failed to understand how the attraction to automobiles stimulated economic growth in the South. In a consumer economy, automobile sales and registrations become one of the indicators for a rebound. The use of cars creates economies of scale in the need for gas, service, places to stay, and travel destinations (tourism). The South had become dependent on the automobile prior to the Depression, so that during the decade of the 1930s cars were a necessary part of life and presented opportunities for change. Like Americans more generally, southerners drove throughout the Great Depression. For Thomas Doyle, who saw his financial success expressed in buying power, the freedom to drive to church would one day lead his children and grandchildren to leave home and explore their own success in places that would not limit them based on their complexion.

Several factors unrelated to the South led to this shift. Automobile affordability moved the car away from being just a faddish trend of the wealthy. With more vehicles on the road, the automobile industry and the general public began to clamor for better roads. Earlier in the century, entrepreneurs in bicycle and foundry shops had made automobiles as a side business, a venture requiring a master blacksmith and creative engineering. The sheer cost to build a car meant that only the wealthy could possess one. Local newspapers across the country would highlight the moment one such vehicle came to town. Macon, Georgia, had its first automobile, likely owned by Henry J. Lamar, in 1899. By 1903 the Macon City Council set the speed limit at "eight miles per hour."[13] Municipal governments had to navigate the problems caused by technical advances in the early part of the twentieth century, as roadways became congested with cars and horses/mules. As one WPA interviewee noted, talking about early travels to his grandmother's house twenty-five miles away, "Both me and the mule saw our first automobile on one of these trips and she ran away and nearly wrecked the wagon. I just stared at it wide-eyed."[14]

Henry Ford changed the nature of the conversation by making automobiles affordable, at least in terms of opening markets to middle-class Americans. An early racecar driver, Ford became interested in production techniques. His philosophical predisposition to democratic ideals married to his interest in production efficiency found expression in the assembly-line process. Mechanized movement held greater promise for economic efficiency by freeing the farmer from the care and upkeep of farm animals like horses or mules.[15] Urban developers and political progressives saw the health benefits of removing farm animals from the market centers in cities, where animal waste created numerous health issues and dead animals might lie in the roadway for days before city workers could remove the carcasses. Ford's massive plants, first in Highland Park, Michigan, and later at Red River, unleashed a significant number of cars and trucks across the nation.[16] As manufacturers such as General Motors rapidly adopted the plant model, automobiles became affordable to larger numbers of families whose greater disposable income helped propel the industry forward. Automobile registrations almost doubled in every southern state from 1915 to 1916. Tennessee's registrations jumped from 7,600 in 1915 to 30,000 in 1916 without a similar kind of increase in individuals holding licenses.[17] The industry continued to see sharp increases in sales across the United States through 1930.

General Motors introduced a financing plan during the 1920s that made it even more affordable to purchase a car. Ford resisted such a plan, emphasizing the need for families to make prudent financial decisions. General Motors outpaced Ford Motor Company in total sales throughout the 1920s and 1930s in part because of their payment plan model. Though this kind of credit would help place the nation in a precarious position when world markets fell, it also meant that individuals who earlier could not afford automobiles were purchasing at significant rates. As noted through the Eastons' and Turners' experiences, limited financial success did not mean continued success, which always put possessions in tenuous positions. By 1929 southern states held nearly a quarter of all US auto registrations, with more than 21 million vehicles.

Data on car ownership in individual states show how much southerners came to rely on their cars and trucks. In 1915, Tennessee had 7,600 automobiles; by 1929 that number exceeded 294,000. Showing a less modest increase, Georgia went from 25,000 registered vehicles in 1915 to over 277,000 in 1929. Texas estimated its 1915 numbers at 40,000 but by 1929 held over 1 million vehicles registered.[18] Between modernizing assembly plants for greater efficiency, which pushes total prices down, and financing plans that allowed purchasers to buy on time, what had been a trendy fad at the beginning of the twentieth century had become a consumer necessity and part of the American dream, even during the Depression.

Increased vehicle numbers required a reconceptualization of infrastructure. While road traffic had always had to deal with difficult conditions, such as washouts, farm animals did the work of overcoming the elements. But if a car got stuck because a road was bad or the driver tried to take a shortcut through a field, the drivers and passengers had to take corrective measures. Early automobiles were built from horse carriages, which helped overcome some issues of travel but created others. The carriage could overcome deep ruts in the road, but in order to do so the ride was stiff and uncomfortable. By the 1910s, it had become clear that advocates of good roads could attach their needs for road improvements to farmers' need to get their produce to markets.

The Good Roads movement, as it became known, played a significant role in focusing attention on road improvement and construction. In Thomson, Georgia, the editorial position at the *McDuffie Progress* embraced road improvement as a way to enhance farm life. In connection to a Good Roads tour, sponsored by the Atlanta Automobile Association, that circled Georgia in October 1910, the *McDuffie Progress* reprinted a "special" report from Atlanta, which noted that good roads were needed for farmers more than for automobiles. The note suggested that any benefit to motorcars was "incidental" to the benefit to the farm. In this way, the road boosters overplayed buying trends at the beginning of the century. Within one decade of the Georgia tour, the mass production system created by Henry Ford and implemented by almost all the other manufacturers made car ownership affordable and shifted the balance of power in the Good Roads movement away from farmers' interest to that of the general public. Roads would continue to benefit the agricultural life of the South, but the main use of roads would be for automobiles. By the time the US economy exploded in the mid to late 1920s, factors outside the region's economic interests had laid the groundwork for southerners' widespread adoption of automobiles.

This emphasis on improved roads also found expression in WPA projects. One of the first programs to receive funding through the New Deal involved "shovel ready" projects like road construction or improvement. Though the Federal Writers' Project is often understood apart from these road programs, they shared a common assumption. Individuals with cars like to drive them. As the FWP worked through how to include writers in the New Deal relief programs, the national directors settled on creating state guides. Every state guide contained a list of driving tours as a way to see important sites or to understand a particular place's contribution to the state. In this way, these guides served a US tourism industry that was in its early stages. This kind of tourism would be built on automobiles and the understanding that if someone had enough free time and disposable income they should take to the nation's roads in an automobile, especially since trips to Europe or anywhere abroad were prohibitively expensive.[19]

By the late 1930s when the state guides began to be published, automobile sales had exceeded pre-Depression percentage increases. While car ownership was limited to folks who could afford them or who had enough assets to use as collateral for credit, the marriage of the idea of the automobile to the idea of freedom had created space for the car-culture explosion in the United States after World War II. By now, southerners were fully aware that the automobile had changed their lives and the region, and they were comfortable with those changes, even in the face of large numbers of deaths from car accidents. Even Caldwell's use of the automobile in *Tobacco Road* highlighted the odd tension the car created. Dude's "new" automobile, which kills Grandma Lester, is the same vehicle he, Sister Bessie, Lov, and Ellie May climbed into after his parents' fiery death in their home. The novel ends with Dude planning to buy a mule and seed to plant cotton—his father's dream—as he drives away from the destroyed family home.

Automobiles created disastrous consequences for people and the environment. Alabama had 375 deaths due to automobile accidents in 1928. From 1930 to 1933, the state counted more than 400 car-related deaths each year. Kentucky had a similar pattern, with 342 deaths in 1928 and 514 in 1933. In 1931 alone, Virginia had 656 auto-related deaths. Georgia charted similar trends during the first four years of the decade. Texas had 1,292 deaths in 1933.[20] In 1938 the number of fatalities on southern roads climbed in direct proportion to registration increases. Alabama and Kentucky nearly doubled the number of deaths caused by automobiles. Although Virginia numbers stabilized by 1938, Texas exceeded 1,700 deaths.[21] The increased fatalities did nothing, however, to diminish the obsession with automobile ownership. The economic expansion that occurred in the post–World War II era found a strong car culture in place and added to it. Whatever fear southerners had about losing their past because of automobiles never materialized in purchasing decisions. Even when road construction worked against different groups' interests—as when construction of the interstate system in the late 1950s through the 1970s destroyed African American neighborhoods across the southern landscape—automobile consumption within those groups continued to climb during the same period. The subtle nature of the change often went without notice.

Jonathan Daniels's *A Southerner Discovers the South* serves as a good example of this remarkable adaptation to automobiles. In his journey, Daniels used a car to explore southern cities and byways. He was never self-conscious about the vehicle. The closing paragraph of the opening chapter makes two references to the automobile—nothing else listed gets more than a single mention—when he notes that he had "a tank full of gas" as "I rode out to find [the South]."[22] The reader knows the trip will be by car, but there is no mention of what kind it is or how the mechanical processes of both the manufacturing of the road he would take and the car that would carry him through "the South" help propel the story. The car just exists.

The journey, as Daniels recounts it, began in Washington, DC. He stopped on Memorial Bridge, which crosses the Potomac River and sits below the high bluff where Arlington Cemetery sits along with the Custis House. "This was undoubtedly the front door of the South," Daniels wrote, "but it ran directly into the past and a graveyard though I knew that somewhere beyond it were the living. I sought them." The ability to move beyond both literal and metaphorical realities was an important part of why automobiles mattered to southerners. "I had nothing against history," he continued, "but I was more interested in the mixture of hunger and hilarity from which has been compounded so much of the life and drama of the South. I pressed on the accelerator, hastening through the parkways and suburbs below Washington, deeper into truer Virginia."[23] The car appeared in the narrative through its instrumental nature; pressing the accelerator allowed him to move past something he claimed he did not want to think about anymore. The long circuit of the South that he traversed meant that he could always drive past what he did not want to engage. Daniels was free to move beyond spatial limitations, not unlike Thomas Doyle on his Sunday drives to church.

Daniels's memoir of the South reveals how automobiles became an extension of southern life and caused southerners to live in a paradox. Some one thousand miles southwest of Washington, DC, and significantly farther by Daniels's route, he visited a large cotton plantation north of Greenville in Scott, Mississippi. Daniels's engaged a plantation manager, Oscar Johnston, in a discussion about the state of tenant farmers in the "Cotton Kingdom." With more than four thousand tenants and thirty-eight thousand acres of cotton production under his management, Mr. Johnston oversaw a vast enterprise and apparently made it profitable for the corporate owners and the tenants. Daniels wondered if the advent of the cotton picker would displace the tenant farmers. Johnston argued that he had seen all cotton pickers on the market and none could do the work of the tenants. Even if cooperatives like Hillhouse used the Rust Brothers Picker, the process of cotton production meant that a human being needed to go through and remove the ready bolls while leaving the rest. While Daniels was suspicious of Johnston's paternalism, he believed Johnston had the best interest of the tenants in mind. The Agrarian writers appear in this chapter, as they do in several chapters, but in this case Johnston appeared to be advocating against mechanized farming practices, even as he added to the plantation "modern" features like a community refrigeration unit and a hospital.

The entire discussion about mechanization occurred as Daniels and either a subordinate of Mr. Johnston or Johnston himself drove a car all over the plantation. Again the car was present but unnoticed. "As we rode over the exquisitely tended earth," Daniels noted, "I was interested in uncovering the opinion that a good unit manager must have in him the stout, earthy qualities of the redneck . . . We passed by gin and lake and church and cabins, the last far less impressive than the dwellings at Dyess [the government-backed cooperative] but seeming stouter than the cabins in the white row and the black row at Hillhouse [the Christian socialist experiment]. We moved on past the big central barns at which on each unit a black hostler under the unit manager presides over all the stock and tools." Daniels saw the plantation from the moving automobile, but the use of the car never appeared to Daniels to be part of the conversation about mechanization. He wanted to know what Johnston thought about the perfected picker and its effect on tenant farmers. Both men engaged the discussion without noticing the irony of how mechanization had already changed the plantation. Central units, refrigerated containers with electricity, and automobiles had modernized and mechanized the southern farm by the late 1930s. The change was clear even as it went unnoticed. Mr. Johnston was wrong about the cotton picker, but it would take another decade and a half for the mechanized farm to displace workers. By that time, the black tenants were showing signs of a willingness to take matters into their own hands and liberate themselves from the racial paternalism of folks like Johnston. Daniels observed that a "new freedom threatened and men shivered at the thought of it."[24]

The rural South of 1930 was similar to the rural South of the 1940. The distance covered in that decade by automobiles suggests that we have not completely understood the decade or how the Great Depression provided opportunities for some while stripping others of their one chance. Automobiles continued to populate the southern landscape, and they suggest a way to understand how people navigated the decade. While the changes that Ella Gooding and Johnny Haselton feared would occur did not come to pass in the ways they thought they would, changes did come. Rather than seeing the automobile as a symptom of those coming problems, most southerners adopted the car in their own image. It broke down some social barriers, even as its financial costs could set a family back. Even during the Great Depression, cars held out the promise of freedom and status. By looking to how people sought and used automobiles to their advantage, especially during tough economic times, we might discover how much the region changed in the process.

## NOTES

1. Thomas E. Watson displayed his wit when he described to readers his journey by car to Jacksonville, Florida, over the course of two issues. He discussed the travails of the automobile breaking down frequently and the impossibility of finding "roads" in rural areas, which often went through a farm property with no visible markings. Ultimately, Watson gives up on the trip by car and secures a train to Florida. The fluid prose is full of insight about the potential for cars and how it is limited by the lack of access to good roads. See Thomas E. Watson, "Our Trip to Florida," *Jeffersonian* 8, no. 11 (Mar. 16, 1911): 1, 12; "The End of Our Trip to Florida," *Jeffersonian* 8, no. 12 (Mar. 23, 1911): 1, 12.

2. Thomas E. Watson, "Scout Cars and Good Roads," *Jeffersonian* July 1, 1909, 8.

3. Michael L. Berger, *The Devil Wagon in God's Country: The Automobile and Social Change in Rural America, 1893–1929* (Hamden, CT: Archon Books, 1979); James J. Flink, *The Car Culture* (Cambridge, MA: MIT Press, 1975), 4. Berger noted that there had been little work done prior to the 1970s on the effects of automobiles on American culture (p. 10). While there are now more monographs on the subject, it is still a fertile field of study.

4. The WPA interviews with Ella and Robert Gooding are available at www.loc.gov/resource/wpalh3.30c82108 (accessed June 17, 2015).

5. South Carolina Writers' Project, Life History, *A Hell Hole Farmer, American Life Histories: Manuscripts from the Federal Writers' Project, 1936–1940*, https://www.loc.gov/item/wpalh002161/ (accessed Mar. 4, 2012).

6. Cynthia Golomb Dettelbach, *In the Driver's Seat: The Automobile in American Literature and Popular Culture* (Westport, CT: Greenwood, 1976), 4.

7. Erskine Caldwell, *Tobacco Road* (1932; Boston: Beehive, 1974), 163–64.

8. Ibid., 179.

9. Dettelbach, *Driver's Seat*, 21.

10. "You're Going to Have Lace Curtains," in *These Are Our Lives: As Told by the People and Written by Members of the Federal Writers' Project of the Works Progress Administration in North Carolina, Tennessee, and Georgia*, ed. W. T. Couch (New York: Norton, 1939) 9.

11. "Tore Up and A-Movin'," in *These Are Our Lives*, 22.

12. "I Has a Garden," in *These Are Our Lives*, 51, 52.

13. *History of Macon: The First One Hundred Years, 1823–1923* (Macon, GA: Williams and Canady, 1996; reprint of supplement to *Macon News*, July 10, 1929), 195.

14. "What I Wanted to Be," in *These Are Our Lives*, 382.

15. "The Automobile," editorial, *Southern Mercury*, July 20, 1899.

16. Flink, *Car Culture*, 40–41.

17. *Statistical Abstract of the United States*, 1918 (Washington, DC: Government Printing Office, 1919), 301.

18. *Statistical Abstract of the United States*, 1929 (Washington, DC: Government Printing Office, 1930), 388.

19. Monty Noam Penkower, *The Federal Writer's Project: A Study in Government Patronage of the Arts* (Urbana: University of Illinois Press, 1977), 25.

20. *Statistical Abstract of the United States*, 1930 (Washington, DC: Government Printing Office, 1931), 390; *Statistical Abstract of the United States*, 1935 (Washington, DC: Government Printing Office 1936), 358.

21. *Vital Statistics of the United States*, 1938, Part II, Fatality and Mortality Data for the United States Tabulated by Place of Residence (Washington, DC: Government Printing Office, 1940), 158–63.

22. Jonathan Daniels, *A Southerner Discovers the South* (New York: Macmillan, 1938), 11.

23. Ibid., 12–14.

24. Ibid., 183–84, 187.

# A Forward Glance

## *TVA Modernism and the Regional Designs of National Progress*

TED ATKINSON

When President Franklin Delano Roosevelt sent a message to the US Congress in April 1933 to recommend passage of legislation authorizing the Tennessee Valley Authority (TVA), he made the case that resources earmarked for a relatively small geographical space would yield substantial benefits to the rest of the nation over time. The president cited the planned repurposing of a facility in Muscle Shoals, Alabama—the initial phase of the TVA project—as a harbinger of the "potential public usefulness" that the Tennessee River could provide if managed effectively. Roosevelt reasoned that this value would prove measurable beyond the kilowatts of electric power generated because "it enters the wide fields of flood control, soil erosion, reforestation, elimination from agricultural use of marginal lands, and distribution and diversification of industry." Consistent with the rhetorical flair that Roosevelt deployed early in his first term to combat widespread despair and anxiety, the statement brimmed with confident ambition in declaring that the plan "touches and gives life to all forms of human concerns." The expansive scope framed the enterprise with universal appeal and bolstered a teleological claim about the validity of the agency's mission and purpose by evoking fundamental components of American mythology. In this vein, Roosevelt described the TVA as "a return to the spirit and vision of the pioneer" from which it is possible to "march on, step by step, in a like development of other great natural territorial units within our borders."[1] The authorization of the Tennessee Valley Authority by a congressional charter passed on May 18, 1933, designated the agency in paradoxical terms as a federal corporation.

While the legislative action was an important milestone, it provided no guarantee that the TVA blueprint would come to fruition. The precariousness of the design became all the more apparent as the authorization had the immediate effect of galvanizing the opposition. Powerful utility interests determined to maintain the dominant market share they enjoyed were the most formidable opponents. The vocal and tactical response was championed by industry lawyer and anti–New Deal crusader Wendell Willkie, whose high-profile stance on this issue contributed to rising political fortunes that eventually garnered him the 1940 Republican presidential nomination. Recognizing a threat to the industry's bottom line, power companies challenged the TVA in the courts and in the court of public opinion, arguing that the heavy costs incurred in one small part of the country could not possibly yield the far-reaching benefits promised by the Roosevelt administration and more aggressively contending that the very formation of the agency was unconstitutional. The specter of loss also supported a claim about lost cultural treasures rather than wasted federal largesse. Critics asserted that the wholesale transformation of the Tennessee Valley amounted to the erasure of local traditions and customs by the inexorable forces of modernity, channeled through the bureaucratic machinations of central planning. Such sharp criticism fueled the highly charged political debate centered on the TVA in the public sphere—a controversy that has figured centrally in historical accounts and cultural portrayals of the large-scale impact that the project has had on the region.

In a 1948 historical narrative of the Tennessee River, Donald Davidson takes this stand, as it were, by deploying the trope of cultural erasure in characteristic fashion. Davidson traces signal developments from the Civil War to the implementation of the TVA and the crucial role it played in the US mobilization for World War II. The prevailing tones are nostalgia and hostility toward the sweeping changes brought to the valley by the TVA, though Davidson does acknowledge some of the benefits to residents as a result of the comprehensive array of agency programs, particularly those designed to make small farms sustainable in a modern economy. Still, his lack of faith in the philosophy of central planning and in the capacity of officials in the federal government to check bureaucratic overreach frequently shows his anti-TVA hand. Davidson was the most vociferous opponent of the agency among his cohort of Southern Agrarians, who did not present a united front on this particular matter, despite sharing a general sense that the New Deal was detrimental to a distinctive regional identity and culture.[2] Accordingly, Davidson casts the vast infrastructure as "the Great Leviathan" unleashed on the bucolic valley by "the calculating eyes of TVA directors and their staff of experts" envisioning "great engineering works, with whatever might be added of social engineering." For Davidson, the resulting losses due to the TVA's "encroachments" are extensive and do irreparable damage to local history and the revered "way of life" in the region. He bemoans families uprooted "from homes where, in symbol or in fact, the Revolutionary sword or the pioneer rifle still hung above the mantel." The sweeping change extinguishes fires burning in the hearth, "as old as the Republic itself," and effaces "old graveyards" along with other historical landmarks.[3]

Davidson's narrative enacts the posture that Allen Tate famously describes in "The New Provincialism," his 1945 essay identifying a recent burst of literary achievement in the South that he marked as already a thing of the past. Using World War I as a line of demarcation between the modern and premodern epochs, Tate writes that in the aftermath of the defining conflict, "the South re-entered the world—but gave a backward glance as it skipped over the border," thus remaining entranced by the spell of a mythic history while planted in the midst of an alienating modernity.[4] As a special effect of this backward glance, the presence of the past became a preoccupation in what Tate identified, and scholars establishing the field of southern literary studies later endorsed, as a bona fide "renascence." This outpouring of literary expression tapped modernism as a source of formal and thematic properties for rendering the melancholia and alienation felt by the Agrarians and others similarly inclined (whether in reality or in fiction) as representative of a whole southern consciousness. The subsequent installment of the Southern Agrarians as the fulcrum of a regional response to the forces of modernity shaped the literary history of US modernism, as the influence of the New Criticism on the post–World War II formation of the American literary canon obscured or erased other encounters with modernism in the region. In recent years, scholars in southern studies have been working to recover the losses and to rethink southern modernism.[5]

The ongoing project of rethinking southern modernism stands to reap substantial benefits from paying close attention to the cultural productions of the Tennessee Valley Authority in the 1930s and early 1940s. This specialized body of work testifies to the intricate relationship between the federal government and the culture industry that formed during the Depression. As Michael Szalay points out, "The New Deal's massive and often bureaucratic engagement with the consumption and production of art . . . makes it difficult to separate out questions of modernist form from the institutional apparatus of the state."[6] Emerging from this arrangement, a subset of TVA modernism consisted of work by writers, filmmakers, photographers, and artists enlisted to promote the agency by figuring the valley as a site of rehabilitation, a productive space for imagining what regional planning and technological progress might mean for the future of the nation. David Lilienthal, one of the initial triumvirate of TVA directors, applied this strategy to the composition of *TVA: Democracy on the March,* a text that combines memoir and advocacy, standing in contrast to Davidson's paean to the imperiled landscape and folkways of the valley. "This is a book about the future," Lilienthal writes in the opening line. Nevertheless, he soon turns to the mythic past for evidence to back a teleological claim that the TVA has remained faithful to the core principles of American democracy while proceeding on a course toward regional planning as the ideal (read: New Deal) model of federal governance.[7]

The temporal scope forged by Lilienthal is characteristic of the cultural work that the TVA commissioned in that it is fitted for casting the preferred "forward glance"—a gesture that takes an alternative approach to modernism staged by agency-enlisted artists. This approach was no less ideologically circumscribed than that of the Southern Agrarians, given that, as Szalay observes, "during the thirties and forties, accounts of form did not aspire to be anything but ideological."[8] For artists involved in the TVA endeavor, the properties of modernism served as tools for working to impose an aesthetic of formal resolution, whether applied to material problems or to the temporal divide between the premodern and the modern used to distinguish the region from the nation. Two standout examples from different mediums evince how artists worked along these lines, exercising creativity within a clearly defined purview that enabled TVA modernism to flourish: *Power,* a play written by Arthur Arent and originally produced in 1937 by the Living Newspaper Unit, a part of the Federal Theatre Project (FTP), and *The River,* Pare Lorentz's influential 1938 documentary film outlining the history of severe flooding in the Mississippi River Valley and touting TVA flood-control projects as the most effective measures of prevention.

When *Power* premiered at the Ritz Theatre in New York City on February 23, 1937, it presented the audience with an ambitious spectacle of theatrical innovation and pointed commentary shaped by earnest political intentions. The script by Arent, who had served as the managing editor of the Living Newspaper Unit since its formation in 1935, was the basis of a production comprising thirty-three scenes and featuring eighty-eight actors, many of whom were nonprofessionals recruited in a desperate attempt to fill empty roles in time for the play's opening night. The production design included a loudspeaker and bright spotlights combined with a multimedia display of text slides, photographs, and film footage projected onto a large scrim. By this time, such outsized theatricality was a trademark of the Living Newspaper Unit—an approach established by influential director Joseph Losey and stage designer Nicholas Ray, who had collaborated on the controversial productions of *Triple-A Plowed Under* (1936) and *Injunction Granted* (1936). They found the theory and practice of experimental Soviet director and producer Vsevolod Meyerhold an inspirational alternative to the naturalistic style of the Stanislavsky school that was taking root in the famed Group Theatre, founded in 1931. Losey and Ray wound up having to resign their posts under political pressure from opponents of the Federal Theatre Project who complained that its plays were little more than leftist mouthpieces funded by federal tax dollars. Despite the controversy, the FTP pressed forward with *Power,* a project that weighed in on the debate surrounding the TVA in real time, even as it eschewed conventional realism as a matter of course. As opening night approached, the US Supreme Court was poised to issue a key ruling on whether or not the TVA charter was constitutional—a potential outcome that had Arent on call to make a quick revision that would answer the question about judicial action left hanging at the play's end. To heighten the sense of urgency, the director, Brett Warren, called for the actors to dispense with theatrical realism by breaking the illusion of the fourth wall. It was a move designed to confront the audience with the argument that electric power should be a fixture of the commons available for the greater good rather than a commodity produced and sold for corporate profit. In making a strong case for the TVA, *Power* incorporated a blend of elements taken from seemingly disparate sources, ranging from the theatrical traditions of vaudeville and agitprop to the aesthetics of cinema adapted for the stage. Jane de Hart Mathews succinctly describes the result: "It was exuberant theater—melodramatic and exciting. It was also propaganda."[9]

The presentation of a united front in *Power* took shape from a complementary mission and shared beliefs among officials in charge of the FTP and the TVA. As Kurt Eisen notes, the key aims of the two agencies were compatible, since the TVA was working to provide light while the FTP endeavored to spread enlightenment in the form of "cultural enfranchisement."[10] The interagency alliance gained additional strength from an abiding faith in technological progress, as well as a firmly held commitment to regional planning as the most effective structure for enabling federal agencies to deliver essential public services. Hallie Flanagan, the FTP director, sided with the TVA triumvirate in viewing affordable electric power as an issue capable of moving public discourse beyond the entrenched politics of the New Deal. The play's successful opening in New York, as demonstrated by brisk advance ticket sales and meaningful critical acclaim, suggested that this theory might be grounded in more than just wishful thinking.[11] Indeed, the initial run spawned a revival at the Ritz in 1938 and five more productions by regional companies of the FTP from 1937 to 1938, including runs in the Northeast, Midwest, and Pacific Northwest. The most notable of these productions was in Seattle, where the portrayal of the Tennessee Valley under transformation gave backers of a similar project proposed for Washington's Columbia River a hand up in a heated public debate.

It is important to note that the production of the South in *Power* was never staged in the South for several reasons—foremost among them the FTP's commitment to integrated casting and, as Eisen suggests, the challenge of gaining a foothold in a region with a dominant culture resistant to storytelling in the service of federal intervention.[12] If *Power* had played in the South, audiences likely would have found its initial foray into the region—the turn to the Tennessee River Valley setting late in the first act—not at all surprising. As the script shows, Arent's project of mapping a geography of uneven development according to access (or the lack thereof) to electric power relies initially on standard coordinates. A prologue that opens scene 15 describes the valley as a place cast in amber for far too long—an anachronistic locale on the periphery far removed from the rapidly expanding conveniences of modernity available in urban centers. The stage direction calls for film footage of the valley projected onto a scrim as a loudspeaker voice describes "a region blighted by misuse of land," populated by people working—if they can find work at all—in vocations deemed "primitive, a throwback to an earlier America," and suffering from social ills proclaimed in an ominous litany. "Meanwhile, the entire country seeks cheap electric power," blares the loudspeaker, the introductory adverb making the spatial transition from a regional to a national framework and establishing a temporal split exposing the preexisting condition of a wide gap in modernization.[13] In establishing the valley as one of *Power*'s multiple settings, then, this prologue uses the standard formulation of "the problem South." Natalie J. Ring explains that this commonly held view of the region from the late nineteenth to the mid-twentieth century defined it as "backward and a potentially catastrophic space," set against the spatial and temporal domain of the progressive nation-state.[14] On these grounds, *Power* anticipated another text that soon emerged under the auspices of the New Deal: the 1938 special report commissioned by the Roosevelt administration that identified the South as "the Nation's no. 1 economic problem—the Nation's problem, not merely the South's."[15]

Though Arent's script evokes a hidebound and debilitated South, it does so only fleetingly and in the service of charting an alternate course—a deviation from the familiar cultural script that plays out boldly and experimentally in subsequent scenes. As Ring documents, the paradigm of the region as the nation's problem tended to go hand in hand with the idea that it served as "the custodian of tradition"—at once a site of authenticity" and an object of "nostalgic yearning for the past."[16] Contrastingly, however, *Power* portrays the TVA's steady hand in guiding southern traditionalism into productive harmony with the newfangled ideas and inventions associated with technological progress. One sequence of related scenes involves a farmer struggling to read by the dim light of a kerosene lamp while resigned to the belief that power companies will never "string lights" to the countryside because they have decided that rural electrification is cost prohibitive. In response, the farmer's wife issues a call to action by urging her husband to channel the fighting spirit of "Andy Jackson": "Tell 'em you're an American citizen! Tell 'em you're sick and tired of lookin' at fans and heaters and vacuums and dish-washin' machines in catalogues, that you'd like to *use* 'em for a change!" Here, as in other scenes, Arent constructs citizens as consumers, making them popular (and populist) mouthpieces for the play's endorsement of public utilities as engines of economic expansion. By this time, the South was familiar ground for staging an appeal to the ideal of the yeoman farmer, but in this case the mythic past reinforces the demand for access to modernity. "We need light!" declares a small farmer late in the play, channeling the titular force in a material and symbolic statement that frames consumer choice and participation in the march of technological advancement as logical extensions of the basic rights of the "common man" trumpeted in the populist tradition of Jacksonian democracy.[17] While Davidson's people of the valley mourn the loss of objects that symbolize an endangered material culture measured in units of rustic value—the Revolutionary War sword disappeared from the mantel, for example—Arent's would-be rural consumers seek access to a mass culture flush with gadgets that promise a new and more convenient southern "way of life."

Although *Power* underlines a rural/urban divide in dramatizing the history and current conditions of electrification, the play is at pains to make the case for a rural-urban alliance against the power companies forged in response to industry practices that are portrayed as exploitative of customers in the city and dismissive of people in the country who aspire to customer status. Through a theatrical effect reminiscent of montage in film, *Power* weaves these experiences separated by distance together into a dramatic rhetorical fabric that posits access and affordability as compatible issues with the potential to inspire solidarity across the modernization divide. The scene featuring the farmer urged to channel the spirit of Andrew Jackson, for instance, is composed of a sequence of sub-scenes (labeled "A-E" in the script) that move back and forth between rural and urban settings in an attempt to impose a formal reconciliation. As the action unfolds, small farm families contend with the inadequacy of kerosene lamps, while their urbanite counterparts in an apartment lit bright with electric bulbs express outrage over a bill that they see as evidence of price gouging. One farmer urges a company to install power lines, only to be met with the answer that the residents themselves must bear the cost of the infrastructure; another farmer fends off workers installing lines on his land, without permission and by cover of darkness, as part of a deceitful, preemptive industry ploy to corner the market before the local municipality starts providing electric service at a relatively low cost. In a parallel urban sub-scene, meanwhile, a character designated only as "City Man"—the name is indicative of how Arent renders individuals as abstractions in service of the play's agenda—appeals to a public official overseeing practices in the utilities industry to work on lowering rates for customers rather than ensuring high-profit margins for power companies.

Eventually, these common causes find a means of uniting in the form of the TVA: the loudspeaker heralds the founding of the agency as a banner day for the country and sets the stage for a parade of enthusiastic supporters singing "The TVA Song." The stage directions describe a "motion picture of TVA activities and water flowing over Norris Dam," a key component of the dam system, projected onto a scrim. This visually engaging backdrop contributes to an innovative mixture of media and agitprop touting the agency as a crowning achievement in the history of electrification depicted in the play. The script calls for "The TVA Song" to start at the moment an actor playing the Clerk of the Senate recites the phrase "social and economic rehabilitation" as he reads from the congressional act authorizing the agency. That prompts a native of the valley, now a TVA worker, to proclaim that "Tennessee's gone wild. / The Government means business—/ It's working like a charm." But the note of triumph struck near the end of the first act is short-lived, as the legal challenges to the TVA by the power companies call into question the future viability of the project.

The politics of the moment imbue the living newspaper with heightened drama and embolden the turn to agitprop. Declaring that the issue of constitutionality hangs in the balance, the loudspeaker voice ends the play by defining what is at stake—no less than "the social and economic welfare of the people of the Tennessee Valley . . . and the character of future legislation for Boulder Dam and other projects through which the people seek to control their water power, to save their soil, and to obtain cheap energy."[18] Arent's reaching and urgent narrative strategy calls to mind the Shakespearean adage that "what's past is prologue," especially when considering how quickly the nod to the problem South in the prologue to scene 15 gives way to a redirected gaze that envisions the valley from a different perspective. This point of view looks away from a history of backwardness derived from uneven development to present an imagined future of electrified consumerism and egalitarianism guided by the principle of controlled consumption. A dramatic heavy hand forces the view away from the chronic social ills and economic stagnation that have plagued the region and made it a cautionary tale of sectionalism set against the dominant narrative of national progress. Instead, the portrayal of the TVA in *Power* positions it as an idealized emblem of historical and cultural continuity and a model of New Deal–style regionalism—a "solution South" signaling the potential down the line for an expanded grid, coursing with publically owned electric power, as a source of technological advancement, economic recovery, and national unity.[19]

In 1938, the year following *Power*'s successful run, Pare Lorentz released his documentary film *The River,* another work that sings the praises of the TVA (though never as literally as in *Power*'s rendition of "The TVA Song").[20] Lorentz, the writer and director, had already made a name for himself as a skilled filmmaker with a clear stake in the cultural politics surrounding the New Deal. In 1936, he wrote and directed *The Plow That Broke the Plains,* a documentary about the devastating effects of the Dust Bowl; the film was produced by the Resettlement Administration (RA), a New Deal agency charged with relocating displaced and dispossessed families to planned communities run by the federal government. After the RA became the Farm Security Administration (FSA), Lorentz worked for the newly formed agency on *The River,* turning to severe flooding for the subject matter and thus addressing the causes and effects of another type of natural disaster much on the minds of the American public in the wake of major floods in 1927, 1936, and 1937.

The focus on flooding meant that *The River* participated in a prevalent cultural trend that arguably reached its apex with the publication of John Steinbeck's novel *The Grapes of Wrath* in 1939 and the release of John Ford's film adaptation in 1940. Michael Denning explains that conservative commentators were turning to natural history to define the social and economic conditions of the Depression in cyclical terms for those faced with relentless hardship. Meanwhile, New Deal advocates favored state intervention in the ailing economy through relief and recovery designed to ease the pain and ultimately to reverse the dire economic course. The ensuing "tensions between these rhetorics of 'the people,'" Denning adds, contributed to an increasingly common practice across the political spectrum of using natural disasters as figurative expressions of economic fluctuation and hardship, so much so that these metaphors eventually became "deeply embedded in popular discourses about the depression." In this context, artists inclined to lend their support to the New Deal, as Arent did in *Power,* or enlisted to engage in outright promotion, as Lorentz was in *The River,* deployed the "trope of prefiguration" to cast agencies and programs as more than isolated, temporary responses to economic or ecological crises. "For the left," Denning argues, "the New Deal programs were celebrated not as solutions in themselves but as prefigurations of a future democratic and collective social order."[21]

*The River* evinces this long-term perspective despite a problem-solution format that would seem to suggest more immediate concerns. It maps complementary riparian and historical paths along the Mississippi River and its tributaries that eventually converge in the Tennessee River Valley to present the TVA system of dams and soil conservation practices as the most effective measures for achieving sustained flood control and thus for averting further loss of life and property.[22] Lorentz's advocacy of the TVA in visual culture was an extension of a strategy that the agency had been using since its inception to cast its designs in a favorable light.[23] In the hands of Lorentz, the emergent genre of documentary filmmaking could render the programs and monumental infrastructure of the TVA—the massive dams, engines, and turbines—so as to reconcile in aesthetic terms seemingly contradictory assertions made in public discourse by agency proponents: that this project was at once an extension of natural history in the region and evidence of "a new order of things" coming under the auspices of the New Deal to function as a unifying force in the nation.[24]

The aura of historicity forms at the outset of *The River,* with images of majestic sky and the introduction of a stentorian voice-over that announces the refrain of "down, down, down" as the film's guiding aesthetic principle. The phrase initially references the Mississippi River currents moving toward the Gulf of Mexico but subsequently describes the relentless economic and anthropogenic flows that navigate and reshape the river in a *longue durée* of intertwined modernization and commerce. Similarly conceived montage sequences alive with kinesthetic imagery and a rhetorical strategy informed by the idea that history repeats itself chronicle an unchecked profit motive driving exploitative labor practices and failures in environmental stewardship over time. Lorentz's skillful editing lends formal expression to the idea of historical repetition—a prime example of how "*The River* makes effective use of cutting to reinforce thematic messages," as Peter Rollins observes.[25] Despite a short runtime of thirty-two minutes, the film manages to cover a wide geographical and historical expanse, as Lorentz centers attention on the Mississippi River Valley and its inhabitants and then pans outward at strategic instances to illustrate connections to broader historical developments and social and economic patterns.

In setting the regional focus and defining the issue of severe flooding Lorentz draws on the stock narrative of the problem South, relying on it far more extensively to set the stage than Arent does in *Power.* This approach early on lays the groundwork for the solution to come by the film's end: the presentation of the TVA with an air of both viability and inevitability and with the contention, as in *Power,* that the project is worthy of future emulation and thus has far-reaching applications and implications. At the outset, the narration references not the water but the settlers and planters who flooded the Mississippi River Valley, staking claims and clearing land in hopes of accumulating wealth in a cotton economy rapidly expanding on a global scale. Portrayals of enslaved people operating mule-driven plows in cotton fields give way to shots of steamboats chugging downriver to deliver the precious cargo, as the narrator explains that they "sent our commerce out to sea." Footage of laborers working mechanistically to load cotton bales onto steamboats illustrates how the forces of supply and demand "rolled them down the river." With this sequence, *The River* opens a concise chapter on the major role of the cotton trade in shaping economic and environmental factors that contributed to the severe flooding crisis in the future.

A scrolling shot featuring a newspaper reprint of the official statement of surrender delivered by Robert E. Lee at Appomattox marks the Civil War section of the chapter and makes the specter of sectionalism loom large for obvious reasons. "We fought a war and kept the west bank of the river free of slavery forever," intones the narrator, "but we left the Old South impoverished and stricken—doubly stricken." Focused on the devastating effects of cotton monoculture and war, Lorentz presents the South as a stage where "the tragedy of land twice impoverished" had its premiere in the nineteenth century and continues its run unabated in the twentieth. This point becomes clear later with a sequence documenting what the voice-over describes as "sharecroppers down on their knees, a share of the crop their only security—no home, no land, aimless, footloose, and impoverished" and illustrating in stark fashion the structural problems and social ills entailed in the system of sharecropping that replaced chattel slavery but retained the guiding principle of brutal labor exploitation. Black-and-white footage of the wan, haggard faces of poor white families staring into the camera with a mixture of exhaustion and resilience projects what was at the time, and certainly is by now, the familiar documentary aesthetic fostered by the FSA. The effect gives new meaning to the term "motion picture," making it appear that the subjects of a Walker Evans or Margaret Bourke-White photograph have broken the arresting spell of the medium to gain some measure of mobility. Nevertheless, these subjects remain fixed by the gaze of Depression documentary, which is characteristically unsettled by the fine line between ethical exposure and prurient fascination, between recognizing subjects as human beings in need and objectifying them as exoticized Others on display in a visual spectacle of abjection.

The tension that arises from trying to incorporate regionally inflected history and images of abjection into the broader narrative of progress under construction is detectable in the fraught pronoun usage in the voice-over. The "we" that the narrator imposes on the account struggles to signify a unified point of view, a national subjectivity, due to the heavy emphasis placed on southern exceptionalism in defining the roots of the problem in need of a solution. But, like Arent in *Power,* Lorentz attempts to steer *The River* away from sectionalism by way of formal tactics that convey an overriding impression of connection between disparate parts of the country, especially the divide between a putatively rural South and distant hubs of urban industrialization. Toward this end, Lorentz intersperses the sequences focused on the history of the cotton economy with images and narration that define the Mississippi River and its tributaries as channels giving rise to industrialization and modern commerce in the nation. The focus shifts to massive deforestation by the timber industry as it moves its product down the Mississippi and to mountaintop removal practiced by mining operations that send coal downriver on a journey to worldwide markets. The images of denuded and defaced landscapes and of vast floodscapes engulfing communities call to mind works of modern art with their abstract, uncanny distortions of the natural world. Shots of factories in which machinery churns and molten steel poured into giant vats sends sparks spewing into the air replicate both the mechanistic labor demanded by the cotton economy and the increasingly unchecked momentum and volume of the river as anthropogenic erosion worsens and flood stages rise to alarming levels. "We built a hundred cities and a thousand towns," proclaims the narrator, "but at what a cost." In this instance, panoramic views of city skylines appear onscreen, only to have their awe-inspiring effects diminished by the dose of reality that comes with the sobering subordinate clause. Where *Power* uses a staged variation on montage to envision a rural-urban alliance powered by a common interest in widely accessible and affordable electricity, *The River* employs the original cinematic technique to bridge the gap with an emphasis on the effects of an insatiable materialism that seemingly knows no bounds.[26] Along these lines, the parallel montage sequences cast the cotton economy not as precapitalist but as proto-capitalist, linking the plantation in the South to the factory in the North, so as to expose a shared profit motive driving chronic environmental degradation over time.

The related currents that *The River* traces visually and narratively comprise what might be termed a stream of historical consciousness—a pattern that trends downward as spatial and temporal flows merge in the problem section to illustrate how the contemporaneous moment of crisis in the Mississippi River Valley has come to pass. With the transition to the solution, however, it becomes apparent that this historical approach has been carefully shaped to run along a tributary path toward the Tennessee River Valley and to the crux of the argument for the TVA—the same narrative strategy used in *Power.*

The coordinates appear in graphic form as an animated map onscreen locates the region within the Greater Mississippi Valley and the vast network of waterways feeding into the Mississippi River. "First came the dams," says the voice-over, inserting the TVA chapter into the broader narrative as a sort of modern creation myth. Shots of explosives detonated on construction sites resemble earlier images of sparks flying from molten steel and footage of raging floodwaters with crashing waves, except that the ominous tones of the narration and score have been replaced by a soothing sense of order reinforced by the scenes of tranquil reservoirs formed as part of the dam system. The subsequent description of flood-control projects, reforestation initiatives, and soil-conservation practices—accompanied by illustrative shots of colossal dams, workers planting trees, and planned communities with all the modern conveniences—supplants the litany of past labor exploitation, rampant materialism, and environmental degradation. The film thus conveys the impression that the control exerted by the TVA is not only prudent but also perfectly "natural" in striking a balance between economic and ecological concerns to achieve the goal of controlled consumption.

*The River* ends on essentially the same note as *Power*—an outcome that is not surprising, given their shared interest in trumpeting the benefits of the TVA. "Where there is water, there is power," declares the voice-over, casting hydroelectric plants as multipurpose generators with the capacity to produce light, fuel sustainable economic expansion, and promote greater social mobility. Low-angle shots of newly installed power lines in the valley reveal the logistical means to such ambitious ends. The fetish of modern technology and infrastructure on display in the solution section of the film specifically is characteristic of TVA modernism generally. As representative texts, *The River* and *Power* project the vision of a widening grid coursing with material and symbolic possibilities, not least the prospect of making regional planning and rural electrification conduits of national unification and progress. As the TVA continued to pursue this goal, it followed the course of the utilities industry by relying increasingly on coal plants to meet the heavy demand for electricity as the Depression gave way to postwar economic expansion and the ideal of controlled consumption was lost to the rise of mass consumption. In retrospect, this future that the artists could not see has exposed the limited scope of the forward glance of TVA modernism—a reason that makes it all the more worthy of study in the contemporary moment. From this standpoint, it is apparent that the dream of an expansive grid enabling greater access to power that the artists creatively imagined on behalf of the TVA did come true—but at what a cost.

## NOTES

1. Samuel I. Rosenman, *The Public Papers and Addresses of Franklin Delano Roosevelt: The Year of Crisis, 1933* (New York: Random House, 1938), 122, 122-23.

2. See Shapiro, "The Southern Agrarians and the Tennessee Valley Authority," *American Quarterly* 22, no. 4 (Winter 1970): 791–806, for an overview of the scholarly consensus on Southern Agrarian antipathy toward the TVA and compelling evidence for a nuanced understanding that allows for division in the ranks.

3. Donald Davidson, *The Tennessee*, vol. 2, *The New River: Civil War to TVA* (1948; Nashville: J. S. Sanders, 1992), 251, 237. Davidson's sense of profound loss and displacement resonates in later cultural depictions of forced flooding conducted by the TVA. See, e.g., Robert Penn Warren's novel *Flood: A Romance of Our Time* (1963; Baton Rouge: Louisiana State University Press, 2003). In it, Warren tells the story of Bradwell Tolliver, a writer who returns to his hometown of Fiddlersburg, Tennessee, to work on a film script about the community before it is inundated for dam construction. Tolliver becomes immersed in melancholia as he experiences alienation mixed with deep feelings of anticipatory loss.

4. Allen Tate, "The New Provincialism," *Essays of Four Decades* (Chicago: Swallow, 1968), 545.

5. See, e.g., Leigh Anne Duck, *The Nation's Region: Southern Modernism, Segregation, and U.S. Nationalism* (Athens: University of Georgia Press, 2006). This scholarship has also involved questioning the centrality of the Agrarians and the paradigm of the Southern Renascence in defining southern literature beyond modernism. For an example of this approach, see Martyn Bone, *The Postsouthern Sense of Place in Contemporary Fiction* (Baton Rouge: Louisiana State University Press, 2005).

6. Michael Szalay, *New Deal Modernism: American Literature and the Invention of the Welfare State* (Durham: Duke University Press, 2000), 6.

7. David Lilienthal, *TVA: Democracy on the March* (New York: Harper and Brothers, 1944), xi. Roosevelt appointed Lilienthal, along with Arthur Morgan and Harcourt Morgan, to serve on a board of directors responsible for overseeing the TVA. For more on Lilienthal's influence on the TVA, see Edwin C. Hargrove, *Prisoners of Myth: The Leadership of the Tennessee Valley Authority, 1933–1990* (Princeton: Princeton University Press, 1994), and C. Herman Pritchett, *The Tennessee Valley Authority: A Study in Public Administration* (Chapel Hill: University of North Carolina Press, 1943).

8. Szalay, *New Deal Modernism*, 7.

9. Jane de Hart Mathews, *The Federal Theatre, 1935–1939: Plays, Relief, and Politics* (Princeton: Princeton University Press, 1967), 113.

10. Kurt Eisen, "Circulating *Power*: National Theatre as Public Utility in the Federal Theatre Project," *Theatre Symposium* 9 (2001): 39.

11. In New York City, sixty thousand people purchased advance tickets. The production got an added boost from a favorable review by Brooks Atkinson, the influential theater critic for the *New York Times* (Mathews, *The Federal Theatre,* 113).

12. Eisen, "Circulating *Power,*" 41.

13. Arthur Arent, *Power,* in *Federal Theatre Plays,* ed. Pierre De Rohan (New York: Da Capo, 1973), 61, 62.

14. Natalie J. Ring, *The Problem South: Region, Empire, and the New Liberal State, 1880–1930* (Athens: University of Georgia Press, 2012), 15.

15. National Emergency Council, *Report on Economic Conditions of the South* (Washington, DC: US Government Printing Office, 1938), https://archive.org/details/reportoneconomicoo nati (accessed Aug. 15, 2015).

16. Ring, *The Problem South,* 15.

17. Arent, *Power,* 63, 84.

18. Ibid., 68, 69, 91.

19. Advocates of regional planning tended to use the terms "sectionalism" and "regionalism" as defined by the influential sociologist Howard Odum: the former term connotes a line of thinking that privileges local or regional authority, as in the trumpeting of "states' rights," while the latter refers to the view that national interests should guide decisions at the local or regional level. See Howard Odum, "Regionalism vs. Sectionalism in the South's Place in the National Economy," *Journal of Social Forces* 12 (Mar. 1934): 338–54. For more on the material and symbolic implications of electrification in the context of national identity, see David E. Nye, *Electrifying America: Social Meanings of a New Technology* (Cambridge, MA: MIT Press).

20. *The River,* directed by Pare Lorentz, *Our Daily Bread and Other Films of the Depression* (1938; Chatsworth, CA: Image Entertainment, 1999), DVD.

21. Denning, *The Cultural Front: The Laboring of American Culture in the Twentieth Century* (New York: Verso, 1997), 265, 266–67.

22. For a detailed description of the film's structure as a rhetorical strategy, see Robin Murray and Joe Heumann, "Environmental Catastrophe in Pare Lorentz's *The River* and Elia Kazan's *Wild River:* The TVA, Politics, and the Environment," *Studies in Popular Culture* 27, no. 2 (2004): 47–48.

23. In addition to documentary film, photography was a medium that the TVA relied on heavily in its promotional efforts. At the time *The River* was produced, Charles Krutch was serving as the official TVA photographer, mixing the eagle eye of a social documentarian with the abstract perspective of a high modernist to capture compelling images of TVA infrastructure and residents of the valley employed or assisted by the agency. The influence of Krutch's photography on *The River* is readily apparent in the shots of dams that present them as emblems of modern design fitting into and working in harmony with the natural landscape. See R. L. Duffus, *The Valley and Its People: A Portrait of TVA* (New York: Knopf, 1946), which blends Krutch's photography with a laudatory narrative of the TVA in the "picture book" format that became popular during the Depression.

24. The phrase comes from Roosevelt's second inaugural address, delivered in 1937. John Gabriel Hunt, ed., *The Essential Franklin Delano Roosevelt* (New York: Random House, 1995), 82.

25. Peter Rollins, "Ideology and Film Rhetoric: Three Documentaries of the New Deal Era (1936–1941)," in *Hollywood as Historian: American Film in a Cultural Context,*" rev. ed., ed Peter. Rollins (Lexington: University Press of Kentucky, 1983), 41.

26. Rollins draws on Sergei Eisenstein's concept of "intellectual montage" to explain how Lorentz makes rhetorical use of the cinematic technique, especially in the solution section of *The River* that endorses the New Deal philosophy of technological innovation geared toward "controlled consumption" ("Ideology and Film Rhetoric," 42).

# IV

# RURAL REPRESENTATIONS AND REALITIES

# We Shall Not Be Moved

## *Highlander Folk School's Cultural Radicalism in the Great Depression*

EMILY SENEFELD

In 1932, Don West and Myles Horton, two former seminarians turned activists, established the Highlander Folk School in Grundy County, Tennessee, one of the poorest counties in the nation. From the outset, its founders identified two primary goals for the school—"to conserve and enrich the indigenous cultural values of the mountains" and "to educate rural and industrial leaders for a new social order." During the 1930s, staff members such as Ralph Tefferteller and Zilphia Horton developed cultural programs that reflected the convergence of these goals; they taught folk music and dancing to southern workers at their workshops in order to build solidarity for the labor movement, for example. In March 1937, Tefferteller and Zilphia Horton produced a live broadcast for the British Broadcasting Corporation (BBC), narrated by Felix Greene, the North American Representative for the BBC. The broadcast captures Highlander's strategy for its cultural programs at a crucial turning point—not only were its musical directors developing an increasingly radical interpretation of folk culture, but they were also collaborating with fellow activists by authoring labor songbooks, teaching folk dances, creating labor dramas, and producing the documentary *People of the Cumberland*. In early 1937, the Highlander Folk School's role in the national labor movement was also expanding, as its activists participated in the Textile Workers Organizing Committee's (TWOC) unionizing drive in the South. In the broadcast, as in Highlander's real-life activism of the period, its staff used the appeal of "Appalachian" folk culture's apparent traditionalism to build support for their radical ideology.[1]

Highlander Folk School played a central role in the "cultural front" of southern activists that emerged during the Great Depression.[2] Its cultural programs reinforced the activists' relationships with other radical organizations developing working-class cultural forms. Labor unions and labor colleges had used music in their activism for decades, and the International Workers of the World (Wobblies) had published songbooks of labor music as early as 1901. By the late 1930s, folk music was becoming increasingly popular within the Old Left as an element of the Popular Front–era focus on "indigenous peoples' cultures." Much of the scholarly attention and public interest in the folk music of this period has focused on figures such as Alan Lomax and the performers Woody Guthrie and Pete Seeger, who were based primarily in the Northeast. This broadcast demonstrates how southern activists such as Highlander's staff and their colleagues in Arkansas—Claude Williams, John Handcox, and Lee Hays—utilized "indigenous" musical forms to gain the support of workers. Two decades later, civil rights activists successfully revived these cultural strategies in their grassroots organizing.[3]

Highlander's staff began incorporating folk music into their programs within the school's first year in order to gain the support of skeptical neighbors in rural Grundy County. The broadcast's depiction of a square dance was hardly coincidental, as the school hosted the dances regularly for visiting union members and residents of the village of Summerfield. The staff opened a music center and library as forms of outreach, for, as Myles Horton suggested, "Supplying food, clothing, and shelter ha[d] sapped [the local people] of any interest in cultural things." The folk-culture programs built on the educational model of the Danish folk schools, which West and Horton separately had traveled to Denmark to observe during the early 1930s. Bishop Nikolai Grundtvig had first created this model in the mid-nineteenth century, and the schools taught peasants Danish music, mythology, and language as a means of collective political empowerment. Horton later described why he admired the schools' cultural emphasis: "Through songs and poetry, students could grasp truths that might otherwise escape them, and . . . singing in unison was an effective way of inspiring people and bringing them closer together."[4] However, Highlander's cultural programs also served the political goal of counteracting the harsh criticism and accusations of Communism the school received from nearby residents, newspaper writers, and leading industrialists throughout its three decades in this location. Much like Highlander's promotional materials of the period, the broadcast depicts the dance as "wholesome recreation." Narrator Felix Greene depicts a multigenerational group—"young boys and girls, old wrinkled men and white-haired old women, and little children." He likely exaggerates the size of the crowd as "hundreds of people . . . from all over the countryside" in order to present Highlander's significance as the social center of the community. As shown in the broadcast, Highlander's square dances provided an effective vehicle for its radical message precisely because they avoided the negative connotation of contemporary labor conflicts.[5]

In the "Broadcast to England," Highlander's staff and Greene attempt to connect with their British listeners by invoking a sense of shared tradition between the two countries. In his narration, Greene directly invokes the apparent ties between Appalachian and Anglo-Saxon culture: "Mothers still tell their children stories passed down through three centuries . . . old and young still sing the ballads sung in Scotland in Queen Elizabeth's time; still dance the old square dances." This interpretation of Appalachia was by no means limited to Greene. Having likely spent little time there, he appears to draw from the interpretation of authors such as Cecil Sharp, a British scholar of American folk music who in 1917 published the influential book, *English Folk Songs from the Southern Appalachians.* Sharp popularized the existing theory that natives of the southern mountains were "the conservators of the essential culture of America," which he narrowly defined as white and Anglo-Saxon. In the decade that followed, American public interest in the nation's British roots only increased, as a result of the country's military alliance with Great Britain.[6] Popular culture of the Great Depression reflected a growing interest in the American "folk"; as historians have argued, the concept of "tradition" was especially appealing because of the political and economic uncertainty that marked the 1930s.[7] Greene and his BBC colleague Alistair Cooke both explored American folk culture in programs of this period; Cooke produced the radio program "I Hear America Singing" with collector Alan Lomax, using new recordings from the Library of Congress. In his narration, Greene emphasizes the authenticity of the music in the broadcast as Anglo-Saxon: "This isn't a make-believe tradition carried on merely for old time's sake, but it's how they still live and feel today." In this way, he attempts to draw listeners into the broadcast's music by building on existing public interest in the cultural links between America and Great Britain.[8]

The broadcast emphasizes the "authenticity" of the folk music in order to present the southern mountaineers as modern-day Anglo-Saxons. Historians have shown that authors such as Cecil Sharp, along with the educators of settlement schools, narrowly defined "authentic" Appalachian music as folk ballads, excluding more modern genres such as vaudeville, ragtime, and minstrel songs. As in Sharp's scholarship, the songs in the broadcast—"The Old Man Who Lived on a Hill," "The Brave Volunteer," "The Crawdad Song," and "The Young Man Who Wouldn't Haul Corn"—present the residents as a "'leisurely and cheery people'" in a "primitive" region, a prevalent stereotype of Appalachia in American art, literature, and music of the Great Depression.[9] Although Greene highlights the poverty of the region, he also exaggerates the cultural and political isolation of the local people: "The march forward of American civilization has swept by them. Industrial advances hardly touch them." Similarly, he states, "These folks may be poor . . . may be hopelessly ignorant, it's true that many of them have never seen a train, or a town larger than their local village." In fact, a section of the Dixie Highway, which ran from Chicago to Miami, had been constructed nearby more than a decade earlier. Greene's portrayal was by no means accurate, but it served to appeal to listeners by presenting the view of the region that predominated in cultural depictions of Appalachia during the early twentieth century.[10]

In their activism, the directors of Highlander's cultural programs depicted themselves as "reviving" a "dormant" Appalachian folk culture. Zilphia Horton collected over a thousand southern folk songs during her twenty-year tenure as musical director. A 1935 article from the school's newspaper, the *Highlander Fling,* expresses the school's interpretation of Appalachian culture: "The Southern mountains have one of the richest folk cultures of any Folk group in America . . . With the coming of radio, the concrete highway, modern industry, and commercialized recreation, much that is best in this tradition is fast passing away."[11] As evidenced by the folk songs in the broadcast, Highlander's cultural program to some extent drew upon the definitions of "Appalachian" folk music developed in earlier folk schools. However, Highlander's staff eschewed those educators' interpretation of culture as a means of moral reform. Institutions such as the Hindman School in Kentucky and the John C. Campbell School in North Carolina had sought to improve local residents' economic position through agricultural training and the production of folk handicrafts such as baskets.[12] In contrast, Highlander's staff increasingly treated folk music and dancing as tools for expanding the southern labor movement. Although its musical directors viewed themselves as restoring an indigenous folk culture, much like the Danish folk schools had done, they were likely aware that they were teaching these "folk" forms to the local people. For example, the school's 1934 Annual Report boasts that "long forgotten folk dances have been retaught." Ralph Tefferteller and Zilphia Horton led folk songs and dances not only in their union workshops but also on the picket line to "[keep] the morale of the strikers at a high level." Highlander's 1938 Annual Report described how folk dancing contributed to labor organizing: "As part of our program for developing cultural activities around the labor movement, a wide-spread interest in folk dancing has been stimulated . . . we have not found a recreational medium to compare with square dancing as a means of developing solidarity and group loyalties." This statement suggests that, by the time of this broadcast, Highlander's staff were conceptualizing folk culture as a means to build working class "solidarity."[13]

In their activism of this period, Highlander's educators employed music that they viewed as particularly appealing to southern workers. Beginning in 1937, Highlander's activists, and especially Myles Horton, began to collaborate closely with the Textile Workers Organizing Committee campaign, which aimed to strengthen the bargaining position of workers throughout the country by unionizing those in the South, where many industrialists had moved their factories to take advantage of lower wages. While compiling a songbook for the TWOC in the late 1930s, Zilphia Horton wrote "Increasing requests for workers' songs for union groups in the South has called to our attention that there are comparatively few Southern workers' songs available with familiar tunes and content." By including labor songs that borrowed tunes from well-known hymns, patriotic songs, or ballads, such as "Rock-a-bye Baby," "Red River Valley," and "Dixie," Horton and other labor activists fulfilled a practical need of accommodating members who could not read music. They also enabled singers to relate to what Myles Horton described as the "emotional content" of the movement. By combining "familiar tunes" with labor-themed lyrics, they aimed to connect southern workers to the political goals of the national labor movement.[14]

In the "Broadcast to England," Highlander's staff used many of the songs from their songbooks and activism. The hymns exemplify how labor activists invoked workers' regional identities to develop support for the union movement. Harp songs such as "Wondrous Love," which is featured in the broadcast, took their name from the 1860s songbook *The Harp of Columbia,* published in East Tennessee. In his correspondence with Greene, Tefferteller emphasizes the authenticity of harp singing as an indigenous musical form in Appalachia: "These songs and this type of singing have been a real part of the lives of these people here in the mountains for well over one hundred years." Although the broadcast avoids directly mentioning race, the producers' inclusion of what Greene calls an "old white spiritual" dramatizes the severe poverty of Appalachia's workers in the Great Depression. Having previously described this "poverty" as "one that keeps them always within sight of starvation," Greene encourages the listeners' sympathy by arguing that the "mournful and discordant song . . . reflects something in these people's natures." Like African American spirituals, "Wondrous Love" draws heavily on the language of God's salvation from earthly tribulations, and the performers repeat the phrase, "What wondrous love is this / O my soul! / O my soul!" The producers' inclusion of "Wondrous Love" would no doubt surprise critics who viewed the school as communist, yet more radical organizations, including the Wobblies, socialists, and communists, had all emulated religious groups when they included songs and portable songbooks in their activism. Highlander and other southern activists similarly employed hymns as tunes for labor songs, including "(Give Me Those) Sixty Million Jobs," set to the tune of "Give Me That Old Time Religion," and "Solidarity Forever," set to "The Battle Hymn of the Republic." The activists' use of hymns likely "legitimiz[ed]" their activism because they avoided overt political messages in favor of broad religious themes.[15]

The producers' inclusion of songs in the "spiritual" mode—"Wondrous Love" and "No More Mourning"—embody the radical theology of Highlander's founders and other notable activists in the South. Don West had attended seminary at Vanderbilt under the tutelage of Alva Taylor, who encouraged students such as West and future Arkansas activists Claude Williams and Howard Kester in their support of the labor movement. Myles Horton studied at Union Theological Seminary in New York, which was a center for student activism. This was a radicalizing experience for Horton, as he interacted with communists, socialists, and with activists from unions such as the International Ladies Garment Workers Union. Horton had studied under Reinhold Niebuhr, a socialist who argued that many religious and political leaders had failed to address the uneven ownership of property which drove social conflict. Niebuhr supported an array of social causes in the 1930s and became one of Highlander's earliest and most vocal supporters. Prior to her arrival at Highlander from her native Arkansas, Zilphia Horton worked closely with Claude Williams, who had become highly controversial for espousing an interracial interpretation of Christianity that emphasized brotherhood and unity. Whereas some scholars would label these hymns "propaganda," they actually demonstrate how the activists' interpretation of Christianity bolstered their support for the labor movement.[16]

The song "No More Mourning" reflects how Highlander and its fellow activists were by the late 1930s already using southern hymns to build interracial cooperation in the labor movement. Highlander's activists had learned "No More Mourning" via John Handcox, a sharecropper in the Southern Tenant Farmers Union (STFU) who collaborated musically with Lee Hays. In 1939, Hays argued in an article for *New Masses* that "spirituals were ideal weapons for working class organization," as these songs had already been incorporated into the interracial STFU. Religion played a major role in STFU meetings, in part because both African American and white members shared a cultural knowledge of hymns and an emphasis on the scripture. Songs such as "No More Mourning" (also known as "Oh, Freedom") had become a rallying point for striking sharecroppers during the 1936 STFU strike. Felix Greene introduces the song in the broadcast by stating, "This song they're singing is one of the many old spirituals that have changed their words to meet new conditions." In the context of this broadcast, it dramatizes the labor conflict by utilizing the spiritual's context of slavery. Sung collectively by a large group, the first verse of "No More Mourning" opens with the repetition of the title phrase, allowing singers to join in: "No more mourning, no more mourning, / No more mourning after a while, / And before I'll be a slave, I'll be buried in my grave, / Take my place with those who loved and fought before." Decades later, civil rights activists such as Guy Carawan, who succeeded Zilphia Horton as musical director, included the song in mass meetings for the sit-in movement. These songs demonstrate how labor activists in the 1930s developed the very tactics for group singing that later spread through civil rights organizations in the late 1950s and early 1960s.[17]

By incorporating songs from the interracial union movement, Highlander's staff expanded their conception of the southern "folk" to include African Americans. Authors such as Cecil Sharp commonly had depicted American folk culture as Anglo-Saxon, a view that consciously excluded African Americans and immigrant groups. Even in the 1930s, organizers of events such as the White Top Folk Festival rejected African American performers.[18] Highlander's inclusion of African American culture represented broader shifts in the ideology of the Old Left. Beginning in the early 1930s, the Communist Party in particular had promoted African American music in their activism. In the same period, Alan and John Lomax recorded African Americans in southern prisons, most notably, Leadbelly. Although they to some extent "exoticized" these performers, they also used the apparent authenticity of this music to present African American folk culture as equal to Anglo-Saxon culture. In this way, such influential scholars and activists redefined America's "folk."[19]

Highlander's interest in African American music likely reflected these outside influences, but it also mirrored the school's increasing support for civil rights issues. Prior to the founding of Highlander, Myles Horton had argued that African Americans were "a 'new racial type created in America and thus more distinctively American' than other 'racial or national groups' in the country." However, in the early 1930s, Highlander's staff members still debated whether to invite African Americans to the school, out of fear of harming the relationship they were building with local residents. By 1936, they were calling attention to the need for interracial cooperation in the labor movement, and they hosted members of the STFU and an African American gospel group. Despite the inclusion of Handcox's song in this broadcast, the producers' failure to mention race indicates that Highlander's staff had yet to fully embrace the civil rights causes it would later champion.[20]

"We Shall Not Be Moved," which features prominently in this broadcast, is one example of a labor song from this period which was later revived by civil rights activists. Highlander staff and fellow activists in Arkansas played a significant role in popularizing the use of "zipper songs" in the labor movement. "Zipper songs" featured lyrics that were largely the same in each verse, with just a few words altered, and they built on the model of hymns. They also allowed activists to adapt lyrics and characters to local contexts, making them all the more persuasive. From 1936 to 1937, Lee Hays and Claude Williams collaborated with Handcox in creating "zipper songs" for the movement, including the labor song "Roll the Union On," which Highlander's labor chorus recorded and which became the title of People's Songs, Inc.'s first album. Hays argued that, "because they are very rhythmic and full of bounce, they're inviting." Among the songs in the broadcast, "We Shall Not Be Moved" is particularly upbeat, its tempo driven by hands clapping. Using this positive tone, the song evokes a universal language of workers' rights as citizens, rather than referencing individual strikes or unions. In general, Highlander's ideology projected the idea of workers' "freedom" as citizens. In one promotional letter from the period, a Highlander staffer argues that the school's role was to provide southern workers "those basic rights which they have been cheated out of in their desperate struggle to survive." The song evokes these same sentiments by linking the phrases "we're fighting for our freedom" and "we're fighting for our children" to the song's labor message—"we're backed up by the union." The prevalence of these same songs in the civil rights movement illustrates the continuity between the Old and New Left.[21]

The song "We Shall Not Be Moved" also demonstrates the key role that southern labor activists played in developing a repertoire of labor songs for the Old Left. The fact that it is introduced with the phrase "Let's sing one everybody knows!" may well indicate its prevalence in the labor movement of the Great Depression era. Zilphia Horton asserted that "Perhaps this song, more than any other one song, has held workers together when opposition was greatest." Communist organizers had carried the song "We Shall Not Be Moved" from miners in West Virginia to Brookwood Labor College in New York as early as 1931. Tefferteller wrote to Greene that the song was "being used all through the highlands where cotton textile mills have located and out into the cotton country itself." By the year this broadcast was produced, "No More Mourning" and "We Shall Not Be Moved" had been sung by members of the STFU at their convention in January 1937, performed in the Highlander play *Gumbo* by Lee Hays, and included in Hays's 1937 documentary, *America's Disinherited*. Hays and Handcox were each major influences on Pete Seeger, one of the best-known folk singers of the twentieth century. Seeger credited John Handcox's recordings with introducing him to southern labor music. After serving as Zilphia Horton's assistant at Highlander, Hays teamed with Seeger in New York to form the Almanacs, and later the Weavers and People's Songs, Inc.[22] The history of songs such as "We Shall Not Be Moved" suggests that their success lay in their circulation among radical organizations collaborating to create a usable working-class culture for America's labor movement.

During the 1930s and early 1940s, Highlander was a central element of a network of organizations, including labor unions such as the Congress of Industrial Organizations (CIO) and the STFU, which aimed to promote a working-class culture that would bolster support for the labor movement in the South. "Broadcast to England" includes many of the songs that Highlander used in songbooks, workshops, and on the picket line during this period. As the music and narration of the "Broadcast to England" illustrate, Highlander's cultural programs drew upon both conservative and radical interpretations of American folk culture. In their activism in general, they built on the existing appeal of music that would likely be viewed as "traditional" within the context of the Great Depression. Highlander's cultural radicalism contributed to the gains made by the school and the southern labor movement during the late 1930s, but its influence declined in the wake of the Red Scare that followed World War II. When Highlander shifted its focus to civil rights during the 1950s, Guy Carawan revived many of Zilphia Horton and

Ralph Tefferteller's cultural programs. Songs that Highlander had shared with workers and fellow activists in the late 1930s and early 1940s, such as "We Will Overcome" and "We Shall Not Be Moved," were once again being used as tools for grassroots organizing in the South. Although Highlander is perhaps best known for its civil rights activism, its successes built directly on the music and tactics developed in the southern labor movement during the Great Depression.[23]

## NOTES

1. "Highlander" is a term used colloquially by both scholars and those connected to the school. In 1961, the school was rechartered in a new location in Knoxville under the name Highlander Research and Education Center, and it remains in existence in New Market, Tennessee. John Glen, *Highlander: No Ordinary School,* 2nd ed. (Knoxville: University of Tennessee Press, 1996), 1–5, 27, 46–47; "Broadcast to England, 1937," FD 729–32, in the Highlander Research and Education Center Collection #20361, Southern Folklife Collection, Wilson Library, University of North Carolina at Chapel Hill. Felix Greene was the top BBC executive for the United States and Canada during this period, as well as a producer. In planning the broadcast, Tefferteller intended for it to be carried by Tennessee radio stations, yet, according to a contemporary account in the *Knoxville News-Sentinel,* the broadcast was carried only by the BBC. Jeremy Lewis, *Shades of Greene: One Generation of an English Family* (London: Vintage Books, 2010), 181; Bill Roberts, "It's in the Air," *Knoxville News-Sentinel,* Mar. 12, 1937; Ralph Tefferteller to "Hamp," Feb. 27, 1937, Zilphia Horton Folk Music Collection, Tennessee State Library and Archives (TSLA), IV-D-3, box 7:2.

2. This analysis builds on the scholarship of Michael Denning, who has argued that the radical activists and authors of the Great Depression era represent a "cultural front" that "reshaped American culture" by making labor a central concern. Michael Denning, *The Cultural Front: The Laboring of American Culture in the Twentieth Century* (London: Verso, 1996), xvi–xvii, 71–72.

3. Robert S. Cantwell, *When We Were Good: The Folk Revival* (Cambridge, MA: Harvard University Press, 1997), 88–90, 104–5; Michael Honey, *Sharecropper's Troubadour: John L. Handcox, the Southern Tenant Farmers' Union, and the African American Song Tradition* (New York: Palgrave Macmillan, 2013), 110–12, 142. While scholars such as Denning mention Highlander Folk School in their analyses, on the whole, the contributions of southern activists to the folk-song movement have not received sufficient scholarly attention. The most extensive recent analysis of Highlander's position within this movement has come from sociologist William Roy, who contends that music played only a minor role in Highlander's activism prior to the late 1940s and that Highlander's success in promoting music in the civil rights movement derived from its rejection of what he views as the Old Left's emphasis on individual performers. William Roy, *Reds, Whites, and Blues: Social Movements, Folk Music, and Race in the United States* (Princeton: Princeton University Press, 2010), 3, 159–62, 178. Much of the scholarship on the

folk-music movement of this period has focused on well-known musicians and collectors based primarily in New York and Washington, DC. See, e.g., Robert S. Cantwell, *When We Were Good: The Folk Revival;* Ronald D. Cohen, *Rainbow Quest: The Folk Music Revival and American Society, 1940–1970* (Amherst: University of Massachusetts Press, 2002); Benjamin Filene, *Romancing the Folk: Public Memory and American Roots Music* (Chapel Hill: University of North Carolina Press, 2000).

4. E. F. Fain, "Grundtvig, Folk Education, and Scandinavian Cultural Nationalism," in Rolland Paulston, editor, *Other Dreams, Other Schools: Folk Colleges in Social and Ethnic Movements.* (Pittsburgh: University Center for International Studies, 1980), 51–53, 60–61, 65, 68; Glen, *Highlander,* 18–21; Myles Horton, with Judith Kohl and Herbert Kohl, *The Long Haul: An Autobiography* (New York: Doubleday, 1990), 51–52; Myles Horton, quoted in Aimee Horton, *The Highlander Folk School: A History of Its Major Programs, 1932–1961* (Brooklyn, NY: Carlson, 1989), 34, 36–37.

5. Frank Adams, *Unearthing Seeds of Fire: The Idea of Highlander* (Winston-Salem, NC: John F. Blair, 1975), 30–40; Glen, *Highlander,* 52–55; "Broadcast to England."

6. "Broadcast to England"; Sharp collaborated with educators at the Hindman School, and his research was funded by Olive Dame Campbell, founder of the John C. Campbell Folk School. David Whisnant, *All That Is Native and Fine: The Politics of Culture in an American Region* (Chapel Hill: University of North Carolina Press, 1983), 113, 117, 121–24; Henry D. Shapiro, *Appalachia on Our Mind: The Southern Mountains and Mountaineers in the American Consciousness, 1870–1920* (Chapel Hill: University of North Carolina Press, 1986), 218, 256–61.

7. The historian Jane Becker has argued that the Great Depression reinforced a romantic view of the region which contrasted to modern industrialization, but she cautions that the appeal of this image lay in its ability to project an idealized past onto the present day, one which erased political and labor conflicts, racial divisions, and debates about American immigration and modernization. Jane S. Becker, *Selling Tradition: Appalachia and the Construction of an American Folk, 1930–1940* (Chapel Hill: University of North Carolina Press, 1998), 5, 25.

8. Michele Hilmes, *Network Nations: A Transnational History of British and American Broadcasting* (New York: Routledge, 2012), 78–79, 101; "Broadcast to England"; According to William Stott, the American public embraced "documentary medium[s]" such as photography, film, and radio because, unlike newspapers, they trusted that they were providing a "direct" source of information about current events. William Stott, *Documentary Expression and Thirties America* (New York: Oxford University Press, 1973), 80–84.

9. Bill C. Malone, "Music," in *High Mountains Rising: Appalachia in Time and Place,* ed. Richard A. Straw and H. Tyler Blethen (University of Illinois Press: Urbana, 2004), 116–17; Shapiro, *Appalachia on Our Mind,* 256–61; Whisnant, *All That Is Native and Fine,* 117; Becker, *Selling Tradition,* 6–7, 210–11; Anthony Harkins, *Hillbilly: A Cultural History of an American Icon* (Oxford: Oxford University Press, 2004), 103–4.

10. "Broadcast to England"; Leslie Sharp, *Tennessee's Dixie Highway: Springfield to Chattanooga* (Charleston, SC: Arcadia, 2011), 7; Shapiro, *Appalachia on Our Mind,* 117–19; Becker, *Selling Tradition,* 7, 15.

11. Annual report for 1934, box 1:3, Highlander Research and Education Center Collection, Wisconsin Historical Society. Aimee Horton, *The Highlander Folk School,* 36; *Highlander Fling,*

May 1935, 1, *Highlander Folk School Collection,* TSLA, box 12:9; Report for the year 1936, HFS, TSLA, 14:8.

12. Whisnant, *All That Is Native and Fine,* 150–60; Shapiro, *Appalachia on Our Mind,* 109–10.

13. Ralph Tefferteller led the folk-dancing program from 1936 to 1939 before leaving to develop cultural programs for the Amalgamated Clothing Workers. "Teffie Is Working with Amalgamated," *Highlander Fling,* Jan. 1939, 1, HFS, TSLA, box 12:9; Ralph Tefferteller, "Folk Dance Organizations," Zilphia Horton Folk Music Collection, TSLA, IV-D-3, box 5:2; Zilphia Horton, editor, *Labor Songs* (Atlanta: Textile Workers Union of America, 1939), in Zilphia Horton Folk Music Collection, TSLA, IV-D-2, box 3:11; "Summary of Activities for 1938," HREC Collection, WHS, MSS 265, box 1:3.

14. John A. Salmond, *The General Textile Strike of 1934: From Maine to Alabama* (Columbia: University of Missouri Press, 2002), 1–4; *Let's Sing!,* Highlander Folk School, 1938, in Zilphia Horton Folk Music Collection, TSLA, IV-D-2, box 3:4; Myles Horton interview with Ben Sweet, 1965, Myles Horton Collection, WHS, MSS 831, box 12:7.

15. Ralph Tefferteller to Felix Greene, Feb. 24, 1937, Zilphia Horton Folk Music Collection, TSLA, IV-D-3, box 7:2; "Broadcast to England"; *Let's Sing!,* Highlander Folk School, 1938, in Zilphia Horton Folk Music Collection, TSLA, IV-D-2, box 3:4; R. Serge Denisoff, *Sing a Song of Social Significance* (Bowling Green, OH: Bowling Green University Popular Press, 1972), 50–51, 57.

16. Aimee Horton, *The Highlander Folk School,* 19–23; Richard Pells, *Radical Visions and American Dreams: Culture and Social Thought in the Depression Years* (New York: Harper and Row, 1973), 140–43; Myles Horton, *The Long Haul,* 35–36; Anthony Dunbar, *Against the Grain: Southern Radicals and Prophets,* 1929–1959 (Charlottesville: University of Virginia Press, 1981), 28–30, 40–41; Frank Adams manuscript notes on Reinhold Niebuhr, HREC Collection, WHS, MSS 265, box 22:1; Honey, *Sharecropper's Troubadour,* 106–7; Doris Willens, *Lonesome Traveler: The Life of Lee Hays* (New York: W. W. Norton), 27–31; Glen, *Highlander,* 21, 73; Denisoff, *Sing a Song of Social Significance,* 50–51, 57.

17. Honey, *Sharecropper's Troubadour,* 76–87; "Broadcast to England"; Lee Hays, "Let the Will Be Done," *New Masses,* Aug. 1, 1939, 15, cited in Denisoff, *Sing a Song of Social Significance,* 55; "Song Notes," Zilphia Horton Folk Music Collection, TSLA, IV-D-3, box 5:3; Roy, *Reds, Whites, and Blues,* 3, 159, 178.

18. Shapiro, *Appalachia on Our Mind,* 111, 117–20; Whisnant, *All That Is Native and Fine,* 244–246.

19. Denisoff, *Sing a Song of Social Significance,* 54–55; Filene, *Romancing the Folk,* 50–59.

20. Glen, *Highlander,* 18, 38, 45; "Broadcast to England."

21. "Song Notes," Zilphia Horton Folk Music Collection, TSLA, IV-D-3, box 5:3; Ralph Tefferteller to Felix Greene, Feb. 24, 1937, Zilphia Horton Folk Music Collection, TSLA, IV-D-3, box 7:2; "Broadcast to England"; Honey, *Sharecropper's Troubadour,* 56–59, 112, 141; Willens, *Lonesome Traveler,* 45–47, 57. People's Songs, Inc. was an organization of labor songwriters, such as Pete Seeger and Lee Hays, that recorded and promoted labor songs during the late 1940s. Willens, *Lonesome Traveler,* 79–82, 107.

22. Seeger's father Charles directed a unit that recorded Handcox's music and poems for the Library of Congress in early 1937. In the 1940s, Zilphia Horton taught Pete Seeger the song

"We Will Overcome," which she had learned from union member in South Carolina. Seeger would later advise the young folk singer Guy Carawan to visit Highlander, where he played a key role in popularizing "We Shall Overcome" as the anthem of the civil rights movement. Honey, *Sharecropper's Troubadour,* xvii–xviii, 106–7, 112. According to Tefferteller's records, Gracie Blackstone, a member of the Southern Tenant Farmers, led the singing of "We Shall Not be Moved" in the broadcast. "Highlander Folk School short wave broadcast from Monteagle to England," Publicity Radio Broadcasts, HREC Collection, WHS, MSS 265, 66:9; "Song Notes," Zilphia Horton Folk Music Collection, TSLA, IV-D-3, box 5:3; Ralph Tefferteller to Felix Greene, Feb. 24, 1937, IV-D-3, 7–2; Cantwell, 89; "Broadcast to England"; Willens, *Lonesome Traveler,* 28–29, 37, 40, 46–47, 50–51, 65–66.

23. Honey, *Sharecropper's Troubadour,* 142; Glen, *Highlander,* 154, 176–77.

# A Fierce Contest Over Images

## Collier's *Magazine and the Fight Against Documentary Reportage in Greene County, Georgia, during the Great Depression*

SCOTT L. MATTHEWS

In January 1938, a piece of documentary reportage started a firestorm in Greene County, Georgia, that would, in a matter of weeks, spread to the floor of the US House of Representatives. The spark was an article in *Collier's* magazine titled "Devil in de Cotton," written by Owen P. White and featuring photographs by Lawrence Monahan. White documented the poverty that tenants and sharecroppers, white and black, endured in the Deep South's crumbling cotton economy. He also emphasized the beneficial role the Farm Security Administration (FSA), a New Deal program, played in providing opportunities for land ownership and stewardship. White did not focus exclusively on Greene County and its farmers. Nevertheless, a black sharecropper and his large impoverished family provided the dramatic hook into a story of destitution and helplessness, and the necessity of government intervention and supervision. Monahan's photographs of Greene County's rural poor, including the Sheldons and their decrepit home, spread across the lead article's opening page. White and Monahan presented Greene County as a place of exceptional poverty, of human and environmental waste, that only the federal government, not local leadership, could remedy.

Greene County's leading white citizens responded by launching a vigorous defense of their home. The county's civil grand jury fanned the flames of local resentment by denouncing the article and its photographs during its January term. Other residents wrote briefs on behalf of Greene for the local paper, the *Greensboro Herald-Journal,* as well as for the *Atlanta Constitution.* Some also called upon their Democratic congressman, Paul Brown, to read one of their defenses of Greene's image into the *Congressional Record.* Greene County's agricultural plight was not exceptional in the 1930s, but the impact of the documentary work that occurred here, and the fierce reactions some of it provoked, was.[1]

The controversy created by "Devil in de Cotton," reveals the contentious political and cultural stakes involved in documentary expression in the Depression-era South. It lays bare the connections between representational, political, and social power that had local and national implications. "The fierce contest over images and counter-images of places is an arena of action in which the cultural politics of places, the political-economy of their development and the accumulation of a sense of social power in place frequently fuse in indistinguishable ways," argues geographer David Harvey.[2] During the 1930s, magazines like *Collier's, Life,* and *Look* brought images and stories of suffering and endurance during the Great Depression into the homes of middle-class Americans who mostly had never heard of a place such as Greene County, Georgia, until they read an article like "Devil in de Cotton." Because of the national scope of the Depression and the national circulation of publications like *Collier's,* Greene County's once-local struggles became public. Consequently, the concerns of federal policy makers and those of leading residents demanded a public response, including one entered into the congressional record.

"Devil in de Cotton" came out during a pivotal point in Greene County's history that also explains why the article produced such an impassioned backlash. In early 1938, the county, like many in the rural South, was on the cusp of a rural reconstruction at the hands of New Deal programs like the Farm Security Administration. At the same time these new federal initiatives seemed to threaten local economic power and racial relations, particularly the old paternalistic relationships between the white landowners and black and white tenants, an article like "Devil in de Cotton" undermined local representational power. Fears of distant forces—federal policies and northern magazines—fused and exposed a struggle to maintain power at the local level in the 1930s South. The documentary reportage of White and Monahan publicly subverted the authority of elite whites, like Judge James Park and local historian and bank president. Dr. T. B. Rice, to define the county's image. If the New Deal's dominance in Greene County's cotton fields seemed like a fait accompli by early 1938, there was still a war to be won against a national publication. The story of "Devil in de Cotton" and Greene County's response reveal that the decade's famed documentary impulse produced not only iconic images of rural America during the Depression but also intense debates over who gets to define the identity of a place for a national audience while in the midst of a national depression, and why.

Greene County stretches across 416 square miles of gently rolling lower Piedmont land midway between Atlanta and Augusta. Formed in 1786, the county had fertile soils that lured migrants from Virginia and the Carolinas who carved out farms and plantations for tobacco and indigo cultures. By the early nineteenth century, cotton had conquered the local economy. Slave-grown cotton made the place renowned for its prosperous plantations, which by 1837, produced more bales than the plantations of any other county in Georgia. The wealth generated by slave labor also supported the creation of three cotton mills along the Oconee River by the end of the 1830s. The fortunes made in a thriving cotton economy turned Greene County into what sociologist Arthur Raper called an "early cultural center." Residents founded numerous academies that educated the children of the planter elite, while the founding of Mercer University here in 1838 and the Greensboro Female College in 1852 made the county into a center of higher learning second only to Athens.[3]

The planters who reaped the rewards of slave-grown cotton in the early and middle nineteenth century also sowed the seeds of the crop's collapse in the 1920s. By the 1930s, the depth of Greene County's demise would lure a long line of sociologists, journalists, and government photographers who used documentary expression to promote reform. But well before outside writers and photographers made the place synonymous with the Depression South, local farmers turned a critical eye on themselves. In 1851, Greene County's Judge Garnett Andrews warned of the "fearful deterioration of our soil" and foresaw a bleak future after farmers "swept off the virgin soil from the face of the earth, as the famine licks up the stubble." A decade before the Civil War, Andrews saw the signs in a wounded landscape. "These bleak hills, with their gullied mouths, speak more eloquently and convincingly on this subject than I can." His critique stopped there, though. He could not condemn a culture beholden to cotton. National and international demand for the crop made the area's acreage some of the most valuable in the nation. The logical conclusion of his argument led to an indictment of the slave economy itself, which was also out of the question. Andrews's status as a local leader and a southerner made his grim portrayal of Greene County's landscape and the farmers' folly possible. It did not, ultimately, represent a threat to the authority and expertise of the slaveholding class. His speech, printed in the County Agricultural Society report, also circulated among friends, not a leering national audience. Unlike the images and descriptions created by reporters and photographers in the 1930s and 1940s, Andrews's picture of Greene County and the South was a product of wise local leadership, not a northern press or the federal government. But when representational power shifted in the 1930s to outsiders, including professional sociologists, national journalists, and New Deal photographers, who spotlighted the rural South as the source of so much of the nation's depression, Greene County's elite became warier of critical views of local problems.[4]

The roots of Greene County's status as a kind of documentary laboratory or studio—a mecca for social scientists, journalists, and photographers—reach back to the 1920s, when the bottom fell out of the local economy, and many residents fled. Beginning early in the decade, a confluence of disasters "left the county economically prostrate." Falling cotton prices due to declining international demand and overproduction occurred alongside boll-weevil infestations and severe soil erosion that left many of the county's lands scarred with gullies. A mass exodus followed. In 1920, three thousand farmers worked the county's land. A decade later, a little over fifteen hundred remained.[5] Into this agricultural crisis stepped Arthur Raper. In 1927, when he began his dissertation, which examined the collapse of Greene County's cotton economy and the large out-migration of its residents, he was one of sociologist Howard Odum's star graduate students at the University of North Carolina at Chapel Hill. The product of seven years of intensive fieldwork, Raper's book *Preface to Peasantry* was published in 1936. "The Black Belt plantation economy," Raper argued, "whether regnant or declining, prepares the land and the man for the emergence of a peasant rather than for the appearance of the traditional independent American farmer. . . . As the plantation crumbles, most of the erstwhile owners and some of the more alert tenants abandon the scene, leaving in the decadent area plantation families schooled in dependency, unaccustomed to responsibility, without experience in community leadership."[6]

The exodus left behind a rural landscape dotted with deteriorating homes. Paltry cash income meant that farmers could not keep up with repairs. By 1938, almost 50 percent of the houses in Greene County had been abandoned and "were unfit for human occupancy," according to an FSA report. Raper described the majority of inhabited houses as badly run down and dilapidated. The land also bore the scars of the county's devastated cotton economy. The soils that once had sustained the area's livelihood had been worn away by exploitative single-crop agriculture, leaving behind a landscape gashed with gullies. It seemed as though Judge Andrews's prophecy from the 1850s was coming to pass in the 1930s.[7]

By the late 1930s, Greene County seemed like a microcosm of the rural South's social, economic, and environmental woes. If the South, in the words of the Roosevelt administration's famous 1938 report, was the nation's primary economic problem, then Greene County became the emblem of the problem. Raper's pioneering research and fieldwork that resulted in *Preface to Peasantry* opened the door for a stream of social scientists, journalists, and photographers, who came to Greene County to document the sources and effects of these problems. Their work resulted in iconic images of the Depression-era South. For example, in 1937, the same year White and Monahan visited the county for their *Collier's* piece, FSA photographer Dorothea Lange took nearly fifty photographs of Greene County while traveling across the country with her husband, the economist Paul Taylor. Some of her photographs later appeared in their 1939 book, *An American Exodus: A Record of Human Erosion*.[8] FSA photographers Marion Post-Wolcott, Russell Lee, and, most notably, Jack Delano, would work in the county in their wake during the late 1930s and early 1940s.

When White and Monahan arrived in Greene County, they were not only following in the footsteps of other documentarians, they were visiting a place in transition. "The old order was passing," according to Raper. The last generation of landed elites was dying off or reluctant to relinquish power. The system of paternalism and dependency the old landed elites had maintained was crumbling, while calls for federal assistance and supervision increased. In the summer of 1937, a few months before White and Monahan stopped in Greene, the Bankhead-Jones Act passed in Congress. The act created the FSA, the successor to the Resettlement Administration, whose purpose was to implement programs that brought tenant farmers out of dependency and made them into an independent, self-sufficient yeomanry. The FSA created homestead communities, provided low-interest and long-term loans, and introduced government planning and supervision in agronomy and other facets of farm life. Government supervision weakened local paternalism. For the old elite, the New Deal "jeopardized a power that rested on the control of property, labor, credit, and local government," writes George Tindall. "As the old went out, the new came in," Raper wrote about Greene County during the 1930s: "And down underneath were the land and the people, the seasons and the pines and the gullies, new forces and old ideas, pleasure, pain, politics."[9]

The increase of government intervention into local politics and economics generated conflicting responses between a desire to maintain local control and power and a recognition of the immediate benefits federal farm programs provided to farmers and their families. During this time, local leaders worried about relinquishing power to federal programs, but they also, as the case involving White and Monahan's reporting for *Collier's* would make clear, feared a loss of control over their county's image. As the New Deal began to transform life in Greene County during the late 1930s, the old guard made a fierce stand to take back a modicum of control over how the place was portrayed by strangers with cameras and pens. The white elite might have had to concede to federal relief programs, but they were not about to cede representational power to outsiders, especially ones who did not curry their favor or focus on the scenes they thought defined Greene County during the 1930s.

When Owen P. White arrived in Greene County in 1937, he was employed as an assistant editor and staff writer at *Collier's,* where he had worked since 1926. He was a native Texan, born in El Paso, and identified as a westerner, not a southerner. In the 1920s, he wrote three books about west Texas's frontier culture, including *Out of the Desert,* a history of El Paso, before moving to New York and turning his attention to investigative journalism. In his pieces for *Collier's,* a magazine that gained notoriety during the Progressive era for its reporting on political and corporate corruption, he appeared as a kind of modern-day muckraker who exposed unscrupulous businessmen and politicians, particularly in his home state of Texas. He was also no stranger to the South's agricultural woes and viewed the region not as a homeland in need of defense but as a national problem in need of reform. He had visited portions of Georgia and South Carolina in 1934 for his *Collier's* article, "All Washed Up," which documented the deterioration of the region's soils. In the fall and early winter of 1937, in the wake of the Bankhead-Jones Act, White and Monahan traveled through the Deep South, including Greene County, "not in search of picturesque backgrounds, but to find out what is happening to the people in those sections where poor farming is ruining the land," wrote a *Collier's* editor. "In 'Devil in de Cotton,' he shows you the dismal picture and what the government is doing to make it a brighter one."[10]

During the 1930s, documentary reporters like White canvassed the country in large numbers for national publications out of a desire to see and experience the Depression for themselves rather than read about it in government reports or tables of statistics. White could and did cite in his article the figures that suggested human suffering. But during the 1930s, as William Stott points out in his book on the decade's documentary impulse, many suspected that statistics like these had been manipulated by government officials, businessmen, radicals, or reformers for their own ends. "If a man didn't trust the publicized facts and generalizations," writes Stott, "the only way for him to approach the awful truths of a broken economy was to go out on his own and see what he could see with his own eyes. . . . The Depression stimulated, even compelled, a documentary approach." Like the legion of other social observers crisscrossing the country, particularly the South, White fit squarely into the mode of documentary reportage. "Frankly, the first thing that struck me was that the foregoing facts and figures couldn't be true," White wrote in "Devil in de Cotton." "I couldn't believe that here in the United States we have any such farm misery as they represented, and so . . . I went to look for it. I found it; it's there, inside the shacks and cabins of sharecroppers, tenants, and even owners, in the shape of hunger, dirt, filth, ignorance and disease, all combined into such a concentrated medium for the destruction of human values as to be almost indescribable."[11]

But describe it he did. White and Monahan's story ran as the lead article in the January 1, 1938, issue of *Collier's*. Greene County, its people, poverty, and deteriorated land, provided the human-interest case study that characterized the style of the decade's documentary reportage. The story of the county and its poorest farmers drew readers into White and Monahan's "dismal picture" of the rural South's woes. Greene County, as White noted, was once one of the most prosperous places in the cotton South, a former "garden spot," but "it went to seed." Its fall from Edenic grace was remarkable if not necessarily representative. "Now, of course, as a reporter, I am not trying to convey the impression that Greene County, with its poor land and poor people, represents a condition that prevails generally throughout Alabama and Georgia. Both states still contain tremendous acreages that are very fertile and being farmed by happy, prosperous people. But, once upon a time, Greene County itself was like that, and so the question arises as to how long it will be before many other counties in the two states, due to unchecked soil erosion and poor farm and home economy, will be in the same sad condition." The poverty he and Monahan saw and documented was a cautionary tale for other places to heed. Unchecked ignorance and hubris had brought the county low. Local leaders and farmers, rich and poor, black and white, appeared incapable of saving themselves. The only hope for a "brighter day" was federal intervention and expertise. It was an assessment and picture of a place not substantively different from what Raper had presented in *Preface to Peasantry* and would later expand on in 1943 in *Tenants of the Almighty*. The difference was that some Greene County residents believed that White focused only on "sensational" scenes and people and excluded anything that did not align with his article's premise. Most decisively, White, unlike Raper, did ingratiate himself to local leaders like Judge James Park and Dr. T. B. Rice. It seemed the *Collier's* journalists took advantage of a place "unschooled in deception," according to Raper.[12]

The human face of Greene County's collapse, according to "Devil in de Cotton," was a black sharecropper named Pote Sheldon and his family.[13] "Down in Greene County, Georgia, which was once one of the richest counties in the state but which now boasts that it is the poorest, away off on a side road, I came across Pote and Lily Sheldon," White wrote in his article's opening lines. Pote Sheldon, at sixty-seven years old, "can still pick cotton but is so full of de rheumatic dat he kain't drive de mule no mo'." His wife, Lily, had given birth to fifteen children. "They have been married for forty-two years, have share-cropped for some landowner in Greene County every year of that time, and today, except for their cheerful indifference to hunger and nakedness, own nothing of any value whatsoever. I never saw a more destitute family." White described an equally desolate landscape. As he traveled the county's backroads into a section called the "Badlands," he observed abandoned "mansions and shanties" that occupied the same "bare ribs of red earth from which almost every vestige of topsoil has been washed away." Gullies—one forty feet deep and a mile long by his estimation—cut sad swaths into a region whose fertility had once attracted prospecting planters from Virginia and the Carolinas. The land was "so sterile that in all that section only one family lives. And what it lives on nobody knows. Wild game and firewood, perhaps."[14]

White's descriptions, particularly his use of dialect when quoting Sheldon, and Monahan's photograph of the family standing shoulder to shoulder outside their dilapidated home, many of them smiling, are suggestive of the style adopted by Margaret Bourke-White and Erskine Caldwell in their documentary book, *You Have Seen Their Faces,* which was released in 1937. For middle-class white audiences picking up the January 1, 1938, issue of *Collier's,* some who perhaps had seen or read about *You Have Seen Their Faces,* White's descriptions and Monahan's photographs would seem to confirm an image of the South as a place beset by pathology and backwardness. "I saw people who are miserably sick and yet so ignorant that they don't know they are sick. I saw slatternly, barefooted, filthy, tobacco-chewing women; and scabby-headed babies who have never had a bath . . . and shifty-eyed, shiftless men, so tired all the time that they'd lie down on the ground to talk to me." For readers, the power of such pathos-infused descriptions came from the author's first-hand experience of having seen these people with his own eyes and then described them with something akin to photographic realism. In this way, documentary realism trumped literary realism in its ability to convey human actuality and suffering. The urge to document reality explains why so many writers of fiction—Sherwood Anderson, Erskine Caldwell, Owen P. White—turned almost exclusively to documentary reportage as the Depression deepened during the 1930s. "There is a profound significance in the fact that this need to search out the land, to compile records, to explain America to itself, found its most abundant expression in a literature of formal social exploration and descriptive journalism," Alfred Kazin wrote in 1942. During a time "when society is changing too rapidly and too violently for literature even to command the necessary detachment for imaginative truth, the serious novel itself will suffer in its effort to dominate what is not yet really known. In times of crisis people prefer to take their history straight, and on the run; and the documentary journalist who writes it on the run will give them history in terms which they are prepared to understand."[15]

The vehemence of the response of Greene County's elite to White and Monahan's piece was due in part to a recognition of the power of documentary reportage to make a story about destitution and deterioration in Greene County seem like incontrovertible truth. White's words and Monahan's images demanded a response commensurate with such a mode of representation, one that was grounded in an even more authoritative position: that of the insider, the local, and the elder leader who know their home the best. A story like "Devil in de Cotton" called into question the power of enlightened white leadership in Greene County. It not only damaged the image of their county but suggested a failure on their parts to manage local social and economic affairs in a way that befitted elite white men. At the same time, the increasing influence and presence of New Deal farm programs threatened to undermine long-standing paternalistic relationships as federal supervisors took the place of the landed elite in providing contracts, loans, credit, and land. The local power structure seemed under assault by distant forces: bureaucrats from Washington, journalists from New York. Back in the 1850s, critiques of Greene County's deteriorating soil and poor farming practices were tolerated because they circulated locally. Now, during a national economic calamity that demanded a national government response and generated documentary stories for a national readership, two of Greene County's leaders, Park and Rice, crafted responses aimed at local, regional, and national audiences. Their counterattack against "Devil in de Cotton" began in the local newspaper and civil grand jury, moved on to a regional paper, and then culminated on the floor of the US House of Representatives in Washington.

The fusillade from Greene County began almost immediately after the *Collier's* issue came out. The December 31, 1937, edition of the *Greensboro Herald-Journal* alerted readers to White's story and suggested they "secure a copy of Collier's Weekly and read the entire article and also see the display of pictures used in connection with the article." The response by the newspaper's young new editor, Carey Williams, reflected the transition and tension between old and new in the county that Raper had detected during his time in the county. On one hand, Williams was a supporter of Georgia governor Eugene Talmadge, who was fervently anti–New Deal. "Devil in de Cotton" defamed Greene County in Williams's eyes. He castigated White and Monahan for "Parading Our Poverty" and blamed them for putting "the devil in the cotton patches of Greene County," rather than revealing him as already there. One the other hand, Williams grudgingly admitted White's story contained "much truth" that locals ignored at their own peril. "No good can come from burying your head in the ground like an ostrich." He realized Greene County was unfortunately "clinging to ante-bellum days" and advocated for more and not less federal support, despite his Talmadge loyalty.[16]

Perhaps sensing the insufficiency of Williams's response, with its acknowledgement of "truth" in the article and support for increased federal presence in the county, two of the most esteemed men of the old order crafted their own defenses of Greene County, which they aimed at regional and national audiences. Park's article for the Atlanta *Constitution* and Rice's defense, which Congressman Brown would read into the record of the US House of Representatives, tended to resemble the position of the ostrich Williams warned about. *If* Greene County had struggles, Park and Rice claimed, they were products of individual failings rather than forces intrinsic to the county's economy and social structure. Not only did Park and Rice never acknowledge any deep-rooted problems in Greene County, but also, notably, they never mentioned the New Deal programs beginning to transform their rural world. For them, the county's savior was not federal intervention but time-tested paternalism. The specter of the federal power, however, hovered over their passionate defenses of Greene County. While trying to take the reins of representational power from documentary reporters from the North, they also made a related case for retaining local, rather than federal, supervision of agricultural affairs. Outside documentarians and federal authority were two sides of the same coin for Park and Rice in 1930s Greene County.

Park launched his attack on White and *Collier's* just a week after Williams's article. Park and his family had deep roots in Greene County. He was a judge for the Ocmulgee Circuit that comprised the heart of middle and eastern Georgia's old plantation belt. He initially told the *Herald-Journal* that "the White article did Greene County 'a great injustice.'" White, he said, did not do a "proper investigation." In an attempt to undermine White's authority as an eyewitness, Park told the paper that the journalist drew on his "imagination" rather than personal observation. In the meantime, Park crafted his own response for the *Atlanta Constitution,* which appeared in the paper on January 9, 1938. According to Park, the person White and Monahan chose to lead off their article with—Pote Sheldon—was widely known to lack industriousness. The family's poverty and squalor, they claimed, were the by-products of a lack of virtue. Most importantly, though, Park wanted to make clear that had whites only known of the Sheldons' dire circumstances, they would have assisted: "Yet I desire to say that had the white people of this county had knowledge of the fact that his children were suffering for food and clothing, they would have gladly contributed to these necessities." White's description of the Sheldons as the "most destitute" family he had ever seen, a family who lived in deep debt to their landlord, called into question the supposed paternalism of local whites that Park had to take pains to defend in his article. But, according to Park, there was little he or any other person could do for people "who are constitutionally opposed to work." "If you would place this class of people in the Garden of Eden," he wrote, "they would soon destroy all of its beauties, and would not have the energy of Adam and Eve to cover their nakedness with fig leaves."[17]

Park concluded by framing his defense of Greene against the depredations of documentary workers in regional and racial terms that harkened back to fears of a loss of local control and white supremacy during the sectional crisis before the Civil War. "In conclusion, I wish to say if the fanatics of the north would attend to their own communities and cease meddling with affairs of the south, it would redound to the mutual good of the white and negro race of our fair southland."[18] On February 4, 1938, the *Herald-Journal* reported that when the Greene County Grand Jury convened for their January term they not only wished to "condemn in strongest terms, the scurrilous, unwarranted, and most unnecessary article appearing in Collier's Weekly magazine of January 1, 1938, written by one Owen P. White" but to commend "His Honour, Judge James B. Park for his masterful reply to this unworthy attack on the good county of Greene, as appeared in The Atlanta Constitution on January 9, 1938."[19]

The final challenge to White and Monahan was penned by Rice, who framed his response as a closing argument by a defense attorney. The case involved not just Rice, Greene County, and two documentary journalists, but the nation. Accordingly, Greene County's Democratic congressman, Paul Brown, would read Rice's statement into the congressional record. On February 9, 1938, Brown stood on the floor of the US House of Representatives and declared, "This article is strongly resented by our citizens." He then read the defense, which Rice titled "Greene County, Georgia on Trial With Collier's As Prosecutor, the Nation as Jury and Owen P. White As the Star Witness."[20]

Rice seemed to be the ideal person to defend Greene County's image and reputation, despite being a nonnative. He was the county's official local historian and possessed a deep well of pride for his adopted home. According to one resident, "If you will just give Rice time, he will prove that Noah's Ark landed in Greene County." Rice was also the president of a local bank, a pharmacist, and director of the county welfare program and the local Red Cross. In all of these positions, he developed relationships with residents black and white, rich and poor. "I believe I have had the opportunity to survey conditions far better than a 'snooper,'" Rice wrote referring to White, "who sneaked in and photographed a few of the very worst specimens that could be found in order that he might 'cash-in' on his sensational story regardless of any harmful effect it might produce."[21]

White's mistake, his snooping without the consent of a local leader like Rice, was something Raper avoided the moment he arrived in Greene County. "Raper's research was a matter not only of science," writes Raper's biographer Louis Mazzari, "but of personal diplomacy, too, and he tried to keep an eye out for trouble." When he began his own sociological and ethnographic study there back in the 1920s, Raper knew he had to establish a rapport with as many local people as he could in order to conduct effective research. Raper eased his way into the community by striking up casual conversations with locals at the courthouse, country stores, and lunch counters. By introducing himself and letting residents hear his southern accent as he told them about his background and research interests, local people usually ended up liking the amiable and unpretentious sociologist. One of the most important of these local people was Dr. Rice, who "for some reason . . . took a liking to me," remembered Raper. He opened up his files of local history for the UNC sociologist and offered "counsel and encouragement" as Raper completed his work on *Preface to Peasantry* and *Tenants of the Almighty*. One year after the release of *Preface to Peasantry*, a book that Secretary of Agriculture Henry Wallace carried with him during his travels through the South in late 1936 and that influenced future New Deal farm policies, Rice now faced another kind of documentarian, one he had not vetted, one who, along with his photographer, had seemingly slipped undetected into Greene County from the North in the night.[22]

According to Rice, the danger of a story like "Devil in de Cotton" was its ability to dupe impressionable minds and create a distorted image of a people and place. If a central theme of White's article was the necessity of reform, then his descriptions of poverty and waste in Greene County seemed to justify a regime change that put power in the hands of the federal government. The story seemed "calculated to do us much harm among those who do not know better, and are ready to swallow the effusions of sensational vermin hunters who are paid to shun the whole truth and thereby, create prejudice against a section of country that contains as fine people as there is to be found upon the face of earth; and a county that contains as much good land as to be found in Georgia, or any other state." Despite the fact that the journalists' "candid camera" did in fact "correctly" portray a few isolated cases, these sensational examples, particularly Sheldon and his family and a white tenant named Mr. Jones, were by no means representative of Greene County as whole.[23]

If Rice had to acknowledge the ability of the camera to communicate a portion of truth, then, it seemed, he had to turn to his own method of documentary verification to make his case. In his written defense, Rice also presented sworn affidavits from Greene County residents who either knew of the people and places White and Monahan documented or who could provide evidence that refuted their claims. For example, Rice tracked down the Sheldons' landlord, T. A. Wilson, who enumerated all of the generous advances and furnishes he provided the family in 1937, including a new tin roof on their house, clothing, and a $144.37 cash loan with no interest. According to Rice, the well-meaning and paternalistic Wilson, by doing his duty, came out "$200.00 poorer by feeding, housing and tolerating Pote's trifling crowd during the year COLLIER'S used them as exhibit A." Rather than being an image of labor exploitation in the cotton fields, the story of Pote Sheldon and his landlord was evidence of an enduring paternalistic relationship misunderstood by snooping journalists and "sob-sisters of the North," according to Rice. "Did Mr. Wilson kick them out as a 'yankee' landlord would have done?," he asked. "He most assuredly did not. On the other hand, he moved them to another farm where he could watch him more closely, and 'Pote' needs watching, and will furnish him supplies again for the year 1938."[24]

In another section of his defense, Rice reinforced the theme of paternalism in Greene County by highlighting the case of Jim Brown, "a thrifty colored man who has worked, saved and paid for his land." According to Rice, "You could not pull Jim away from Greene County because he knows it is a good place for both negroes and white folks to live, and his rights are respected and are as secure as any white person in the county." During a time when Greene County was still hemorrhaging its people, particularly its black population, to Atlanta and northern cities, Rice offered a vision of prosperity, stability, and racial harmony. A new image of Greene County thus emerges from Rice's pen and the personal testimonies he collected. Here in the face of increased New Deal intervention and supervision, the solution to local agricultural problems was the old plantation tradition of enlightened paternalism that benefited both races. To reinforce the point, Rice offered up "Put" and Anna Callaway, black farmers and "shining examples of what thrift, work, and determination can do for tenant farmers." They turned their backs on the New Deal and embraced the local way. "They had faith in Greene County land; so they bought a farm on credit—not on 'Uncle Sam's' credit but their own—and it is now fully paid for." Here was the real Greene County. Those who would think otherwise had been deceived by the "sensational vermin hunters."[25]

In keeping with his desire to present an image of a place with a dignified culture, Rice called attention to the monuments of power, culture, and beauty that existed in Greene County and that White ignored. "Had Mr. White cared for some artistic pictures that would elevate the thoughts of his readers," Rice wrote, "he would have trained his candid camera on the old Mercer buildings that constitute one of Georgia's most sacred shrines." He also suggested the county's courthouse in Greensboro, the seat of local political power, as a fitting subject for a photographer. "As I look out of my office window I can see our handsome brick Courthouse that was built in 1849. Its massive Doric columns, three stories in height, and its beautiful surroundings all testify that neglect and decay are not, and have not been the order of the day." Rice's emphasis on the architectural symbols of social and political power clearly clashed with White's "dismal picture" of Greene County, which highlighted the plight of the black poor and included images of the Sheldons' deteriorating house as symbolic of a lapse in local paternalism. Recognizing, again, the national implications of White's documentary reportage during the Depression, Rice finished up his case by arguing that *Collier's* also could have balanced its portrait of poverty by looking around the country. The South might have been a problem in the national consciousness, but problem places abounded in the 1930s. "Yes, Mr. White's candid camera told the truth insofar as he pointed it at the very worst that he could find; and if he will do some 'snooping' in the wealthy cities of New York, Philadelphia, Baltimore and other cities—rural sections too—in the North, he will find far more poverty and suffering than he found in Greene County, Georgia."[26]

Summing up for the defense, Rice concluded his case with the following recommendation: "Therefore, we feel that both our defamer and his mouthpiece deserve a good spanking." It was a more modest proposal than the one White received in the mail a few weeks earlier from an Ohio resident whose ancestors had once lived in Greene County. "Skin the dirty muckrakers for defaming the county where my ancestors lived," wrote Devereaux Lake, president of a foundry company in Sandusky. According to Rice, Lake was the first person from "'Yankeeland' to raise his voice in protest."[27]

The irony of the fight against "Devil in de Cotton" is that by 1942 Greene County had received more attention from government photographers, sociologists, and journalists than any other county in the South and, perhaps, the nation, precisely because of curiosity about how New Deal farm programs were transforming a rural community in the region. FSA photographer Jack Delano collaborated with Raper between 1940 and 1942 and took more than one thousand photographs of seemingly every facet of life in Greene County. No other FSA photographer documented a place in such depth, and no other county in the South was as heavily photographed as Greene during the Depression and New Deal.[28]

Nevertheless, the legacy of the fierce response generated by "Devil in de Cotton" shaped, even in unspoken ways, how Raper and Delano carried out their documentary work in Greene County. The collaboration between Raper and Delano was also a collaboration between documentarians and the documented during the New Deal. Raper acknowledged that since the strength of his fieldwork depended on community collaboration, locals should also have a say in his findings. To engage locals, Raper published in the *Herald-Journal* weekly installments of his work, titled "Greene's Going Great," and invited comments from readers. In a similar spirit of community engagement, Raper brought along Rice on some of Jack Delano's photographic excursions into the countryside. And, in October 1941, Delano created an exhibition of his FSA photographs that traveled from community to community in Greene County and allowed residents to see images of their home before they appeared in print. It appears that Delano and Raper's local exhibit was one of kind among FSA photography projects during the New Deal. It lasted about two months and attracted a fair number of local residents. While there is no record of how they responded to the photographs, their engagement in the documentary process, even as readers and viewers, seemed to ease anxieties about the potentially progressive goals of Raper and Delano's federally supported work. They had at least been given the opportunity to vet the documentarians and their words and images, and therefore they did not feel as though they had been deceived by unscrupulous journalists who criticized their home behind their backs.[29]

The ties to Greene County and its residents that Raper had established for more than a decade, the frequent and prolonged trips Jack Delano made there, and the FSA's active role in the county all fostered more intimate interactions between documentarians and locals than existed anywhere else during the New Deal. Raper later wrote to Roy Stryker, director of the FSA's photographic division, that the "local people here are expressing a genuinely hopeful interest in our Study." Raper told Stryker that he "remained convinced that we can say what needs to be said in such way that they will recognize it as dynamic truth; that is, the facts can be presented in such way [*sic*] to be helpful in the furtherance of the farm program here." All that was left to do now was present the "facts" in an "acceptable manner" that garnered community support for federal intervention and reform.[30]

Their collaboration culminated in *Tenants of the Almighty,* a documentary book that wove Greene County's history together with ethnographic description and sociological analysis of New Deal farm programs. It contained 101 of Delano's photographs, including images of Dr. Rice and Judge Park. Rice and Park may have ceded control over their county's image to outside documentarians during the New Deal, but their looming presence and influence played no small role in determining how far someone like Raper could go in calling out the county's exploitative racial and economic systems of oppression. The benefit of Raper and Delano's close cooperation with the Greene County community was that they largely avoided the resentment and feelings of exploitation that erupted after the *Collier's* article was published. Their diplomacy gave them unprecedented access to nearly every cross-section of the community. On the other hand, by insisting on local acceptance, particularly from white leaders, Raper and Delano produced a sanitized and idealized image of Greene County in the *Tenants of the Almighty,* one that even Park and Rice could endorse. Indeed, the first photograph that appears in *Tenants of the Almighty* is Delano's photograph of Rice sitting in a rocking chair in his home surrounded by framed pictures of his ancestors. "Here is a book for the people of Greene County, Georgia," Raper wrote in the caption. "It is dedicated to the County Historian, Dr. T. B. Rice, who is most at home among his heirlooms."[31]

## NOTES

1. Owen P. White, "Devil in de Cotton," *Collier's,* Jan. 1, 1938, 9–11, 42.

2. David Harvey, *Justice, Nature and the Geography of Difference* (Malden, MA: Blackwell, 1996), 322.

3. Arthur Raper, *Tenants of the Almighty* (New York: Macmillan, 1942), 19, 33, 36; *Preface to Peasantry: A Tale of Two Black Belt Counties* (Chapel Hill: University of North Carolina Press, 1936), 13, 15. For an assessment of Greene's nineteenth-century history, see Jonathan Bryant, *How Curious a Land: Conflict and Change in Greene County, Georgia, 1850 to 1885* (Chapel Hill: University of North Carolina Press, 1996).

4. Raper, *Tenants of the Almighty,* 54–55.

5. Ibid., 157

6. Raper, *Preface to Peasantry,* xxxix, 3–4.

7. "Greene County, Georgia: The Story of One Southern County," 4–6. https://archive.org/details/greencountygeorg1940unit (accessed Aug. 1, 2015).

8. Daniel T. Rodgers, "Regionalism and the Burdens of Progress," in *Region, Race, and Reconstruction: Essays in Honor of C. Vann Woodward,* ed. J. Morgan Kousser and James M. McPherson (New York: Oxford University Press, 1982), 23.

9. Raper, *Tenants of the Almighty,* 191–92, 196–97; George Tindall, *The Emergence of the New South, 1913–1945* (Baton Rouge: Louisiana State University Press, 1967), 424–25, 618; Jack Temple Kirby, *Rural Worlds Lost: The American South, 1920–1960* (Baton Rouge: Louisiana State University Press, 1987), 57.

10. Cynthia Farah, "Owen Payne White," Handbook of Texas Online, Texas State Historical Association, www.tshaonline.org/handbook/online/articles/fwh26 (accessed Sept. 10, 2015); Owen P. White, "All Washed Up," *Collier's Weekly,* Sept. 29, 1934, 12–13; *Collier's Weekly,* Dec. 25, 1937, 4.

11. Owen P. White, "Devil in de Cotton," *Collier's Weekly*, Jan. 1, 1938, 10–11; William Stott, *Documentary Expression and Thirties America* (Chicago: University of Chicago Press, 1986), 71–72.

12. White, "Devil in de Cotton," 10–11; Raper, *Tenants of the Almighty*, 197.

13. Census records indicate that his actual name was Porter Shelton.

14. White, "Devil in de Cotton," 9–10.

15. Ibid., 11; Alfred Kazin, *On Native Grounds: An Interpretation of Modern American Prose Literature* (New York: Harcourt Brace, 1995), 489–90.

16. *Greensboro Herald-Journal*, Dec. 31, 1937.

17. *Greensboro Herald-Journal*, Feb. 4, 1938; "Misleading Magazine Article Denied by Greene County Leader," *Atlanta Constitution*, Jan. 9, 1938, 11.

18. "Misleading Magazine Article Denied by Greene County Leader," *Atlanta Constitution*, Jan. 9, 1938, 11.

19. *Greensboro Herald-Journal*, Feb. 4, 1938.

20. Representative Brown, "Greene County, GA," *Congressional Record* 83, part 2 (Feb. 9, 1938): 1737. See also Rep. Brown, "Greene County, Ga.—Extension of Remarks," *Congressional Record* 83, part 9 (Feb. 8, 1938): 531–32; T. B. Rice, "Greene County, Georgia on Trial With Collier's as Prosecutor, the Nation as Jury and Owen P. White as the Star Witness," folder 110, Arthur Franklin Raper Papers #3966, Southern Historical Collection, Wilson Library, University of North Carolina at Chapel Hill.

21. Rice, "Greene County, Georgia on Trial"; Thomas Brockett Rice, *The History of Greene County, Georgia* (Macon, GA: J. W. Burke, 1961), 476.

22. Raper, *Tenants of the Almighty*, viii; Louis Mazzari, *Southern Modernist: Arthur Raper from the New Deal to the Cold War* (Baton Rouge: Louisiana State University Press, 2006), 114, 346n18; Patricia Sullivan, *Days of Hope: Race and Democracy in the New Deal Era* (Chapel Hill: University of North Carolina Press, 1995), 2, 59.

23. Rice, "Greene County on Trial."

24. Ibid.

25. Ibid.

26. Ibid.

27. Ibid.; Rice, *The History of Greene County, Georgia*, 476.

28. I have taken my statistical information here from two websites that maintain digital collections of the FSA photography file: The Library of Congress, www.loc.gov/pictures/collection/fsa/, and Photogrammar, http://photogrammar.yale.edu/.

29. Raper, Tenants of the Almighty, viii; "'Greene's Going Great' New Feature for Herald-Journal," *Greensboro Herald-Journal*, Jan. 9, 1942, folder 121, Raper Papers; "Delano Photographs Greene County," *Greensboro Herald-Journal*, Oct. 31, 1941.

30. Arthur Raper to Roy Stryker, Nov. 29, 1941, folder 970, Raper Papers.

31. Raper, *Tenants of the Almighty*.

# Inside the Farmhouse

## *Ruth Allen and Margaret Jarman Hagood Confront Rural Realities*

REBECCA SHARPLESS AND MELISSA WALKER

A car jounces down a rutted dirt road and stops near a rickety board-and-batten farmhouse. A young woman emerges from the car, mounts the broken steps, and knocks at the screenless door. A tired-looking woman answers the door and eyes the stranger warily. For the next hour or so, an extraordinary encounter occurs, as the university researcher gains the trust of the farm woman, who then shares the most intimate details of her life.

In Texas and in North Carolina, at opposite ends of the South, such meetings occurred hundreds of times at the behest of economist Ruth Alice Allen and sociologist Margaret Jarman Hagood. The two conducted studies of southern farm women—Allen in the late 1920s and Hagood in the late 1930s—which paralleled to a surprising extent. Whether the women were farming tobacco or cotton, whether they were white, African American, or Mexican, their lives were marked by hard work and hard times. Reformers had been worried about conditions in the rural South since the 1870s, but they rarely had concerned themselves with the farm family. Allen and Hagood insisted that farming was more than the dealings of men—mules and staple crops and liens—and that women, with their battered farmhouses, shabby clothes, and, particularly, their many babies, ought to be a part of the discussion of rural poverty in the South. If the South were to progress, Allen and Hagood believed, women and the things that mattered to them had to be included in the equation. In their insistence on including gender analysis in the broader discussion, the two researchers became pioneers in their respective areas of social science.[1]

From the Progressive era up through the New Deal, American policy makers became increasingly convinced that the key to solving social problems was the application of data gathered through the rational study of the interpersonal relationships and institutions of human society. Regional and federal officials turned to scholars in the expanding social sciences for data to shape their policies, and social scientists eagerly accepted their growing influence on efforts to solve national problems. Nowhere was the influence of social scientists more important than the rural South, a region plagued by uniformly high levels of endemic, deep poverty. Into this milieu came Allen and Hagood, embracing the idea that a complex interplay of history, custom, and systemic constraints shaped individuals' economic and personal decision making. Both rejected the proposition held by many of their contemporaries, particularly the eugenicists who held considerable sway over public policy in the South, that poverty was a result of the inferiority and failings of individuals. Instead, they argued, the poverty that gripped the rural South came from entrenched economic and social systems and particularly the way those systems disempowered women.

Allen and Hagood likely never met, being in different fields and different states, but they shared much in common. Both were the daughters of professional educators, and both were shaped by their upbringings in the rural South. They also had similar professional training by social scientists who sought to link research to reform efforts.

Ruth Allen was born in Cameron, Texas, in 1889 to Jennie Adams Allen and Thomas Franklin Allen, a teacher and school superintendent. Her family's political sympathies tended to the left. They subscribed to the *Appeal to Reason,* a socialist newspaper, and Allen recalled reading it "rather regularly" as a child.[2] After graduating from high school in Marlin, Allen earned a teaching certificate from Southwest Texas State Teachers College.

In 1918, Allen enrolled at the University of Texas (UT), where economics and sociology shared a department, and received her bachelor's degree in 1921. She then completed a master's degree in economics at UT in 1923, writing a thesis on "The Theory and Practice of a Minimum Wage." At Texas, she was mentored by Professor A. B. Wolfe, who taught courses focused on social change, including "Introduction to Social Problems" and "Sociology of the Women's Movement."[3] Wolfe's colleague, Max Handman, had earned his PhD at the University of Chicago and then taught with Thorstein Veblen at the University of Missouri. Under their leadership and that of their successors, UT became an outpost of the school of economic thought known as institutionalism.[4] Influenced by the German historical school, institutionalists held strongly that economic theory could not be developed "in a vacuum apart from the real working lives of the average person." They were averse to abstractions and relied heavily on examinations of history and custom to explain people's economic decision making. They also believed in the value of collecting empirical data through field work.[5] Allen demonstrated her institutionalist leanings as she "scrutinized actual institutions" to discover how they affected peoples' everyday lives and influenced people's behavior outside of "rational economic behavior." She was an economist but one with a strong sociological bent. For the Texas economists, "theory and policy in the real world were intimately tied together."[6]

Upon the completion of her master's degree, Allen taught as an adjunct at UT. In the late 1920s, she began doctoral study at the University of Chicago under the guidance of Harry A. Millis, a noted institutionalist and later a member of the National Labor Relations Board. Also a former colleague of Veblen, Millis was "no academic theorist" but worked closely with real people, particularly industrial workers.[7]

Being at Chicago brought Allen squarely into the movement to use social science research to affect public policy. The university received substantial support from the Laura Spelman Rockefeller Memorial (LSRM), a fund established to produce through the social sciences "adequate theoretically grounded explanations of human behavior."[8] The University of Chicago and the Brookings Institution, which awarded Allen a fellowship, were among the top recipients from the LSRM. Years later, the LSRM would also indirectly shape the career of Margaret Hagood through funding for her graduate institution. At the University of North Carolina, Howard Odum established the Institute for Research in Social Science in 1924 with LSRM funding, and the University of Texas received one grant from the institute in 1927, establishing the Bureau of Research in the Social Sciences. Allen, who returned to UT after completing her coursework in Chicago, accepted several years of funding from the LSRM to conduct her study of farm women.[9]

Born October 26, 1907, eighteen years after Allen, Margaret Jarman Hagood came from a long line of devout, well-educated Presbyterians. Her maternal grandfather was president of Erskine College, a Presbyterian college and seminary in South Carolina, and both parents were college educated. Her father taught mathematics at the college level and eventually became president of Mary Baldwin College in Virginia. Margaret spent much of her childhood in rural Newton County, Georgia, and from an early age, she demonstrated the concern for the rural poor that would be a hallmark of her later work. For example, family members recalled that at the age of thirteen, she organized a Sunday school for textile-mill children in her community.[10]

Hagood was educated at the Emory-at-Oxford preparatory school in Covington, Georgia, at Chicora College in Columbia, South Carolina, and at Agnes Scott College in Atlanta. After her marriage to dental student Middleton Howard Hagood in 1926, Margaret left school and gave birth to a daughter. In 1929, she returned to college, earning a bachelor's degree at Queens College in Charlotte, North Carolina, and a master's degree at Emory University.[11] She and Middleton divorced in 1936, and Margaret retained primary custody of their daughter. For several years, she taught mathematics, first at Druid Hills High School in Atlanta and then at National Park Seminary, an all-girls school in College Park, Maryland.[12]

Hagood's career path shifted in 1935 when Odum, a long-time Jarman family friend, offered her a graduate fellowship in sociology at Chapel Hill. Like A. B. Wolfe and Max Handman at the University of Texas, Odum trained a generation of researchers to use the social sciences to analyze and address the South's social and economic problems. In an approach similar to that of the institutionalists, Odum advocated studying the section from a standpoint that he called "regionalism." He maintained that careful study of the social, cultural, and economic characteristics of a region, with a focus on links between people, the land they inhabited, and the culture they created, could be a tool for planning that would integrate disadvantaged regions of the United States into the national mainstream.[13]

Not surprisingly, given her skills as a mathematician, Hagood followed Odum's lead in becoming a social demographer. Social demography, a subspecialty within sociology that analyzes the relationships between economic, social, cultural, and biological processes influencing a population, relies heavily on the compilation and analysis of statistics. Unlike many demographers but again like her mentor, Hagood believed that sociologists should use quantitative methods in tandem with qualitative sources. Trends in the demographics of a population, she argued, could only be understood by examining the cultural factors that shaped that demography.[14]

Thus Allen and Hagood were both poised to use their training in statistics to investigate social problems. But both of them moved in a new direction from their mentors, bringing into the study of southern rural poverty questions about the roles of women. In the late 1920s, Allen decided to investigate the part that women played in the disaster that was the southern cotton economy. She wanted to include women, believing that economists ignoring "the strategic position occupied by women in any competitive struggle" led to failure in analyzing many problems of "modern industrial life."[15] Allen summed up the effects of the cotton economy on Texas farm women: "A profit and loss account of a cotton crop raised by the labor of the home maker in the field would show, upon the asset side, labor costs very low; and upon the liability side, poor food, unkept houses, dirty and poorly nourished children, marriage relations which have become worse than commonplace, and the loss of wholesome family life. Who shall attempt to balance the accounts by talk of money equivalent?" (147).

Allen later recalled that she had one overarching question in her study of farm women: "Why wouldn't the cotton grower make a profit after using so much non-paid labor—women and children who worked the fields with no cost to him?"[16] She was aware of the "long-continued depression in the farming industry" and that all aspects of life on Central Texas farms were "tied inextricably to the price of cotton" (12). Allen also knew that women who worked in the cotton fields comprised a third of all employed women in Texas. Ironically, too, Texas was urbanizing faster than any other southern state, save Florida, and rural women, particularly the best and brightest, were heading to the cities in unprecedented numbers, where they would be drawn into the "industrial life of the state." Urban dwellers' knowledge of their lives in rural areas, Allen argued, would enable others to assist and prevent rural women from having to pay "a greater price than is necessary" in their transition to town dwellers (13–14). While attempting to answer an economic question, Allen veered into examining the conditions of women's lives and the circumstances that impoverished many of them.

Allen designed her study to investigate women in five counties of Central Texas, with one in West Texas and two in East Texas as controls. With apparently little reflection, she chose to look at Anglo, African American, and Mexican women, observing that in Texas there existed "three groups divided by barriers of race, of nationality, of economic backgrounds, and of social traditions" (21).[17] She or her assistant personally interviewed 664 "American" women, 238 African American women, and 269 Mexican women, for a total sample size of 1,171 to represent 1.1 million rural Texas women.

Allen created a standardized questionnaire of about 170 questions, gathering information about "the living conditions of women and the work they do." The work she divided into three categories, "rearing a family, housework, and field work," which she further subdivided into work done for family and work done for hire (24). The topics included everything from the use of a midwife in childbirth to the number of pounds of lard rendered per year to the number of items crocheted in a year. Allen and an assistant conducted the interviews between November 1928 and January 1930. She estimated that each interview took about an hour and a half, as "the somewhat antagonistic attitude of farm women toward town women must be broken down" (31). She did not assume any differences between herself and her interviewees because of race, class, or marital status. As an economist, Allen believed in the value of counting, and her completed report bristles with eighty-two statistical tables. But she admitted the limitations of statistics. Regarding the collection of water, for example, she observes, "It would seem that the statement that water is carried 300 yards gives a fairly clear picture of the situation; but if the 300 yards are up and down the steep sides of a creek and under a wire fence, the method of securing water is not in the same class with carrying water 300 yards across a level lot" (32). Nonetheless, she relies mostly on numbers and aggregates to tell her story, with only an occasional illustrative sentence or two. Her work, as economists Alexandra Bernasek and Douglas Kinnear comment, is "fact-based in the extreme. . . . Her emphasis on real-world phenomena comes at a price, though, as Allen displays an aversion to abstract theorizing so extreme that the reader is sometimes left to piece together sections of analysis for herself."[18]

Allen's primary concern was the effect of women's labor on the system of cotton agriculture. Like census workers and other enumerators before her, Allen struggled to define field work and how much of it was statistically significant. What was clear, however, was that the poorer the family, the more likely the wife was to do field work. Eighty-seven percent of the African American women did field work, and many of them worked for wages. Many women received no cash remuneration for their work with cotton, for it became subsumed as part of the so-called family wage, in which all workers' earnings were credited to one account. Allen fumed, "Any labor given by these women to the production of cotton is unquestionably a gift. In most cases they even pay highly for the privilege of making the gift" (157). Further, she found that the so-called family work unit was impracticable, for it forced down the wages of others outside the family (168–69). And even when women did receive pay for their labors, their income, Allen observed, was "almost no wage at all" (199).

While younger women might work for money at little or no cost to their personal lives, married women paid heavily for their participation in field work. Cotton took its heaviest toll in early summer, the period known as "chopping," when the plants were thinned, and in the fall, when the crop had to be gathered by hand before wet weather ruined the mature bolls. Women squeezed in all of their home tasks around their outside work during those peak periods. Allen commented, "It is the mothers who are carrying the two-fold task of bearing and rearing families of three or more children and at the same time doing heavy farm work who call for social questioning" (120). Allen was also concerned about the danger to women's bodies in picking cotton, particularly dragging heavy sacks through the fields and to the weighing station (141), and she remarked that for many women, "her method of self-preservation is neglect" (147).

Field work affected women's home production, for the less outside work a woman did, the more time she had to raise chickens, make butter, bake bread, and grow and can fruits and vegetables—which in turn kept her family from having to purchase food at the store. Allen bluntly remarked, "Women who do not help raise cotton bring in more money than women who do" (92).

Although she was concerned mainly about labor in cotton, Allen carefully documented the living standards of farm families. She argued that since women were remunerated for their labor primarily in goods and services from the farm—their housing, food, and clothing—rather than cash, their low standards of living forced down the cost of cotton production (168–69). Their housework, which Allen defined as cooking, sewing, house cleaning, and washing and ironing, was onerous, mostly done without mechanical conveniences. Allen's data included such details as percentages of water "carried," "hauled," and "piped," with "piped" further subdivided into "to house, "to sink," "to bath," and "to bath and sink." A third of white families had access to "piped" water, while African American and Mexican women were most likely to haul their water from nearby creeks or stockponds (43, 182, 218). Living standards were lowest for Mexican migrant workers. Allen found a group of workers in a house in which a wall had fallen in and been replaced with an old cotton sack, and she observed, "even the poorest Negro tenant seldom has such crude facilities" (217).

Childbearing was a central concern of farm women and to Allen, who wrote, "The unnecessary human cost of bearing children is impressed upon any observer who studies the life of women. Too frequent confinements, bad or no prenatal care, lack of proper care during and immediately following labor; all take their toll on the mother's strength." She diligently counted and tabulated the numbers of children, finding that white farm owners averaged 3.27 children, tenants, 3.74, and laborers, 4.68, while African American women bore 4.8 children and Mexican women 4.82 (63, 177, 225). While Allen made few direct recommendations, she was blunt with regard to childbearing, advocating better and more reasonably priced medical care, "spacing" of children (although she did not openly call for birth control, which was illegal), and protective legislation to shield farm women from excessive hours of work (64–65). Allen disagreed with the old saw that children were an economic asset: "If children be an economic asset, why does a woman who has borne fourteen and lived all her life on the farm find herself at eighty-three without house or land, living in a hovel . . . ?" (70).

The arrival of workers from Mexico caused Allen great consternation, and she condemned the farmers who exploited Mexican labor: "The cotton civilization was built upon the exploitation of an ignorant and helpless race; and one can only marvel at the temerity of a people who, faced with the gravest race problem of all history, insist upon the addition of still a third element, alien in spirit and unassimilable socially" (238). Economically, Allen believed, the Mexican laborers were a disaster, for "with them, we can raise cotton, cheap cotton; in fact, we can meet almost any price the market will pay and still produce cotton." (239).

Allen's casual racism is jarring. While her treatment of African American women was generally even-handed, she openly scorned the women from Mexico, whom she called peons. She found Mexican women frail in comparison with African Americans—"she lacks the Negro's physical strength and ability to care for herself and her offspring" (212)—and she despaired of the women who stood silently while their men talked for them (222–23). The low expectations by Mexican women, Allen believed, would make cotton growing even more exploitative: "It would appear, then, that the Mexican woman has a willingness to accept a lower standard of living than either the Negro or the American white. And, furthermore, her standard is so much lower than even that of the Negro that it will be an important factor in any economic competition" (246).[19]

Allen's solution to the difficulties of cotton agriculture in Texas was to pay women wages for working in cotton. If not paid, Allen believed, the women would go to town to secure income, "simply a shifting of the problem of hard work, long hours, and miserable living standards to the city." (249). Women's work should be brought within market control "as to wages, as to labor supply, and as to price" (265).

Allen's study found a limited audience as a University of Texas bulletin. Beginning in 1882, these bulletins published information ranging from regents' reports to faculty research, and by the 1930s numbered forty-eight per year. The readership for such a bulletin would have been statewide, as about one hundred libraries cataloged the report, in all regions of Texas. The University of Chicago accepted the bulletin, exactly as published and printed down to the title page, as Allen's PhD dissertation in 1933. But a casual reader would likely not have come across the terse, statistic-laden document.

Ruth Allen placed women's labor at the center of her analysis, considering childbearing in the context of that labor. By contrast, Margaret Hagood made childbearing itself the central focus of her studies, first in a dissertation that relied exclusively on demography and later in a book that relied on qualitative field studies. Hagood's dissertation, completed in 1937, was titled "Mothers of the South: A Population Study of Native White Women of Childbearing Age in the Southeast."[20] Noting that native white women in the South had a fertility rate almost twice as high as that of the rest of the nation (108), Hagood studied the implications of the South's exceptionally high rate of population growth "for the definition, determination, and achievement" of an optimal standard of living (iii–iv).

Like Allen, Hagood was an early and articulate proponent of using gender as a category of analysis. She argued that "sex has been considered 'the most fundamental cleavage in society'" and that the distinctive experiences of women shape the larger society in profound ways (v). For example, she pointed out that in the South, several demographic indices that related to women distinguished it from other regions of the country, including the young age at which women began bearing children, the percentage of brides in their early teens, the relatively large family size and high ratio of children to women, the small proportion of women employed outside the home, the number of women engaged in agricultural production, and the fact that the region had the highest rate of population growth in the country (iv, 287–88). She said that women's roles were "central not only in a biological sense because they bear children, but also in a social and cultural sense because they exercise a tremendous influence on these children during their most formative years" (5).

Hagood focused on white women, and she was explicit about her reasons for doing so. She explained that as a white woman, she believed she would not be able to produce a solid study of black women's lives. Acknowledging the barriers that the Jim Crow system placed in the way of honest communication between the races, she said, "the limitation to white is due to the recognition that qualitative material, a necessary supplement to statistical data, could best be secured from Negro mothers by one of their own race" (iv–v). She also chose not to include foreign-born women "because the inclusion of the foreign-born would introduce extraneous patterns not truly representative of the region in which they form such a small proportion of the people" (v).[21]

Admirers of Hagood's masterful 1939 book *Mothers of the South: Portraiture of the White Tenant Farm Woman* might be startled by the statistical nature of the dissertation bearing the same main title. In spite of her insistence on the importance of combining quantitative and qualitative sources, in the dissertation, Hagood did not use the case-study method. She explained that while "there is no adequate substitute for first hand material consisting of case studies . . . such case studies are not within the scope of this thesis, but will compose the content of a projected supplementary study" (iv, n.7). Instead, the dissertation exhaustively charted the demographics of childbearing and fertility in the South and the nation. Hagood concluded that the South lagged behind the rest of the nation in part because of the high fertility rates in the region, and she feared the problem would grow worse in future years because "the supply of people produced by these mothers within the next generation will be greater than the demand for people as forecast by experts in the various occupational fields" (121–22). She attributed this high rate of population growth to the fact that very few women in the South practiced any kind of contraception. The reasons women did not try to limit their family size were complex. Hagood noted that "a common heritage of cultural patterns from frontier, plantation, rural life, and religion . . . have made for an early age of marriage, many children, subjection to husband, and restricted activities" that in turn shaped attitudes about childbearing and the appropriate role of women in society (287). She detailed the persistence of "frontier" conditions and patriarchal attitudes that were a holdover from the plantation South, as well as the practice of nonmechanized agriculture, which placed a premium on child labor. Even in areas where the South had begun to industrialize, the prevalent industry was textiles, which also traditionally employed child laborers. Religious communities also criticized efforts to limit family size (145–51). Unless a woman lives in a community "where the tradition [of having large numbers of children] is at least beginning to break down, she will still feel great hesitancy in seeking a radical departure from the accepted practice unless she is a true pioneer of spirit" (161). Aside from these heritage factors, the poor economic conditions in the South and the relative geographic isolation of many of its rural areas had delayed the distribution of contraceptive knowledge and limited access to health care facilities. She cautioned that policy makers should not assume that women were "free agents" in choosing whether or not to limit their fertility, for they needed the cooperation of their husbands. Hagood warned that social pressures would also mitigate against the rapid adoption of family-planning practices (289).

The dissertation included detailed analysis of four "locational occupational" groups of women: white tenant-farm women, mountain mothers, mill-village mothers, and upper-middle-class working mothers. Hagood concluded her dissertation by calling for case studies focused on these locational occupational types (291–92), and she launched into the fieldwork for one of these case studies almost immediately after completing her doctorate. With Odum's help, she obtained funding from the Julius Rosenwald Foundation to support her fieldwork with white tenant-farm women during the 1937–38 academic year. This fieldwork became the basis for her landmark book, *Mothers of the South.*

*Mothers of the South* is one of many works of documentary expression produced during the Great Depression. Intellectuals and artists from many backgrounds sought to put a human face on the suffering endured by millions of ordinary Americans during the 1930s and to use the documentary records as the impetus for social and economic change. In *Mothers of the South,* Hagood added depth and humanity to the picture of rural southern women that she had summarized statistically in her dissertation.[22]

In her new work, Hagood documented the lives of 254 childbearing women on tobacco and cotton farms in the North Carolina Piedmont, Georgia, and Alabama. Relying on referrals, she assembled a group of interviewees who represented each study region "in three aspects: location, type of farming, and socio-economic level." Hagood outlined her interviewing techniques at the end of *Mothers of the South.* Writing in third person, she said, "The visitor, knowing in advance the name of the woman, found her—as often in the kitchen, striphouse, yard or field as at the front door—introduced herself as Mrs. Hagood from Chapel Hill, stated that she was interested in women who live in the country and their problems in bringing up children, and asked if she might visit for a little while." Sensing that she would gain richer material if she approached the women in a conversational manner, she said, "in general, questioning was avoided," other than a few basic queries about the family size and the state of the woman's health. She also did not take notes during her visits, preferring to write up her observations immediately after the visit so as not to inhibit the conversation.[23]

Hagood quickly built a rapport with most of the women she interviewed. She explained that most women seemed to welcome the break in routine that Hagood's visit offered and that they were eager to "talk of their children, homes, work, and even more intimate matters if certain conventions are observed in approach and phraseology"(68). Hagood's own rural background enabled her to speak knowledgably about elements of the women's daily work lives, encouraging them to share details of family and farm life. She admired their intelligence and their strong work ethic. While few of the women she interviewed had much formal education, she reported that "imagination and ability to talk did not seem to be closely correlated with number of grades completed." She said, "Their knowledge of farming matters is surprising and pertains not only to the immediate condition of the current crop but to details of renting, credit, the sequence of operations, and to the basic data for making an estimate of how they will 'come out this year'" (77).

Hagood dismissed assertions that tenant-farm families were poor because they lacked the ambition or will to improve their own lives. She reported that the women she met exhibited a remarkable "emotional maturity . . . in their acceptance of economic hardship. Such acceptance can not be termed passive for it involves a constant output of labor that even a subsistence living may be obtained. It is mature in the sense that activities are directed toward the objective factors of the situation . . . rather than toward inner goals demanded by inferiority feelings or other internal maladjustments" (63, 68–69, 73, 75).

Rejecting the idea that tenants were poor because of "bad hereditary stock" or a lack of "industry and thrift," Hagood instead indicted the farm-tenancy system. She offered the example of "farm four," a family of cotton tenants: "Here was a family of two parents and four children with good health, with a love of farming and fieldwork, with demonstrated thrift, with self-restraint and temperance, with high motivation toward achieving ownership—and yet the results of their efforts . . . were complete impoverishment" (38, 29–30). Just as Allen had documented in Texas, hard work and large families were not enough to lift a family from poverty in the rural South.

Hagood's opening chapters presented detailed sketches of representative farms and families, providing rich and engaging descriptions of farm families. An example was her vivid description of "farm two," where a disintegrating unpainted shack housed a tenant farmer, his wife, and their ten surviving children. "A visitor will always find the tenant mother . . . at home, for she has not left the immediate neighborhood in a good many years except to go to funerals. But she will not be found in the house unless the call is before breakfast, after supper, or on Sunday. 'Gimme the field every time,'" the woman told the scholar. Hagood went on to describe the family's struggles against weather, insects, malnutrition, and debt. In spite of an ample labor supply, rich farmland, and cash income from tobacco, the family's standard of living did not meet even "minimum standards of adequacy." The family had been in the community for generations and on this farm for years, but "the evidence of care and conservation of land which might be expected from long tenure of one family are missing." She attributed the lack of care to a lack of education, especially education about modern farming techniques. The family, she concluded, "scores an indictment against the 'system'" (14, 17, and 20).

These chapters also delivered an astute critique of the myth of the agricultural ladder, with several case studies demonstrating the near-impossibility of climbing out of tenancy. One example was farm seven, where a young family had managed to build a tidy three-room home on five acres of woodland they had scraped to purchase after ten years of tenant farming. The wife on farm seven had labored full-time in the fields even though she gave birth to a child every two years. The couple had also been able to buy their own mule, but none of these achievements rescued them from tenancy. Their own wooded land was unusable for farming, so they continued to labor on a landowner's farm in exchange for one-fourth of the cotton crop and one-third of the corn. Hagood commented, "This year their share from eight acres of cotton was not sufficient to pay their year's debt for fertilizer and running expenses" (42).

Hagood noted that "the major problems of regional and occupation overpopulation and the bankruptcy of cash crop agriculture intertwine and come to a focus in the life of the tenant farm woman" (127). In the second part of the book, she explored the lives of the mothers—their work lives, childbearing, and childrearing. She found that once she revealed to women that she herself was married and a mother, women were quite forthcoming—albeit usually with circumspect language—with intimate details regarding childbirth and contraception. "It was often interesting to note the immediate shifting to the biological and especially obstetrical features the moment a husband or child left the room and there was privacy. . . . There was almost always a willingness to talk about such matters even though circumlocution made the process of conveying information cumbersome." She noted that women often described the sexual act and contraception with colorful euphemisms. For example, one woman who practiced coitus interruptus with her husband to limit her family size, explained, "If you don't want butter, pull the dasher out in time." Some women expressed approval of efforts to limit family size because it better enabled the family to attend to the welfare of "already-born children" (111, 123, 124).

Southern tenant farm women, Hagood argued,

> compose a group who epitomize, as much as any, the results of the wastes and lags of the Region. They suffer the direct consequences of a long-continued cash crop economy; they undergo extreme social impoverishment from the lack and unequal distribution of institutional services; and they bear the brunt of a regional tradition—compounded of elements from religion, patriarchy, and aristocracy—which subjects them to class and sex discrimination. Moreover, they continue to augment the pathologies of the Region by their very functioning, as they produce, at a ruinous cost to both the land and themselves, the cotton and tobacco by which the rural South still lives, and the children who are simultaneously the Region's greatest asset and most crucial problem. (4)

Hagood warned that the problems of the South's rural people were acute, and it was imperative that policy makers take steps to improve conditions there; otherwise "southern tenant farm mothers will continue to supply a disproportionate share of children who will be disadvantaged from birth." She concluded, "The welfare and functioning of southern tenant farm mothers have consequences of significance not only for the quality of people who shall inherit the Nation, but through them, eventually for the sort of Nation that will be maintained" (243, 244).

Hagood's work was well received at the time, garnering praise for its vivid picture of rural southern life and its scientific rigor in scholarly journals ranging from the *Annals of the American Academy of Political and Social Science* to *Social Forces* to the *Journal of Educational Sociology.* In *Social Forces,* sociologist William E. Cole wrote, "No recent publication on the South is more welcome," adding, "The study reveals the intimate way in which the economy of the South takes its toll in human misery, submarginal lives, and blighted hopes."[24]

What neither Allen nor Hagood could know, of course, was that the world that so concerned them was shifting in the early 1940s as World War II stimulated rural depopulation. While both of them had strong ideas about how to improve the lives of rural women, neither saw their ideas implemented or even seriously discussed. Rather, demographic changes and industrialization moved southern women from their sharecroppers' shacks into the cities. What the two social scientists left, instead of a record of effective change, was a detailed and revealing picture of southern farm life in the interwar years with a special focus on gender. Both researchers forced the inclusion of women into southern rural studies, and both depicted in depth the daily lives of women struggling to make lives despite widespread poverty. What the researchers left, in the end, were historical records rather than treatises effecting social reform. Seventy-five years later, historians remain indebted to Hagood and Allen for their empathy and their eye for detail and for what they reveal about the mostly hidden lives of southern women.

## NOTES

1. While numerous social workers researched the social conditions of farm women in the 1920s, Allen and Hagood's investigations were the most sustained and, in the case of Hagood, the most widely disseminated. Others' work also tended to focus on women only as mothers of children, not as women per se. For an example of other women's work, see Ellen Nathalie Matthews and Ethel M. Springer, *Child Labor and the Work of Mothers on Norfolk Truck Farms* (Washington, DC: Department of Labor, Children's Bureau, 1924).

2. Ruth Allen to Theodore Debs, May 20, 1940, Briscoe Center for American History, University of Texas, Austin (hereafter Briscoe Center), Labor Movement in Texas Collection, box 2E301, folder 12, quoted in Andrew Graybill, introduction to *Chapters in the History of Organized Labor in Texas,* by Ruth Alice Allen (Dallas, TX: William P. Clements Center for Southwest Studies, Southern Methodist University, 2006), viii.

3. Graybill, introduction, vii; "Announcement of the Department of Education," University of Texas Bulletin no. 1718, Mar. 25, 1917, 54.

4. Malcolm Rutherford, "American Institutionalism after 1945," *A Research Annual: Research in the History of Economic Thought and Methodology* 33 (2015): 98.

5. Ronnie J. Phillips, introduction to *Economic Mavericks: The Texas Institutionalists,* ed. Ronnie J. Phillips (Greenwich, CT: JAI Press, 1995), 3–4; Alexandra Bernasek and Douglas Kinnear, "Ruth Allen: Frontier Labor Economist," in Phillips, *Economic Mavericks,* 76–77.

6. Phillips, introduction, 2.

7. "Dr. H. A. Millis Dies," *New York Times,* June 26, 1948.

8. Martin Bulmer, "Support for Sociology in the 1920s: The Laura Spelman Rockefeller Memorial and the Beginnings of Modern, Large-Scale, Sociological Research in the University," *American Sociologist* 17, no. 4 (Nov. 1982): 186.

9. Bulmer, "Support for Sociology," 188–89; 1928–29 Budget for Research in the Social Sciences, box 2N230, University of Texas Bureau of Research in the Social Sciences Record, Briscoe Center.

10. Agnes Riedmann, "Margaret Jarman Hagood," in *Women in Sociology: A Bio-Bibliographical Sourcebook,* ed. Mary Jo Deegan (New York: Greenwood, 1991), 157; Anne Firor Scott, "Margaret Loyd Jarman Hagood," in *Notable American Women: The Modern Period,* ed. Barbara Sicherman and Carol Hurd Green (Cambridge: Belknap Press of Harvard University Press, 1980), 297; Julie N. Zimmerman, "Margaret Loyd Jarman Hagood," in *American National Biography,* ed. John A. Garraty and Mark C. Carnes (New York: Oxford University Press, 1999), 791; James Browder email to author, Mar. 4, 2011, copy in author's possession.

11. Scott, "Margaret Loyd Jarman Hagood," 297; Larry Riddle, "Margaret Jarman Hagood," *Biographies of Women Mathematicians,* Agnes Scott College, www.agnesscott.edu/lriddle/women/hagood.htm (accessed June 6, 2011); *1930 United States Federal Census*; James Browder telephone interview with author, July 14, 2011.

12. Scott, "Margaret Loyd Jarman Hagood," 297; Zimmerman, "Margaret Loyd Jarman Hagood," 791.

13. Scott, "Margaret Loyd Jarman Hagood," 297; Zimmerman, "Margaret Loyd Jarman Hagood," 791; Howard W. Odum, *Southern Regions of the United States* (Chapel Hill: University of North Carolina Press, 1936); Howard Washington Odum and Harry Estill Moore, *American Regionalism: A Cultural-Historical Approach to National Integration* (New York: Henry Holt, 1938), 35–43; George B. Tindall, "The Significance of Howard W. Odum to Southern History: A Preliminary Estimate," *Journal of Southern History* 24 (Aug. 1958): 285–307; John Shelton Reed, "History of the Odum Institute," http://unc.live/2t8KmFQ (accessed June 15, 2015).

14. Margaret Jarman Hagood, "Mothers of the South: A Population Study of Native White Women of Childbearing Age of the Southeast" (PhD diss., University of North Carolina, 1937), iv.

15. Ruth Alice Allen, "The Labor of Women in the Production of Cotton," University of Texas Bulletin no. 3134, Sept. 8, 1931, 250.

16. Bill Warren, "Books," *Austin American-Statesman*, Apr. 2, 1972.

17. Allen was not the first to interview women from three ethnic groups; fieldworkers from the US Children's Bureau had broken that ground five years earlier. See Ellen Nathalie Matthews and Helen Maretta Dart, *The Welfare of Children in Cotton-Growing Areas of Texas,* US Department of Labor, Children's Bureau Publication no. 134 (Washington, DC: Government Printing Office, 1924).

18. Bernasek and Kinnear, "Ruth Allen," 78.

19. Sociologist Elena R. Gutierrez charges Allen with introducing "the enduring construct of Mexican women as hyper-fertile baby machines" and portraying them as "passive, fatalistic, and unquestioning of their life-long service to men." Elena R. Gutierrez, *Fertile Matters: The Politics of Mexican-Origin Women's Reproduction* (Austin: University of Texas Press, 2009), 56–57. Allen published a version of her research on Mexican women as "Mexican Peon Women," *Sociology and Social Research* 16 (1931): 131–42.

20. Hagood, "Mothers of the South: A Population Study." Subsequent references are given in parentheses in the text.

21. In her conclusion, Hagood expressed a hope that a similar study of "Negro mothers" would be undertaken (291–92). Historian Linda Gordon has suggested that Hagood's decision to focus her study solely on white women was a sign of her acceptance of the racist assumptions of the Jim Crow South, and Hagood's mentor had a mixed record on issues of racial inclusion, demonstrating "growth and change" over time. See Linda Gordon, *Dorothea Lange: A Life Beyond Limits* (New York: W. W. Norton, 2009), 272; Tindall, "Significance of Howard W. Odum," 287.

22. For an introduction to documentary expression, see William Stott, *Documentary Expression and Thirties America* (New York: Oxford University Press, 1973). For a study that situates Hagood's work in the documentary tradition, see Daire Elizabeth Roebuck, "Margaret Jarman Hagood's *Mothers of the South* as Sociological Documentary," MA thesis, North Carolina State University, 2004.

23. Margaret Jarman Hagood, *Mothers of the South: Portraiture of the White Tenant Farm Woman* (1939; reprint, New York: W. W. Norton,): 5, 223–25, 227. Subsequent references are given in parentheses in the text.

24. John E. Wills, *Annals of the American Academy of Political and Social Science* 209 (May 1940): 228–29; Review of *Mothers of the South, Journal of Educational Sociology,* 15, no. 6 (Feb. 1942): 380; William E. Cole, *Social Forces* 18, no. 3 (Mar. 1940): 450–51.

# V

# RACE AND INTERRACIALISM

# Redlining Georgia

ELLA HOWARD

"The Color of Credit," a 1988 Pulitzer Prize–winning series of fifteen investigative articles, began, "Whites receive five times as many home loans from Atlanta's banks and savings and loans as blacks of the same income—and that gap has been widening each year, an *Atlanta Journal-Constitution* study of $6.2 billion in lending shows." Using lenders' reports and real estate records, researchers found that mortgage availability was determined far less by residential turnover, home value, and household income, than by the race of a neighborhood's occupants. The reason for this trend was readily apparent to Atlanta City Council president Marvin Arrington, who observed, "It's institutional racism. While we are patting each other on the back about being a great city and a city too busy to hate, they're still redlining."[1]

More than fifty years after the New Deal–era Home Owners' Loan Corporation (HOLC) commissioned its now infamous "residential security maps" to communicate its mortgage-lending recommendations for American cities, the effects of such discriminatory practices continued to be felt even in the city known as a haven for middle-class African Americans. The ensuing investigation resulted in Decatur Federal Savings and Loan being required to pay $1 million for unjustly rejecting mortgage applications from African Americans. More recently, redlining has drawn media attention in the wake of the subprime lending crisis that began in 2007, and the urban unrest following the deaths of Michael Brown in Ferguson, Missouri, and Freddie Gray in Baltimore, Maryland. Americans are increasingly questioning the role of institutional and systemic racism in fostering divided and hostile urban environments. As sociologist Douglas Massey has argued, "Through its deliberate decisions, white America consistently chose to build, support, and maintain a characteristic residential configuration known as the ghetto."[2]

This essay takes Georgia as a case study, tracing the development of residential segregation in five cities from Reconstruction through the formal redlining of the 1930s and beyond. Augusta, Columbus, Macon, Savannah, and Atlanta were surveyed by the HOLC, creating remarkably precise snapshots of the residential patterns that had taken shape by the 1920s. In most of the Georgia cities surveyed, race played a determining factor in the redlining process. In part, this was because African Americans were already clustered in the oldest, shabbiest housing available in many southern cities. Even in those cities and neighborhoods where this was not the case, however, the race of an area's residents largely determined the assessment value given by surveyors and influenced future mortgage lending and economic development.

## SOUTHERN REDLINING AND THE HOME OWNERS' LOAN CORPORATION

Traditionally a rural region, the South witnessed increased urban development in the early twentieth century. During the 1920s, the populations and industries of southern cities grew markedly. While still predominantly rural, the South's cities played an increasingly important role in the region's economic and cultural life. In 1936, sociologist Howard Odum produced a massive study of the South, observing that "the culture of the Southeast is more regional in the sense of a time lag than it is conditioned primarily by physiography or regional culture as a separate entity." The patterns of southern urban development, he argued, followed the broader national norms, albeit on a delayed timeline. Indeed, similar to northern cities, Atlanta, Savannah, and other southern urban centers were dramatically affected by the development of regional transit networks, new patterns of residential development, the increasing use of automobiles, and the rise of industrial production.[3]

Still, for all the parallels between southern urban development and that taking place in other areas of the country, some racial patterns of residential demographics remained regionally distinctive. Historian David Goldfield argued that the South's commitment to maintaining a racially divided society limited opportunities not only for African Americans but also for southern cities overall. Economists Trevon Logan and John Parman have recently found that segregation doubled nationwide between 1880 and 1940. Their research has also determined that while northern cities have been justly criticized for their patterns of racial segregation, southern cities were significantly more segregated, both in 1880 and in 1940. Their findings support earlier research by historian Howard Rabinowitz that documented that black residents of southern cities such as Atlanta, Nashville, Montgomery, Raleigh, and Richmond occupied inadequate housing within undesirable neighborhoods by 1900. Rabinowitz found that as early as the 1890s, areas that were home to African Americans tended toward intense segregation, soon having populations over 90 percent black.[4]

Residential demographic patterns varied throughout the South, however. Old South cities, in particular, have stood out to generations of researchers as exceptions to the broader regional patterns. In the 1960s, sociologists Karl and Alma Taueber noted that cities such as Charleston maintained a surprisingly high rate of residential racial integration. They traced this pattern to the antebellum housing arrangements in which enslaved workers lived close to the homes of white elites. Yet the definition of segregation proves more complex than a simple measurement of the physical proximity of individuals. Sociologists have developed several different indices for measuring segregation in order to capture also the nature of the interactions between individuals of different races.[5]

Throughout the period under study, racial discrimination shaped Georgia politics and policies. The state's 1891 Jim Crow laws mandated the segregation of prisoners and railroad cars, for example. In the realm of education spending, a Works Progress Administration study found Georgia spending nearly six times more per capita for white students than for African Americans. White supremacy transcended policy decisions as well, with murderous results. A recent study identified Georgia as the site of more lynchings than even Mississippi between 1880 and 1940. Southern activists challenged white supremacy but struggled against such entrenched opposition.[6]

The racially segregated residential patterns of the South, in place by the 1920s, became solidified in the decades after the implementation of the Home Owners' Loan Corporation. As part of the first New Deal in 1933, the Roosevelt administration established the HOLC. Over the next three years, it issued new mortgages to approximately 1 million homeowners, in a bid to stabilize the economy. Beginning in 1935, the agency also began an elaborate survey program to study the real estate market in 239 cities. Teams comprised of local real estate professionals, bankers, and HOLC employees compiled intricate data sets documenting home values, racial demographics, and housing conditions in various neighborhoods. Based on these findings, the assessment teams ranked areas into four categories. "A" areas were deemed most desirable for future mortgage lending and were shaded green on the security maps. "B" areas, shaded blue, were desirable for lending, and yellow "C" areas were determined to be declining. Neighborhoods considered downright "hazardous" for lending were graded "D" and were shaded red, giving rise later to the term "redlining." Factors that resulted in danger signs for a neighborhood included poor or dilapidated housing, few homeowners, and the existence of African American or Jewish residents.

Scholars have debated the tangible effects of the HOLC maps. Initially, historians assumed that the maps and survey results were widely distributed and, as a consequence, effectively shut down lending to low-income and, especially, minority neighborhoods. Indeed, many such areas experienced massive disinvestment in the postwar decades; some redlined areas remain today home to impoverished minority communities. As urban studies scholar Amy Hillier has shown through Geographic Information System (GIS) analysis of Philadelphia neighborhoods, both the HOLC itself, in the years prior to the survey, and private lenders, in the years following the survey, offered mortgages on properties within "hazardous" areas. Hillier cautions scholars to avoid overstating the influence of the HOLC surveys themselves, locating their usefulness instead in their documentation of the real estate landscape of the 1930s.[7]

The existing patterns of southern racial segregation were also compounded by related federal initiatives. The rise of New Deal public housing led to the further entrenchment of residential racial segregation across the nation. Moreover, cities like Savannah also felt the striking effects of postwar historic preservation, first in the form of protective legislation limiting demolition and renovation of buildings within designated historic districts, and later in the form of tax benefits to investors in historic properties. The segregation of the Jim Crow era was thus southern in origin, reflecting persistent racial tensions and white resistance to interracial contact in both the social and commercial spheres. As historian Thomas Hanchett noted, those racial divisions would be "frozen" in place by initiatives originating outside the South. Redlining, public housing, and historic preservation would all limit racial interaction in the South.[8]

## AUGUSTA, MACON, AND COLUMBUS

When the HOLC survey team set out to study Augusta, Macon, and Columbus, they faced cities that had spent decades steeped in the bitter and divisive climate of Jim Crow segregation. Race defined many of the cities' residential neighborhoods. The 1938 Federal Writers' Project *Guide to Augusta* described the city's African American neighborhoods as home to an especially broad range of socioeconomic classes. Noting that the city's population was 40 percent African American, the guide's authors painted a portrait of the "average Negro tenant house." Lacking electricity but offering running water, such "shabby wooden houses" rented for approximately eight dollars per month. Their yards were described as "untended," with porches covered in plants, some growing out of "lard cans painted in bright colors." Their backyards contained wash pots for laundry the residents were doing for whites. By contrast, nearby "bungalows of more solid construction" were "home-owned or rented to a substantial class of citizens." These "respectable homes," equipped with amenities such as electricity and porch furniture, were "adjacent to rows of shack-like houses, just as their occupants, college graduates perhaps, must share neighborhoods with laborers and one-time field hands." Due to white hostility, African Americans of varying classes clustered together.[9]

Augusta's journey toward segregation had already begun during the Civil War, when the city enjoyed relatively good fortune. General Sherman opted not to destroy Augusta's downtown business district, leaving the city well positioned for postwar growth, especially given its location on the Savannah River and near the region's major railroads. The city's industries grew quickly after Reconstruction; by 1890, one-third of Augusta's white workers were employed in the city's six cotton mills. The population grew apace, rising from twelve thousand in 1860 to forty thousand in 1900, when Augusta was Georgia's third largest city. The city's infrastructure, however, did not develop quickly enough to meet the needs of its growing population. As a result, low-income African American neighborhoods and homes of white factory workers lacked basic sanitation and access to clean water.[10]

During the 1880s, racial segregation in Augusta was increasing. Transit and public accommodations remained integrated, even as churches, schools, hospitals, and cemeteries, as well as social and fraternal organizations, were clearly divided along racial lines. Economically, as was the case throughout the nation, most African Americans were clustered in low-income occupations and segregated neighborhoods. In Augusta, many African Americans worked as blacksmiths, carpenters, hucksters, and junk dealers, while very few were employed as lawyers, doctors, restaurant owners, or in other professional occupations. Some black elites, however, occupied multiracial neighborhoods.

One such resident was Amanda Dickson, daughter of an enslaved girl and wealthy plantation owner David Dickson. Amanda Dickson inherited much of her father's estate after his death in 1885. She and other black elites struggled to maintain their social status as racial segregation took hold by the turn of the century.[11]

In the early twentieth century, Augusta's economy was driven by cotton distribution and textile manufacturing. Bricks, other clay products, fertilizer, cottonseed oil, and iron and steel goods were also manufactured in Augusta. The largest mills included the John P. King Manufacturing Company and the Sibley Mills. Tourism was also significant to the economy, due in part to the development of five eighteen-hole golf courses by the 1930s.[12]

By 1930, Augusta's population was 40 percent African American and 1 percent immigrant. Several areas of Augusta were found in the HOLC survey to be highly segregated. Areas D-7, D-8, and D-12 were nearly 100 percent African American, while D-11 was above 90 percent African American. Overall, the most desirable areas of the city were located on the west side and to the north. The security survey of Augusta found relatively few areas desirable for mortgage lending; less than 5 percent of the city's dwellings were located in zones coded "A" or "B." The vast majority of Augusta's residential properties (approximately 96 percent of them) were valued below $10,000. The overall homeownership rate for Augusta in 1930 was less than 26 percent.[13]

Columbus developed along related lines, and its survey team came to similar conclusions. The team coded large expanses of Columbus in red and only very small areas in green. The redlined areas were primarily on the city's west side and central district, while the green were all located in clusters on the east side.[14]

Racial demographics were a major factor in the survey of Columbus. All areas that were home to African Americans were designated "hazardous" for lending. Sections D-4 (known as "the Bottoms") and D-5 were 100 percent African American, while D1 and D2 were 50 percent and D3 was 35 percent African American. The team's narrative descriptions of the neighborhoods clarify their "undesirable" factors. Area D2 (made up of sections of Old North Highlands, North Columbus, Beallwood, and Beallwood Heights) had no zoning in place, but property deeds did contain racial restrictions, thus ensuring its segregation. Less than 3 percent of the area's streets were paved. The Beallwood and Beallwood Heights areas offered residents no utilities or fire service, because they were outside the city limits. The area was home to factory workers and laborers, who lived in frame houses in fair to poor condition. The team noted that area D2 was plagued by "obnoxious odors," while D4 was subject to flooding. Vandalism was present throughout the hazardous areas, where homes were up to fifty years old. The newer housing stock of Columbus was found in Section A, where homes were no more than ten years old, and in section B, where homes were up to fifteen years old. In Columbus, the age of the housing stock correlated with the existing racial segregation in place by the 1930s. Whites occupied the newer homes, located in more advantageous areas, with clear amenities, such as large lots, paved streets, and convenient location to schools, parks, and bus transportation, while African Americans lived in the oldest and least desirable areas.

Macon followed a similar trajectory of development. By the 1920s, industrialization had reshaped the city, which was home to eleven textile mills, most notably, the Bibb Manufacturing Company. Banks lent stability and growth to the African American community, including the Liberty Loan and Investment Company and Middle Georgia Saving and Investment Company. Yet poverty continued to grip the majority of Macon's African American population. Eighty-four percent of African American women were employed in domestic service. As was the case in many cities, unemployment in Macon in 1940 was far higher for African Americans (nearly 13%) than it was for whites (just over 7%). The differences between black and white neighborhoods could also be stark. Black neighborhoods in Macon often remained unpaved and lacked adequate water and sanitation.[15]

By the 1930s, 43 percent of Macon's residents were African American. All of the neighborhoods that were home to African Americans were coded hazardous for lending by the HOLC survey team. Several additional areas, either partially or completely occupied by whites, were also coded hazardous. As a result, vast expanses of the city's landscape were deemed unsuitable for mortgage investment. The stark segregation seen in other cities was present in Macon, as well. Several redlined areas were made up entirely of African American residents (D13, D14, D15, and D16). The areas deemed most desirable for lending, by contrast, were located in the northeastern and eastern sections of the city, on higher ground.[16]

The redlining process and the existing segregation it captured would vary across southern cities. Augusta, Macon, and Columbus had developed in similar fashion, and their survey teams also took a similar approach to their analysis. The survey categories for these cities neatly conflated housing conditions, age of housing stock, and race of occupants. Due to Jim Crow segregation, African Americans in each city occupied the oldest and most dilapidated housing units. All areas that were home to African Americans were coded red by the survey team.

## SAVANNAH AND MORTGAGE LENDING IN REDLINED AREAS

Savannah embodied the Old South pattern of residential demographics. During the antebellum era, the city's streets had been lined with grand homes occupied by whites, while its narrow lanes were filled with shacks and modest homes built for African Americans. In many cases, these smaller homes were occupied by enslaved people, some of whom "lived out" in a separate household from their master. Others were home to the city's free African American population.[17]

Some African American neighborhoods in the early twentieth century, such as Yamacraw on the city's west side, had roots stretching back to the antebellum era. By the time of Reconstruction, that area had already been home to impoverished African Americans for decades. Black neighborhoods took hold after the war, sometimes centered on institutions like the Beach Institute, built by the Freedmen's Bureau in 1867 as a school for African American youth. Savannah's black community was internally divided between those of mixed descent and those of darker skin tones, although to a lesser extent than in Charleston, which was home to a larger population of mixed descent.[18]

During Reconstruction, Savannah's African American community had resisted the initial tide of racial segregation, protesting segregated train cars, steamships, theaters, and churches. The black community did not gain economic strength, however. As industry grew in Savannah, white prejudice led to fewer industrial jobs being available to African Americans, who were pushed increasingly into labor and domestic service.[19]

The city had developed in waves, from the river outward. The original four squares mapped out in the colonial era anchored the city's central district. As the decades passed, new areas were added, creating twenty-four squares by the mid-nineteenth century. By the late nineteenth-century, the Victorian district had been developed and was filled with stately homes bracketed by modest neighborhoods constructed for the railroad workers.

One remarkable area that developed in the late nineteenth century was Cuyler-Brownsville. The neighborhood was located within the southwestern area of the city south of Anderson Street, then home primarily to impoverished African Americans. The Brownsville neighborhood developed first, followed by the Cuyler area shortly after. By 1883, the area became part of the city of Savannah, although it lacked reliable fire service, adequate sanitation, and drinking water. Built during the era of Jim Crow, the neighborhood was designed to be segregated, with whites living east of Montgomery, and African Americans to the west. The area's African American workers traveled to work on the streetcars that were in place by the turn of the century.[20]

The HOLC survey of Savannah was never finalized, leaving only the draft map and detailed survey report. Still, this draft offers valuable insights into the thought process of the survey team, comprised mostly of Savannah real estate and banking professionals. The report described Savannah's decline as a city, due to the movement of the rice industry to Louisiana and Texas, the loss of cotton shipping from the port, and the subsequent loss of shipping and storage to improved railroad and highway facilities. As a result, only 20 percent of Savannah families owned their homes.[21]

The surveyors also cited the presence of 42,000 African Americans as a detrimental factor for Savannah. After the loss of the river business, they argued, "the local negro was thrown back on the white people almost as a ward. In other words, the majority of the local negro population is dependent for a living upon the earnings of the white portion of the population."[22] The survey team thus looked warily upon African American Savannah residents, seeing them as a threat to the city's financial stability.

Likewise, the survey team had no patience with Savannah's nascent tendencies toward historic preservation. Within the historic business district, they lamented, "Some of Savannah's oldest white families, for sentimental reasons still live in the original homesteads which are located in this area." The team also found the Victorian district in "urgent need of modernization." Overall, the surveyors described Savannah as being averse to destroying old and "obsolete" homes due to "local custom and tradition,' speculating that outside of Charleston, no other city so resisted modernization. Indeed, in their overall findings, the team cited as detrimental influences the odor from the fertilizer plants, the railroad that cut through the Victorian district, and "the dislike of the monied and older class of Savannah residents to break tradition and move out of old family homesteads into up-to-date, modern homes."[23]

The team issued only three rankings of "A" in their Savannah study. One was awarded to Gordonston, on the city's eastside. The neighborhood was described as an exclusive enclave: "Practically all of the residents of this section are home owners and are the better class of white, occupying single homes, both one and two story, which are in very good condition and which will average ten years old." The second area given an "A," comprised of Chatham Crescent and Ardsley Park, contained early twentieth-century housing developments that had been created as neighborhoods restricted to whites. Those restrictions remained in place. As noted in the HOLC survey: "This is the most desirable white residential property in Savannah and is highly restricted, both as to race and type of construction permitted."[24]

The most striking aspect of the Savannah draft survey was the coding of Cuyler-Brownsville as green. As stated in the report, "Property in this section is the most desirable Negro home-owner residential property and the best type of Negro lives in this section." After noting that the remaining white residents would likely leave the neighborhood within five years, the surveyors suggested that "Negro ownership of property is detrimental to white property owners in this section; but on the other hand, from the Negro standpoint, the best colored schools in Savannah are located in this area." Unlike in other cities, Savannah surveyors rated a predominantly African American neighborhood as highly desirable for mortgage lending.

By contrast, the survey team described the redlined Yamacraw area much differently. "It is adjacent to railroad yards, sidings, shops, drainage canals and steamship lines," the report stated, noting that "the houses are occupied by the lowest class negro tenants." The surveyors went on to describe the area as home to "unpaved streets, poor sanitation, and frame buildings in terrible state of repair." They described the redlined district to the west of Forsyth Park as a neighborhood in transition, commenting that "formerly good, high-class white property, [was] now rapidly declining and [also] changing from a home-owner section to a rental section." The committee offered an especially bleak description of a small area to the east of East Broad Street. Its residents were "the poorest class negroes, who live in one story frame row houses and tin shacks of a make-shift nature." They summarized the general area as having little more than "garbage dumps, poor sanitation, adjoining land subject to overflow, and the presence of extremely bad vandalism."[25]

The Savannah report offers insights into the committee's process. The committee described one interracial neighborhood as home to industrial property and garbage dumps and initially redlined it, but when they considered it instead from the point of view of African American homeowners, they changed the report code to yellow. They described this neighborhood as home to "a fair class of negroes and low type of white." Another interracial neighborhood coded as yellow included a broad swath of the Victorian district. It was described as home to the "middle class of white and the best class of negro," with a mixture of "one story frame negro houses to four story old aristocratic white homes." Using the language of invasion encouraged by the HOLC survey forms, the surveyors noted a "definite infiltration of negroes in certain sections, particularly the southwestern portion along Burroughs, West Broad and Montgomery Streets."[26]

The HOLC survey found that some private Savannah banks loaned money to African American homebuyers. Chatham Savings and Loan Company's secretary and treasurer, Stewart Kraft, reported that the bank had 161 outstanding loans in Savannah. Kraft noted that Chatham loaned money to African Americans at its standard interest rates. While whites could borrow up to 60 percent of a home's appraised value, however, African Americans could borrow no more than 50 percent. Also, for African American borrowers, loans were limited to between $1,000 and $2,000.[27] Although unequal, private funding was, as this example shows, available for lending in minority areas.

Private and public lenders issued loans in redlined areas of some other cities, as well, both before and after the completion of the city surveys. Throughout the country, many HOLC loans were issued before the detailed city surveys were compiled. In Chicago, Memphis, and Newark, the agency made the majority of its loans in areas that were soon redlined or labeled yellow. Loan summaries are available for Savannah as of February 1936. By then, the HOLC had issued 532 loans. Forty-five of these were made in the historic business district, an area that had not been issued a ranking grade. The agency provided 102 loans (19.2% of the total) in green areas, 193 (36.2%) in blue areas, 159 (29.9%) in yellow areas, and only 33 (6.2%) in red areas. Approximately 36.1 percent of the loans issued by the HOLC were in areas that would soon be coded as red and yellow, a lower rate than in Chicago, Memphis, and Newark.

This picture is complicated, however, by the Savannah survey team's aberrant application of the HOLC guidelines. The program intended for interracial neighborhoods to be downgraded, as homogeneity was seen as a desirable trait for area stability. Savannah's team dutifully coded many such areas yellow, including much of the city's west side, near Laurel Grove Cemetery, and the majority of the Victorian District located below Forsyth Park. However, the team not only coded Cuyler-Brownsville green, they also coded several African American neighborhoods blue, marking them as desirable for lending.

Blue areas included B4 (on the west side, west of Yamacraw and the rail yards) and B6 and B7 (on the west side, above and below Cuyler-Brownsville). These areas had also received HOLC loans prior to 1936.

The surveyors' description of these areas lends insight into the process they were following. They described section 4 as "fair negro home-owner property," with a few rental properties scattered throughout. The area's residents were "second and third class negroes" living in homes from ten to thirty years old and in poor repair. Detrimental influences to the area included the odor produced by the nearby fertilizer plants. However, the surveyors noted, "This factor is not a detriment to the type of people occupying the property at the present time." Sections six and seven were home to "middle class negroes" in one to two-story wooden homes. The homes in area six ranged from fifteen to fifty years old, most needing only minor repairs. The houses in section seven were newer, from ten to twenty years old, and in fair condition.

The HOLC redlining process, therefore, was not monolithic. Public loans were issued in redlined areas, both before and after the city surveys were completed. Similarly, private loans were also issued in minority areas both before and after the mid-1930s. The terms of such mortgages could be significantly less advantageous, however, than those offered to whites.

## ATLANTA: REDLINING AND BEYOND

In the decades after the Civil War, Atlanta's legendary growth created a New South city plagued by racial divisions. In 1880, the city was home to approximately nine thousand African Americans; by 1900, that number had risen to thirty-five thousand. As the city's population became larger and proportionally more African American, racial segregation became more pronounced.[28]

Segregation in Atlanta was furthered by the race riot of 1906. In the context of a contentious election, white women's accusations of sexual assault by black men drew intense media attention. Ultimately, white mobs formed to beat, shoot, and otherwise terrorize the city's African American community, violence that would claim the lives of at least ten African Americans and two whites. In the immediate aftermath of the riot, efforts were made to broker greater racial harmony. Soon though, the lasting damage of the riot became apparent, as many African Americans left the city and African American–owned businesses were increasingly consolidated onto Auburn

Avenue. The black residential community, too, clustered more tightly into the enclaves forming on the east and west sides of the city. The African American population became more strictly segregated even before Atlanta's first racial segregation law was passed in 1911.[29]

By the 1920s, Atlanta was a starkly segregated city, in which African Americans made up approximately one-third of the population. During the early twentieth century, middle-class whites had moved to North Atlanta, while African Americans moved from the east side to the west side. Scattered African American enclaves included Johnson near present-day Lenox Square. Although it was a New South city, African American servants continued to live behind the homes of their white employers in some areas.[30]

Middle-class African American business leaders attempting to cooperate with whites became frustrated by the rampant discrimination in the city's allocation of resources. In 1920, the *Atlanta Independent,* an African American paper, challenged such stark inequality. "Haven't our neighbors sense enough to know that filth, lack of lights and police protection in a black settlement is a menace to the health and protection of the white settlement?" editors asked. "It seems that our neighbors would rather die and go to hell with the Negro than to live in heaven with him. These conditions constitute a civic shame to Atlanta."[31]

As the 1920s continued, racial segregation would only increase. The city's first racial zoning law was enacted in 1922, as part of the Atlanta Zone Plan. Planning consultant Robert Whitten developed the plan expressly to separate residents into neighborhoods designated "white," "black," and "undetermined."[32] By the 1930s, the HOLC Atlanta survey team categorized as hazardous for lending all areas whose population was comprised of at least 10 percent African Americans. In some cases, the area's homes were predominantly only six to twelve years old, yet they were already listed in fair to poor condition. Because it was a New South city and had undergone major growth and development after the Civil War, few of Atlanta's surveyed areas contained many old structures. Still, African Americans occupied the oldest housing stock, as was the case in other cities. Most African Americans in Atlanta, however, resided in more recently built, albeit low value, homes.

The area near Atlanta University offers a useful lens through which to understand the priorities of the assessment team. The HOLC survey described this neighborhood as "the best negro area in town." Occupants were African American business and professional men, as well as clerical workers, with an estimated annual family income between $1,300 and $3,000. Homes ranged from one to fifteen years in age and were valued between $3,000 and $8,500, well above the values in most other African American neighborhoods. Advantages to the area included access to African American schools, parks, community centers, churches, and streetcar transportation. The majority of the streets in the area were paved. Yet the area was deemed hazardous for lending, due to the race of its occupants. This decision by the committee stands in stark contrast to that made by the Savannah survey team to code Cuyler-Brownsville as desirable for lending. Scholars have noted that subsequent drafts of the survey maps reflected stricter application of the ranking criteria. Presumably, had the Savannah file been finalized, Cuyler-Brownsville would have been downgraded, particularly after the federal authorities had more input into the process.[33]

After the redlining surveys had been completed, racial segregation continued to solidify in Atlanta. The authors of the 1942 WPA guide *Atlanta: A City of the Modern South* described a landscape of stark contrasts. A visitor seeing the outlying factories might also marvel at the homes of the elite. "On the other hand," they continued, "he could live here for months and see nothing more inspiring than rows of houses indistinguishable from those of any other city. He may see avenues of mansions or dreary back streets, pleasant cottages or tumbledown Negro shanties. Wealth and poverty, beauty and drabness—Atlanta has them all." The guide also described the varying socioeconomic strata within the city's African American community. The Atlanta University "set" enjoyed "attractive homes" and "a good living standard." The authors went on to note, "But the poorer Negroes live squalidly along their own streets which appear abruptly in all parts of the city; here the ramshackle wooden shanties and rooming houses are crowded with many families and the streets are noisy with the cries of little ragged brown children."[34]

In 1946, amid the postwar housing crisis, racial tensions again rose in Atlanta. Whites protested African American arrivals in neighborhoods such as the West End area near Ashby Street. The white supremacist group, the Columbians, recruited members in the textile mills and posted signs declaring neighborhoods "white counties." The group's leader, Homer Loomis, declared Garibaldi and Formwalt Streets the dividing line between the races, calling upon the group's members to enforce it. The Columbians, along with the revived Ku Klux Klan, faded within a few years. As they did, however, the West End Cooperative Corporation was formed to battle the racial turnover on Ashby Street. The group presented itself as a far more respectable organization, but by 1949, they, too, had resorted to bombings to try to terrorize African Americans moving into white neighborhoods.[35]

Atlanta became a city of remarkable African American success, even as it remained racially divided. In the postwar era, Atlanta became known as home to many prosperous African Americans. Black-owned businesses were worth almost $30 million by 1945. In 1956, *Fortune* magazine published a lengthy piece, "The Negro's New Economic Life." The article praised Atlanta as "a model for all the South," famously describing Auburn Avenue as "the richest Negro street in the world."[36]

The *Fortune* article noted that Atlanta's African American community drew strength from its access to credit. By the mid-1950s along "Sweet Auburn," the Atlanta Life Insurance Company held $40 million in assets; the Citizens Trust Company, $7 million; and the Mutual Federal Savings & Loan Association of Atlanta, $11 million. These institutions allowed more black Atlanta residents to buy new homes than was the case for their counterparts in other cities. By this time, Atlanta's white-owned banks were also willing to lend to African Americans, a response to the efforts of the African American–owned banks to publicize the success of their pioneering lending programs. The president of Citizens Trust Co., L. D. Milton, observed, "Our role has been to set up pilot institutions. We have been economic *interpreters* of Negro life addressing a white financial community. We have simply given the needed proofs. This institution can say, 'It is a lie to say that the Negro is a bad bank risk.' The Mutual can say, 'It is a lie to say that the Negro is a bad mortgage risk.' The Atlanta Life can say, 'It is a lie to say that the Negro is a bad insurance risk.'"[37]

Yet for all this economic opportunity, segregation continued to limit African Americans' access to city life. Employment, shopping, and entertainment remained starkly segregated in Atlanta. The *Fortune* article drew a heavy comparison between Atlanta and Baltimore in this regard. The magazine noted that Baltimore had begun to move beyond its segregated past, establishing integrated seating in lunch counters, parks, and classrooms. Despite Baltimore's newly relaxed attitude toward racial mingling, however, desperate poverty plagued the city's African American population. Few black citizens there owned businesses or had access to decent homes, although they comprised nearly 30 percent of the city's population. In the years just before the 1954 *Brown v. Board of Education* decision, racial segregation had become so commonplace in the South that it drew few references in political campaigns.[38]

*Fortune* leveled particular criticism at the "land installment contracts" that were issued in lieu of proper mortgages for African American borrowers. The contracts required "little or no down payment" but offered few details about equity or amortization. The article described these vague and misleading contracts as "flawless designs for bankruptcy, eviction, and foreclosure," noting that "the final results for Baltimore's Negro population are congestion, dirt, crime, and the human despair that knows no measure in decimal points."[39]

As predicted by the *Fortune* article in the 1950s, African American economic development has not always been linked to a subsequent decline in racial segregation. Social scientists have observed that southern racial segregation is so persistent that it does not recede even in the face of broad black economic growth.[40] Home ownership and the lending institutions that support it must be considered alongside patterns of racial segregation in order to assess community development.

Racism, segregation, and poverty have been inextricably linked in America's cities. The relationships between them, however, are far from uniform or static, developing along distinct trajectories in specific locations at certain historical moments. The 1930s proved a critical juncture for southern cities, as the Great Depression's horrific effects prompted a reevaluation of urban development. The South was becoming more urban even as it clung to the racial segregation that had been developing since the end of Reconstruction. Federal oversight would not save the South's African American prospective homebuyers in the 1930s. While they might benefit from other New Deal legislation, their access to credit through midcentury would depend upon decisions made more often at the local level. Such access to economic resources was always relative, however. Even at the peak of lending to the African American community, the resources available would not approach those available to whites.

## NOTES

1. Bill Dedman, "Atlanta Blacks Losing in Home Loans Scramble," *Atlanta Journal-Constitution,* May 1, 1988.

2. Stephen Ross and John Yinger, *The Color of Credit: Mortgage Discrimination, Research Methodology, and Fair-Lending Enforcement* (Cambridge, MA: MIT Press, 2002), 4; Ta-Nehisi Coates, "The Case for Reparations," *Atlantic,* June 2014; Laura Bliss, "After Nearly a Century, Redlining Still Divides Baltimore," *Atlantic Citylab,* Apr. 30, 2015; Ta-Nehisi Coates, "The Racist

Housing Policies That Built Ferguson," *Atlantic,* Oct. 17, 2014; Douglas S. Massey, "Origins of Economic Disparities: The Historical Role of Housing Segregation," in *Segregation: The Rising Costs for America,* ed. James H. Carr and Nandinee K. Kutty (New York: Routledge, 2008), 40.

3. Blaine A. Brownell, "The Urban South Comes of Age, 1900–1940," in *The City in Southern History: The Growth of Urban Civilization in the South,* ed. Blaine A. Brownell and David R. Goldfield (Port Washington, NY: Kennikat, 1977), 123–58; Blaine A. Brownell, *The Urban Ethos of the South, 1920–1930* (Baton Rouge: Louisiana State University Press, 1975), 1; Howard W. Odum, *Southern Regions of the United States* (Chapel Hill: University of North Carolina Press, 1936), 497, quoted in Brownell, *The Urban Ethos,* 10. On Odum, see also David Goldfield, *Region, Race, and Cities: Interpreting the Urban South* (Baton Rouge: Louisiana State University Press, 1997), 17–36, and Michael O'Brien, *The Idea of the American South, 1920–1941* (Baltimore, MD: Johns Hopkins University Press, 1979), 31–93.

4. David Goldfield, *Cotton Fields and Skyscrapers: Southern City and Region, 1607–1980* (Baton Rouge: Louisiana State University Press, 1982), 6–8, 80–132; Trevon Logan and John Parman, "The National Rise in Residential Segregation" (National Bureau of Economic Research, Working Paper No. 20934, issued Feb. 2015); Howard N. Rabinowitz, *Race Relations in the Urban South, 1985–1890* (New York: Oxford University Press, 1978), 97–124, 106-10. On the evolution of segregated spaces nationwide from 1900 to 1940, see Douglas S. Massey and Nancy A. Denton, *American Apartheid: Segregation and the Making of the Underclass* (Cambridge, MA: Harvard University Press, 1993), 17–59.

5. Karl E. Taueber and Alma F. Taueber, *Negroes in Cities: Residential Segregation and Neighborhood Change* (Chicago: Aldine, 1965), 45–49. See also Leo F. Schnone and Philip C. Everson, "Segregation in Southern Cities," *American Journal of Sociology* 72, no. 1 (July 1966): 58–67; Douglas S. Massey and Nancy A. Denton, "The Dimensions of Residential Segregation," *Social Forces* 67 (1988): 281–315.

6. For state-level analyses, see John C. Inscoe, ed., *Georgia in Black and White: Explorations in the Race Relations of a Southern State, 1865–1950* (Athens: University of Georgia Press, 1994); John Dittmer, *Black Georgia in the Progressive Era, 1900–1920* (Chicago: University of Illinois Press, 1977); and Numan Bartley, *The Creation of Modern Georgia* (Athens: University of Georgia Press, 1983). Andrew M. Manis, *Macon Black and White: An Unutterable Separation in the American Century* (Macon, GA: Mercer University Press, 2004), 4, 79; Equal Justice Initiative, "Lynching in America: Confronting the Legacy of Racial Terror" (Montgomery, AL: Equal Justice Initiative, 2015); Patricia Sullivan, "Southern Seeds of Change, 1931–1938," in *The New South: New Histories,* ed. J. William Harris (New York: Routledge, 2008).

7. Kenneth T. Jackson, *Crabgrass Frontier: The Suburbanization of the United States* (New York: Oxford University Press, 1985); Amy Hillier, "Redlining in Philadelphia," in *Past Time, Past Place: GIS for History,* ed. Anne Kelly Knowles (Redlands, CA: ESRI, 2002), 79–92.

8. Thomas Hanchett, *Sorting Out the New South City: Race, Class, and Urban Development in Charlotte, 1875–1975* (Chapel Hill: University of North Carolina Press, 1998), 231.

9. Federal Writers' Project in Georgia, Works Progress Administration, Augusta Unit, *American Guide Series: Augusta* (Tidwell Printing Supply, 1938), 45.

10. Edward J. Cashin and Glenn T. Eskew, eds., *Paternalism in a Southern City: Race, Religion, and Gender in Augusta, Georgia* (Athens: University of Georgia Press, 2012); Kent Ander-

son Leslie, "No Middle Ground: Elite African Americans in Augusta and the Coming of Jim Crow," in Cashin and Eskew, *Paternalism*, 110–34.

11. Ibid.

12. "Report of Survey, Augusta, Georgia," 9, 3-4, box 82, folder "Augusta, Georgia #2," Records of the Federal Home Loan Bank Board, Record Group 195, National Archives and Records Administration, College Park, Maryland. The bulk of the material about redlining in Georgia is in boxes 37, 83, 91, 92, and 93.

13. Report of Survey, Augusta, 21, 25, 37, 38.

14. "Security Map of Columbus, Georgia," box 83, folder "Columbus, Georgia," Records of the Federal Home Loan Bank Board.

15. Manis, *Macon Black and White*, 77, 78, 109.

16. "Report of Survey, Macon, Georgia," 30, 35, box 83, folder "Macon, Georgia," Records of the Federal Home Loan Bank Board.

17. Whittington B. Johnson, *Black Savannah, 1788–1864* (Fayetteville: University of Arkansas Press, 1996).

18. Robert Eugene Perdue, "The Negro in Savannah, 1985–1900" (PhD diss., University of Georgia, 1971), 136–38, 158–63. See also Bernard E. Powers, *Black Charlestonians: A Social History, 1822–1885* (Fayetteville: University of Arkansas Press, 1994).

19. Perdue, "The Negro in Savannah," 37–53, 190–93.

20. Julie L. Oliver, "From Plantation Backroads to City Streets: The Rise of Black Workers' Housing in Savannah, 1870–1900" (MA thesis, Armstrong Atlantic State University, 1996), 62–76.

21. "Report of Survey, Savannah, Georgia," 1, 12, box 93, folder "Savannah, GA," Records of the Federal Home Loan Bank Board.

22. Ibid., 15.

23. Ibid., 12-14.

24. "Analysis of Realty Area Map of Savannah," box 93, folder "Savannah, GA," Records of the Federal Home Loan Bank Board.

25. Ibid.

26. Ibid.

27. "Real Estate Brokers," box 83, folder "Savannah, Georgia," Records of the Federal Home Loan Bank Board.

28. Allison Dorsey, *To Build Our Lives Together: Community Formation in Black Atlanta, 1875–1906* (Athens: University of Georgia Press, 2004), 150, 151.

29. William A. Link, *Atlanta, Cradle of the South: Race and Remembering in the Civil War's Aftermath* (Chapel Hill: University of North Carolina Press, 2015), 169–73; Dorsey, *To Build Our Lives Together*, 150, 161. See also Mark Bauerlein, *Negrophobia: A Race Riot in Atlanta, 1906* (San Francisco, CA: Encounter, 2001).

30. Brownell, *The Urban Ethos*, 13–14; Clifford M. Kuhn, Harlon E. Joye, and E. Bernard West, *Living Atlanta: An Oral History of the City, 1914–1948* (Athens: University of Georgia Press, 1990; published in conjunction with the Atlanta Historical Society), 32, 34–35. See also Karen Ferguson, *Black Politics in New Deal Atlanta* (Chapel Hill: University of North Carolina Press, 2002), 19–45.

31. Brownell, *The Urban Ethos,* 114. *Atlanta Independent,* May 29, 1920, quoted in Brownell, *The Urban Ethos,* 115.

32. Brownell, *The Urban Ethos,* 184.

33. Hillier, "Redlining in Philadelphia."

34. Writers' Program of the Works Projects Administration, *American Guide Series: Atlanta, A City of the Modern South* (Atlanta: Board of Education of the City of Atlanta, 1942), 3, 5.

35. Kevin M. Kruse, *White Flight: Atlanta and the Making of Modern Conservatism* (Princeton, NJ: Princeton University Press, 2005), 42–43, 45–47, 50–51, 53, 54–57.

36. Ibid., 28. Emmet John Hughes, "The Negro's New Economic Life," *Fortune* 54 (Sept. 1956): 248.

37. Hughes, "The Negro's New Economic Life," 248, 251.

38. Earl Black, *Southern Governors and Civil Rights: Racial Segregation as a Campaign Issue in the Second Reconstruction* (Cambridge, MA: Harvard University Press, 1976), 29–47.

39. Hughes, "The Negro's New Economic Life," 252.

40. Wade Clark Roof, Thomas L. Van Valey, and Daphne Spain, "Residential Segregation in Southern Cities: 1970," *Social Forces* 55, no. 1 (Sept. 1976): 59–71.

# Empire on Parade

## *Public Representations of Race at the 1936 Texas Centennial Exposition*

NICHOLAS ROLAND

Dallas department store magnate Stanley Marcus once opined that "modern Texas history started with the celebration of the Texas Centennial." The image that Texas projected during the 1936 Texas Centennial is a familiar one: cattle ranchers, (white) cowboys, rugged oilmen, and the heroes of the Alamo and San Jacinto, all pointing toward economic dynamism. White elites utilized the discourse of progress, employed at world's fairs since the nineteenth century, to push aside the most regrettable features of Texas's southern past and to introduce a new identity for the Lone Star State. In the narrative of the Centennial Exposition, Texas was not a southern state but rather a part of the American West. Anglo-American expansion into the West, and the constellation of ideas and motifs that accompanied this process in the American imagination, formed the essence of both the popular image and the historical memory promulgated by the Texas Centennial Exposition. In 1936, Texas sought to put the march of Anglo-Texan empire on parade for the American public.[1]

With the Great Depression as a backdrop, the organizers of the Texas Centennial Exposition were especially motivated to portray Texas as a state that was business and industry friendly, forward looking, and racially harmonious. These rebranding efforts attempted to surmount a bitter legacy of discrimination and racial violence. Between 1889 and 1918, the three decades marking the height of the racial lynching epidemic in the South, Texas followed only Mississippi and Georgia in the total number of lynchings. Although 1925 marked the first lynching-free year in Texas since at least the 1880s, the practice persisted into the 1930s. Sherman, Texas, located sixty-five miles north of Dallas, was the sight of a 1930 lynching and race riot that required a deployment of the Texas National Guard and drew national media coverage. Though they initially opposed any overt acknowledgment of black culture at the Centennial Exposition, the white leadership of the Texas Centennial Exposition eventually chose to market black participation at Dallas as an example of racial harmony in Texas.[2]

The Centennial Exposition's Hall of Negro Life served as a means to project the ideal "race relations" desired by Anglo-Texan elites: a social structure that made minimal, incremental concessions to nonwhites within the boundaries of segregation. Located between the Hall of Religion and the General Motors building, the single-story, fourteen-thousand-square-foot exhibit hall was operated by an all-black staff and housed educational exhibits on various aspects of African American life and socioeconomic progress in the seven decades since emancipation. Over 400,000 visitors reportedly visited the exhibit hall, and it is cited by *The Handbook of Texas* as "an exposition milestone, the first recognition of black culture at a world's fair." This distinction is repeated in the only book-length study of the Texas Centennial Exposition. The Hall of Negro Life and other aspects of black participation have thus been represented over time as tentative steps forward from the oppression of segregation and racial hierarchy and as an important part of the nascent civil rights movement in the state of Texas.[3]

Yet the physical space of Dallas's Fair Park belies the triumphalist narrative of the Hall of Negro Life. The park is noted as an outstanding example of the Art Deco style and is preserved as a National Historic Landmark. According to the park's website, "Fair Park is the only intact and unaltered pre-1950s world fair site remaining in the United States." Despite this assertion, Fair Park is not "intact and unaltered." A single building in the 277-acre park complex was demolished prior to the exposition's continuance in 1937: the Hall of Negro Life.[4] Appropriately, the concept for a Texas Centennial celebration in 1936 originated within the burgeoning advertising industry of the 1920s. On November 5, 1923, New Yorker Theodore H. Price addressed the Tenth District Convention of the Associated Advertising Clubs of America in Corsicana, Texas. Price's speech, titled "What Texas Has to Advertise and How to Advertise It," exhorted the assembly of ad men to promote, among other things, "your gloriously romantic history" to outside investors. The idea gained the support of the governor at the time but languished for many years before being revived during the Great Depression. Finally, on February 27, 1934, the last day of the year's legislative session, Senate Bill Number 22 cleared the House. The bill established a Texas Centennial Commission, allocated funds for the commission's interim activities, and stated that the city offering the largest financial inducement and support would become the location of the centennial celebration's central exposition. Dallas was eventually chosen over San Antonio and Houston as the location of the Texas Centennial Exposition.[5]

Much like the image-conscious white leadership of the Texas Centennial, the large and well-organized black community in Dallas attempted to utilize the Centennial Exposition to project a positive image of Afro-Texans. A. Maceo Smith and a cadre of black urban businessmen and professionals in the Dallas Negro Chamber of Commerce (DNCC) spearheaded lobbying efforts to ensure significant black representation and participation in the festivities. Smith, a native of Texarkana, graduated from Fisk University and held an MBA from New York University; he completed additional graduate education at Columbia University. A key leader in the black community of Dallas, Smith was, by the mid-1930s, working as a teacher at Booker T. Washington High School, editing the weekly *Dallas Express,* and serving as the first executive secretary of the DNCC. Established in 1926 as an outgrowth of Booker T. Washington's National Negro Business League, the DNCC was the first such organization in Texas. Revived by Smith after a period of dormancy, the DNCC had every expectation that its lobbying efforts would yield state funding for an African American exhibit at the Centennial Exposition site. Every major southern exposition, beginning with the 1884 New Orleans World's Industrial and Cotton Centennial, had contained an exhibit specifically designated to highlight the achievements of African Americans. Smith and other black Texans saw no reason why the Texas Centennial should break with this well-established tradition.[6]

Smith aggressively pursued contacts in the legislature and the white business and political establishment of Dallas to ensure support for an African American exhibit. He traveled to Austin with black architect J. L. Blount to present his idea for an "Africa Museum" before the Joint Legislative Committee on October 23. Smith believed his presentation was "warmly received." The appropriations bill of 1934 ultimately failed to pass, but the DNCC continued to be optimistic that an earmark would be made for "the Negro life feature of the Texas Centennial" in 1935. The *Dallas Express* followed the Centennial Exposition developments closely and reported positively on the DNCC's lobbying campaign. Unfortunately, white support for the DNCC's efforts depended upon Dallas blacks toeing the line on political issues. A state House race proved to be the hinge upon which white support for the DNCC's project swung.[7]

In early 1935, Texas governor James V. Allred appointed Sarah T. Hughes, a state representative from Dallas, to the state district court. This vacancy in the legislature led to a general election in March 1935 to fill the seat. Incredibly, sixty candidates were included on the ballot, one of whom, Ammon S. Wells, was a black Dallas lawyer. As a general election, the obstacle of the all-white primary was avoided, and any black Dallas voters who had paid their poll taxes could cast a vote. With no shortage of candidates, a solid black vote for Wells might have ensured victory in the race. In a later interview, Smith recalled that "key leaders" in Dallas told him that if Wells pulled out of the race, "you'll get your money.'" As campaign manager for Wells, Smith refused to pull his candidate from the race despite the threat to the "Negro life feature." Wells went on to place sixth in the race, and the Texas state legislature responded to what it saw as the Dallas black community's recalcitrance by failing to appropriate funds for an African American exhibit.[8]

After passage of the state appropriations bill, white Texans began to lobby for federal funds to help support the centennial. Not to be deterred by the bigotry of the state legislature, black Texans also turned to federal assistance to secure a role in their state's big celebration. Smith and other black leaders in Dallas began to work through their white contacts in North Texas to ensure federal support. Eventually their requests were passed on to US Representatives Wright Patman and Sam Rayburn, and, most importantly, to Vice President John N. Garner, a native Texan.[9]

Congress passed the Texas Centennial funding bill on July 21, 1935, allocating $3 million in federal money to the celebration. Fortunately, the disbursement was left to a commission headed by Garner. The Dallas black community's lobbying efforts now paid off. Garner continued to support the allocation of funding for a Hall of Negro Life, and the federal commission designated $50,000 to support the construction of a Hall of Negro Life and another $50,000 for the creation of exhibits within the hall.[10]

Successful acquisition of federal funding signaled a major triumph for the black leadership of Texas and especially Dallas. Smith and other leaders had skillfully navigated the channels of political power at the national level, outflanking white opposition at home. The *Dallas Express* proudly ran the headline "Dallas Negroes to Actively Participate in Central Exposition at Dallas" and reported that "$50,000 has been set aside for the Negro Building."[11]

The same issue reported that "the Texas Centennial Exposition is the first World's Fair to extend official recognition to the Negro Race," an action which "sets a new precedent." The article was apparently taken verbatim from a Texas Centennial Committee press release. The committee's claim notwithstanding, both white and black leaders were certainly aware of the well-established practice of erecting "Negro halls" at southern expositions. Jesse O. Thomas, who was named to run the Hall of Negro Life, later claimed that the hall was indeed distinctive because it was completely manned and run by African Americans, in contrast to earlier exhibits, such as the one at the Jamestown Exposition in 1907. Press releases made no such distinction, quickly championing the Hall of Negro Life as a sign of innovation and progress, despite white Texan leaders' refusal to support it. Thus the myth was born that the Hall of Negro Life was an entirely new and Texan innovation.[12]

Several problems arose during construction of the hall. Although the Texas Negro Centennial Committee (TNCC) desired a black architect to design the building, it was instead designed by George L. Dahl, a Dallas-based white architect who served as the principal architect for the exposition grounds. A local contractor disregarded the published plans and painted the interior of the building "deep green and red." When questioned about his actions, the contractor replied that "he understood that Negroes liked loud colors." The contractor also failed to install fire hoses instead of fire extinguishers. Due to these issues the Hall of Negro Life was not ready to open until June 12, six days after the opening of the Centennial Exposition fairgrounds. When construction was finally completed, Thomas was dismayed to find a line of cedar trees planted directly in front of the building, a feature he believed to be a deliberate attempt to screen the hall from public view.[13]

Hall manager Jesse O. Thomas, an Atlanta native and director of the Southern Field Division of the National Urban League, found his role quickly expanded to de facto point of contact for black participation at the Dallas exposition site in general. His interactions with the white leadership of the exposition were often frustrating. Thomas believed that Walter D. Cline, first director of the Centennial Exposition and an oilman who had originally helped secure funding for the hall, was a paternalist who "never regarded Negroes as full grown men." Thomas considered Cline's successor, Walter A. Webb, even less enlightened. Webb ignored repeated requests regarding deficiencies in restroom facilities and concessions for black visitors. When Webb suddenly passed away in July, Thomas recorded that "accompanying the expressions of regret was the sigh of relief in many quarters." Fortunately, Webb's successor, Harry Olmstead, was more open minded or at least more willing to collect gate receipts from black visitors. He authored an August missive to the *Dallas Express* assuring the black community that they were welcome at the exposition, and at his direction the offending trees were finally removed from the vicinity of the Hall of Negro Life on October 18, just in time for the last of the exposition's three "Negro Days" meant to encourage black visitation to the fairgrounds.[14]

Even with these reassurances, black participation at the Centennial Exposition was troubled from the start. Black visitors were constantly reminded that the color line was in force. Smith recalled that "Icecapades would close up, because they didn't want the blacks seeing them little naked white gals," and he admitted that some exhibits wouldn't allow black visitors. Black performers at the National Folk Festival, held concurrently with the exposition, were subjected to humiliating insults by white Dallasites. The stage manager at the festival recalled that at one point in the festival, a group of black singers took the stage, only to become the object of racial slurs by some "ladies of the Dallas music clubs." The white women then interrupted the black singers' performance by singing a Stephen Foster number from off stage. The exposition grounds had few toilets and concessions open to African Americans, and some bus and cab operators refused to offer transportation to black visitors. Thomas pursued a letter-writing campaign to the management of these businesses, and by his account the issues were resolved relatively swiftly.[15]

A series of viciously racist newspaper headlines and articles mocking the Juneteenth celebration and other Negro Days were also major sources of irritation for Thomas. He expressed his outrage in a series of letters to the editors of Dallas and other papers who published these slurs and met with some of them personally. A May 24 letter from Thomas to the *Dallas Morning News* editor took the paper to task for publishing an article entitled "History of the Negro from Jungles Until Now" with a subheading declaring, "Centennial to be Turned Over to Darkies Juneteenth." The *Dallas Morning News* persisted, covering Juneteenth with such headlines as "Dallas Eats Cold Supper and Cotton Patches Emptied as Thousands Inspect Magic City" and "Dusky Beauties Prance; Cab Calloway Does His Stuff for Truckers." The article went on to describe "thousands of dusky merrymakers" who had "left fiddle-faced mules to munch contentedly in idleness, farm work forgotten." The fairgrounds were allegedly the scene of "rolling eyes and flashing white teeth," evidence that "laughter and carefree happiness comes easy to the Sons of Ham."[16]

Dallas papers drew national attention from African Americans for their virulently racist coverage of these events. The *Chicago Defender,* a leading black newspaper, attacked the Dallas press for their actions. Writing for the

*Defender,* A. N. Fields caustically claimed to have "read with interest your various articles on the progress exhibited and the intelligence shown as demonstrated by your hundredth anniversary and Centennial expositions." Fields went on to charge, "Your entire state and white civilization of Texas reflect a hundred years of decadence, prejudice, hate, and bigotry." Apparently unconcerned with this negative publicity, the *Dallas Journal,* the evening edition of the *Dallas Morning News,* carried a headline for October 19 with the byline "One Dead as Negroes Celebrate Here," juxtaposing violent crime with the final Negro Day at the Exposition. This kind of attention was certainly not what Thomas, Smith, or the TNCC desired for an enterprise to which they had committed so much work.[17]

For Smith and others in the black community of Dallas, the Hall of Negro Life offered an opportunity to counter the master narrative of the Texas Centennial and to project a more positive message about black Texans. Utilizing the $50,000 allocated toward exhibits, Thomas and his staff filled the Hall of Negro Life with art and informational exhibits intended to display the economic and social progress of African Americans since emancipation. The building's facade was adorned with a plaster relief sculpture by Raoul Josset of "a Negro with broken chains from slavery, ignorance, and superstitions falling from his wrists." Upon entering the lobby of the hall, visitors found an information desk manned by black Works Progress Administration and National Youth Administration workers and a series of four murals adorning the walls. Executed by Aaron Douglas, a Harlem Renaissance artist, the panels illustrated the progress of black Texans over time. One panel portrayed the exploits of Estevanico, an African member of the Cabeza de Vaca expedition and the first black man to set foot in Texas. A second panel showed the arrival to the New World of Africans in chains, followed by another panel depicting the "Negro's Gift to America." Alonzo Aden, an African American art critic and curator of the exhibits, interpreted the paintings to mean that "Here, 'Human Labor' is the key to a true understanding of the Negro in a new world. Music, Art, and Religion are all a part of the contribution." The final panel portrayed blacks who had been "released from the machine-like state which has been the role of the Negro." Once freed from this state, "it is less difficult for them to enter fields where mentality is a dominant factor."[18]

After viewing an artistic representation of black progress, visitors could proceed into the exhibit areas, equipped with informational booklets: "What the Negro Has Done for the United States and Texas," by W. E. B. Dubois, and

"Progress of the Negro in Texas," by Charles E. Hall, a specialist in "Negro Statistics" for the Bureau of the Census. Dubois's contribution to the exhibit was a concise history of African Americans in Texas, while Hall's pamphlet was a compendium of statistics culled from the latest census returns. The pamphlet contained figures on topics such as "Marital Condition," "Size of Family and Home Ownership," "School Attendance," "Prison Population," and "Retail Stores," categories meant to suggest the conformity of black Texans to American middle-class values. Hall highlighted the importance of black consumers who were "contributing to the productive wealth of the State" due to "the purchasing power of this large group of people."[19]

Exhibits inside the hall were varied but emphasized the educational attainment and cultural sophistication of the black middle class, as well as the vocational skills of black workers. The main categories on display fell under the headings of "education, fine arts, health, agriculture, mechanic arts, and business." The education exhibit contained displays from black colleges and universities throughout the United States and especially in the South, such as Fisk University, Florida A&M, and Bishop and Wiley Colleges in Texas. Accompanying these displays were statistics similar to those found in Hall's pamphlet.[20]

The education hall also contained a large display of books written by African American authors. Visitors could obtain a copy of the bibliography for this collection at the information desk. The fine arts section included works by artists such as Aaron Douglas, Archibald J. Motley, Richard Barthe, Sargent Johnson, James Wells, Hale Woodruff, Samuel Countee, Laura Wheeler Waring, "and many other lesser known." Black musicians were represented in a display, and records from artists such as Marian Anderson, Paul Robeson, William Dawson, Nathaniel Dett, Lillian Evanti, Roland Hayes, H. T. Burleigh, Hall Johnson, "and scores of others" were played "almost continuously." The mechanical arts exhibit showed various African American–created inventions, gathered by the Hall of Negro Life committee. Past the mechanical arts exhibit was a display on newspapers, created by Claude A. Barnett, another Tuskegee graduate and editor of the Associated Negro Press. According to Jesse Thomas, "Many of the visitors to the building had never seen a Negro newspaper and were very much surprised to know that Negroes were publishing a daily paper." The health exhibit related statistics showing the falling rates of contagious illnesses within the African American population, a subtle challenge to racialized notions of disease. The business and social work areas also exhibited various statistics, all painting a picture of progress.[21]

Though they wished to delineate a positive image of the African American community, the administrators of the Hall of Negro Life were careful not to directly challenge white supremacy. A series of dioramas in the agriculture exhibit depicted the progress made by a black-owned farm. Supposedly taken from the story of an actual farm in Texas, the first diorama was set in 1863 and portrayed the farm of a slave emancipated and granted land of his own for loyal service to the Confederacy. The dioramas progressed from the 1860s to the 1930s to show improvements in machinery, tools, and techniques on this model farm. The improbable origin of the Texas farm in question served to couch black progress within the accommodation of white hegemony.[22]

Jesse Thomas, who had been personally mentored by Booker T. Washington while at Tuskegee Institute, sought to advance a narrative of racial uplift through his management of the hall. Racial uplift posited that the black middle class should lead the African American community through a process of gradual advancement with an emphasis on "self-help, racial solidarity, temperance, thrift, chastity, social purity, patriarchal authority, and the accumulation of wealth." Thomas's belief that "interracial relations" would benefit from the didactic possibility afforded by the Hall of Negro Life was an important corollary to racial uplift ideology. White visitors would be imbued with "a higher appreciation of the Negroes' contribution to American culture and with a more tolerant attitude toward the Negroes' effort." Smith's *Dallas Express* concurred, reprinting with approval an item from the *Dallas Morning News* that claimed that "the commemorative exhibit here should serve to improve interracial relations as well as to bring Negro visitors." Through education, reasonable white people would be convinced of the progress of black society toward middle-class norms. Persuading white people in this manner would serve as a prerequisite for the incremental improvement of socioeconomic and political conditions for black Texans. Black patronage of the Centennial Exposition would also serve to make a point about the dollar power wielded by black Texans. Armed with this Washingtonian conviction, Thomas and Smith replicated the kind of African American world's fair exhibit that had been in use for the past forty years.[23]

Virtually every feature of the Hall of Negro Life replicated previous African American exhibits. Criticized from the beginning by those who saw them as symbols of the tacit acceptance of segregation, "Negro buildings" at expositions tended to emphasize education, the importance of black workers to the economy, and the growing economic power of the black community. Thomas diligently adhered to this model. The hall's informational displays mirrored those of the 1890s Atlanta and Nashville expositions almost exactly. Even artistic renderings of African American progress were nearly identical. The Negro Building at the Atlanta Exposition featured "an allegorical pediment that told the story of black progress since slavery" and included *The Negro with Chains Broken but Not Off,* a statue of a former slave rising to a standing position with broken manacles on each wrist. The Hall of Negro Life was clearly more representative of the Washingtonian ideology of racial uplift than of the more politically oriented African American civil rights movement emerging in the 1930s.[24]

Though the Hall of Negro Life offered at most a subtle rebuke to segregation and white racism, an interracial track and field meet put on by the national Amateur Athletic Union (AAU) posed the greatest challenge to Jim Crow at the Centennial Exposition. The Juneteenth event was reportedly "the first time in the history of Texas blacks and whites will compete in the same events on the same track." Outstanding black athletes such as Olympians Ralph Metcalfe and Eddie Tolan competed in the event. White athletes, including shot-putter Jack Torrance and long- and triple-jumper Rolland Romero, also appeared. A number of African American colleges were represented, as well as Booker T. Washington High School in Dallas. White athletes were reportedly in attendance from Woodrow Wilson High School, Loyola University–New Orleans, Northern Texas State Teachers College, and Texas A&M.[25]

Unfortunately, the halting step forward undertaken by the interracial meet was marred by the overt racism of some of the white spectators. The date of the meet, June 19, 1936, was also the date of the highly anticipated Joe Lewis–Max Schmeling boxing match. The fight pitted the champion of the Third Reich against the African American world champion in a highly symbolic and politically charged affair. The track meet was temporarily interrupted to broadcast the boxing match over the loudspeakers of the Cotton Bowl to a crowd of approximately one thousand. "When the German finished Louis," reported the *Dallas Express,* "a great cheer went up from 500 American white throats. It's funny to note that American whites would rather see a white foreigner come in here and take the bacon back home than to keep it here through and by a black boy." The *Express* went on to bitterly question, "Which is bigger anyway—a nation or a race?"[26]

In spite of all the problems they encountered, Thomas and Smith remained enthusiastic about the effects of African American participation in the Centennial Exposition. The Hall of Negro Life drew a total attendance of 403,227 over the course of the exposition, representing, according to Thomas, "a complete cross-section of all race elements and all cultural levels of American citizens." By his estimate nearly two-thirds of visitors to the hall were white, "at least ninety-nine per cent" of whom were enthusiastic enough about it to encourage others to visit. In his account of black participation in the exposition, Thomas included numerous anecdotes of laudatory statements by white politicians, as well as the comments of hall workers and visitors. A librarian working at the information booth claimed that the exhibits were "of untold value to Negroes, measured in terms of respect developed among thousands of white people who never before knew that Negroes help to form the underpinning of past and present day civilization." Thomas also highlighted ignorant remarks by white visitors to show the need for such an exhibit. One woman, experiencing a revelation after viewing the hall, reportedly commented to one of the staff, "You are way ahead of white folk and there's no telling where you will go. We must be careful what we do, because you are too far ahead now."[27]

Thomas and other black leaders argued that the Centennial Exposition had proven the respectability of black Texans both through a demonstration of their financial prowess and through their comportment on the fairgrounds. The *Dallas Express* reported on October 31 that "Negro day figures will be beaten only by July 4, which recorded the highest receipts." In addition to being big spenders, black visitors drew praise for the "orderliness and general character of Negro participation." According to Thomas, the Centennial Exposition had demonstrated "that if and when Negroes are accorded the opportunity of normal expression and self determination they behave very much like other civilized beings." Thomas continued to employ the language of racial uplift in his assessment of the exposition: "The fact that with 70,000 Negroes on the ground . . . there was not an occasion for a single arrest . . . graphically tells the story of the development Negroes have made in the matter of self control since their Emancipation." By these accounts, the twin objectives of improving "race relations" through education and demonstrating the respectability and economic potency of black Texans were achieved.[28]

Beyond making this tenuous claim to success, black leaders were eager to demonstrate that more concrete advances resulted from their efforts in the Centennial Exposition. The opening of Southwestern AAU active membership at a regular membership rate was attributed to "the success of the recent interracial track meet held in Dallas, June 19th." Jesse Thomas also championed the successful negotiation of railroad rates and accommodations for black visitors. The all-white Dallas Police Department was allegedly embarrassed by a Juneteenth parade that was led by black police officers from other Texas cities. Thomas stated that during a city election campaign "within thirty days after the close of the Exposition, several of the candidates pledged themselves to secure the appointment of Negro policemen, if elected."[29]

Besides their personal investments of reputation, time, and effort, Thomas and other black leaders involved in the Centennial Exposition were spurred to defend the success of their endeavors against criticism by segments of the black community. The rhetoric of their critics illustrated the division between proponents of Washingtonian ideas of racial uplift and those who favored more direct methods to break down the barriers they faced in Jim Crow Texas. The most direct criticism leveled at black involvement in the Centennial appeared in the *Dallas Express* as the exposition was winding down. Charles H. Bynum II, a black schoolteacher in Dallas, wrote an article called "The Centennial In Retrospect." After first justifying criticism of the Centennial in black newspapers, Bynum charged that "State, Local, and Centennial officials led Negroes to believe and to work expecting that their rights and privileges would be fully respected." In truth, "the Centennial Exposition never deigned to give Negroes a voice in the Centennial preparations, and used unsportsmanlike tactics to justify policies practiced." He blamed the deficit run by the Centennial Exposition on the lack of "favorable conditions" for black attendance and accused Thomas, Smith, and other black leaders of being either ignorant, incompetent, or apologists for "the 1936 debacle." Bynum concluded his polemic by insisting that in the coming Pan-American Exposition of 1937, the black community of Dallas must be faithfully represented at the Hall of Negro Life.[30]

Thomas, Smith, and several other African American leaders responded to criticism in a number of ways. Their acquiescence to the Centennial Committee's rhetoric about the supposedly innovative Hall of Negro Life was a way to legitimize the hall as progressive. Thomas also fired back with criticism of his own, accusing the black community of failing to take full advantage of the economic windfall to be had from the exposition. According to Thomas, this reflected "the anti-social attitude of the Negro in Texas." Thomas dismissed those who "squawked" about the exposition's segregationist policies. In his view, "the character and type of segregation to which they were subject to on the Grounds they were subject to in their own towns." These critics "made demands upon the Administration to change the whole social pattern of Texas in ninety days," Thomas complained, "or stand guilty of subscribing to segregation." Thomas argued that the segregated exposition grounds and special Negro Days actually ensured that black participation was "concentrated," ensuring higher visibility for the revenue generated by black visitors. Smith acknowledged that "some felt that it was another Jim Crow thing," but he believed that "you got to start somewhere. You can't start on an integrated pattern." Smith felt that the attitude of many newspapers was, essentially, "here's another segregated enterprise that you're creating." Despite this internal conflict, Dallas's black community looked hopefully toward the future in the afterglow of the Centennial Exposition.[31]

Though the exposition had operated at a loss, the decision was made to reopen it from June to November 1937 as the Greater Texas and Pan American Exposition. Black leaders in Dallas assumed that the Hall of Negro Life would be included and were shocked to receive directions in January 1937 to dismantle the exhibits in the hall and return them to their owners. The hall would not be used in the upcoming exposition. In spite of the protests of Thomas and other black leaders, along with the support of some white Dallas leaders, the reason for the "mysterious elimination of Negro participation" was never fully explained. In a letter to a Commerce Department official, explaining the decision, Vice President Garner alluded to the protests of some white Dallas residents.[32]

According to Thomas, the White House launched an investigation to determine why the Hall of Negro Life was being discontinued. A redacted letter was eventually produced which claimed that "there was not sufficient residue in the Federal appropriation of last year to maintain and operate both the magnificent Federal building and the Hall of Negro Life." Black visitors were offered the succor that "we shall offer major special events for them on special days." Thomas denied the lack of funds for the hall, but this time black leaders were unable to wrangle support to continue their exhibit. Not only was the operation of the hall discontinued, but the hall itself was razed, making it the only building demolished prior to the 1937 exposition. Thomas concluded his account of the affair with the sarcastic lament, "There was somebody in the wood pile and he was not a Sambo."[33]

For black Texans, the experience of the Texas Centennial Exposition was ultimately disappointing in many ways. Writing in 1938, Thomas was optimistic that some concrete gains might be realized from black participation in the enterprise. Smith believed the Hall of Negro Life provided "a beachhead for the Negro Civil Rights movement in Texas" and asserted that contacts made in organizing for the Centennial Exposition were important for later "enlarging of the state NAACP, forming a statewide Negro Chamber of Commerce, [and] forming Urban League chapters in Texas." African American leaders earnestly desired to improve the everyday situation for black Texans, but their efforts during the Texas Centennial Exposition were limited by hardened white racial attitudes, the very real threat of white racial violence, and their own reliance upon an ideology of self-help and moral suasion.[34]

Unsurprisingly, white racial attitudes in Dallas and in Texas as a whole were not noticeably affected by the image of black progress put forth by the Hall of Negro Life. While the Centennial Exposition portrayed Texas to the rest of the country as a forward-looking, Western state, Dallasites had paired the opening of the exposition grounds with an homage to the Confederate past. On June 12, 1936, prior to attending the opening ceremonies, President Franklin D. Roosevelt offered remarks at the unveiling of a $50,000, larger-than-life statue of Robert E. Lee in what had recently been renamed Lee Park. Following the Centennial Exposition, Dallas doubled down on its public memorialization of the Confederacy, in 1939 erecting Arlington Hall, a structure in the park modeled after the Lee-Custis Mansion in Virginia. Thomas's optimism about the hiring of black police officers in Dallas also proved premature—the city did not hire its first officers of color until 1947. Perhaps the razing of the Hall of Negro Life in 1937 should have signaled the extent to which white attitudes on race had shifted since the commencement of the Centennial Exposition.[35]

The exposition's most radical element, the interracial track meet, likewise failed to inspire immediate changes in athletics in the state. The Texas Relays, one of the major track and field events in the country, would not integrate until 1962, and Texas high school athletics would not be integrated until the late 1960s. The University of Texas, which had declined to send athletes to the Centennial Exposition meet, fielded the last all-white national champion college football team in 1969 and became the site of a nearly two-decade struggle over full integration of the university.[36]

Looking back in 1968, Smith succinctly captured the dilemma he faced during the Centennial Exposition. "I was as militant and activist as anyone in the U.S. in working for the black man," he exclaimed, "but be practical!" The

Texas Centennial Exposition would ultimately be little more than an interesting footnote in Smith's career. He went on to serve as a key leader in forging a formidable black electorate in Dallas and in gaining incremental concessions through his Progressive Voters League. He was also involved in the NAACP's ultimately successful fight against the white primary and in the long effort to desegregate the University of Texas. Real progress for black Texans in the 1930s and 1940s was driven by the success of Smith and others in grassroots political activism and civil rights litigation. The efforts of a previous generation to win the hearts and minds of whites through claims of respectability were largely superseded in favor of a hardnosed campaign for civil rights and political power. The Hall of Negro Life was not the first of its kind but instead a last gasp of the tactics that had guided black participation at southern world's fairs for the previous four decades.[37]

Michael Phillips writes that Dallas's white leadership "sought to rescue the city from the weight of the Southern past by creating a mythological past that tied Dallas to the larger national frontier narrative." Phillips argues further that Dallas has been caught "in a timeless warp because of its denial of history," a situation that "left the structures of oppression soundly intact." Public sites of popular memory in Dallas remain a jumbled collage, commemorating tragic Confederate heroism, the westward march of the Anglo-imperial frontier, and entrepreneurial can-do spirit. Much the same could be said for Texas popular memory and identity writ large, which often seems to be grounded in a triumphal denial of time and place. The veracity of Texas's deliberately ahistorical origin myth has only recently been seriously challenged by historians, a testament to the Texas Centennial's remarkably successful branding campaign.[38]

Ironically, even though the Hall of Negro Life represented a prominent display of the well-worn narrative of racial uplift, it was appropriated from the beginning as evidence for Texas's secession from its southern past. In fact, the chief innovation of the Centennial Exposition was not in its forward-looking inclusion of the Hall of Negro Life but rather in the efforts of white Texans to exclude any formal recognition of black culture during their state's hundredth birthday party. The eighty-year-old legend of the Hall of Negro Life dramatically underscores the degree to which white supremacy undergirded the Lone Star identity that emerged during the 1930s.

## NOTES

1. Stanley Marcus, quoted in Kenneth B. Ragsdale, *Centennial '36: The Year America Discovered Texas* (College Station: Texas A&M University Press, 1987), 302. On the rebranding of Texas, see Light Townsend Cummins, "History, Memory, and Rebranding Texas as Western for the 1936 Centennial," in *This Corner of Canaan: Essays on Texas in Honor of Randolph B. Campbell*, ed. Richard B. McCaslin, Donald E. Chipman, and Andrew J. Torget (Denton: University of North Texas Press, 2013), 37–57; Leigh Clemons, *Branding Texas: Performing Culture in the Lone Star State* (Austin: University of Texas Press, 2008), 104–7. On the ideology promulgated at nineteenth-century expositions, see Robert W. Rydell, *All the World's a Fair: Visions of Empire at American International Expositions, 1876–1916* (Chicago University of Chicago Press, 1984). Variations of the phrase "Empire on Parade" were frequently used in speeches, promotions, and ephemera during the Texas Centennial. Wallace O. Chariton, *Texas Centennial: The Parade of an Empire* (Plano: Texas Centennial, 1979), 131; Ragsdale, *Centennial,* 231, 247; Franklin D. Roosevelt, "Address at the Texas Centennial Exposition, Dallas, Texas," June 12, 1936, The American Presidency Project, www.presidency.ucsb.edu/ws/?pid=15302.

2. National Association for the Advancement of Colored People, *Thirty Years of Lynching in the United States* (New York: NAACP, National Office, 1919), 7; John R. Ross, "Lynching," and Nolan Thompson, "Sherman Riot of 1930," at *Handbook of Texas Online,* www.tshaonline.org/handbook, Texas State Historical Association (accessed Aug. 31, 2015).

3. Paul M. Lucko, "Hall of Negro Life," *Handbook of Texas Online*; Jesse O. Thomas, *Negro Participation in the Texas Centennial Exposition* (Boston: Christopher Publishing House, 1938), 21; "Texas Centennial," *Handbook of Texas Online*; Ragsdale, *Centennial,* 305; John David Boswell, "Negro Participation in the 1936 Texas Centennial Exposition" (MA thesis, University of Texas at Austin, 1969), 40–42.

4. "About Fair Park," www.fairpark.org (accessed Apr. 4, 2013); Ragsdale, *Centennial,* 305. More than half of the buildings were eventually razed. Lucko, "Hall of Negro Life."

5. Ragsdale, *Centennial,* 6–11, 32–33; "Texas Centennial," *Handbook of Texas Online.*

6. Neil Sapper, "Smith, Antonio Maceo," and Paul M. Lucko, "Dallas Black Chamber of Commerce," *Handbook of Texas Online*; Dale Tomlinson and Dorothy Irwin, "Interview with A. Maceo Smith," Institute of Texan Cultures Oral History Collection, http://digital.utsa.edu (accessed Nov. 26, 2012), 2–5; On black participation in southern world's fairs, see Ruth M. Winton, "Negro Participation in Southern Expositions, 1881–1915," *Journal of Negro Education* 16 (Winter 1947): 34–43; Bruce Gordon Harvey, "World's Fairs with a Southern Accent: Atlanta, Nashville, Charleston, 1895–1902" (PhD diss., Vanderbilt University, 1998); Blain Roberts and Ethan J. Kytle, "Looking the Thing in the Face: Slavery, Race, and the Commemorative Landscape in Charleston, South Carolina, 1865–2010," *Journal of Southern History* 78 (Aug. 2012): 639–84; Nathan Cardon, "The South's 'New Negroes' and African American Visions of Progress at the Atlanta and Nashville International Expositions, 1895–1897," *Journal of Southern History* 80 (May 2014): 287–326.

7. Tomlinson and Irwin, "Interview with A. Maceo Smith," 5–6; Ragsdale, *Centennial,* 65–67; "C of C to Hold Annual Meeting," *Dallas Express,* Dec. 8, 1934; "Negro C. of C. Elects Head," *Dallas Express,* Mar. 7, 1936.

8. Ironically, Hughes was a trailblazing progressive jurist. She was the first woman to serve as a state district judge, as well the first woman to serve as a federal district judge. Hughes sat on the first panel to rule on Roe v. Wade and, perhaps most famously, administered the oath of office to Lyndon B. Johnson after the assassination of President John F. Kennedy. Robert S. La Forte, "Hughes, Sarah Tilghman," *Handbook of Texas Online*; Tomlinson and Irwin, "Interview with A. Maceo Smith," 6–7; William C. Yancey, "Wells, Ammon Scott," *Handbook of Texas Online*.

9. Tomlinson and Irwin, "Interview with A. Maceo Smith," 7–8; Boswell, "Negro Participation," 10–12.

10. Boswell, "Negro Participation" 12–13.

11. "Dallas Negroes to Actively Participate in Central Exposition at Dallas," *Dallas Express*, Feb. 1, 1936.

12. "Dallas Negroes," *Dallas Express*, Feb. 1, 1936; Jesse O. Thomas, *Negro Participation in the Texas Centennial Exposition* (Boston: Christopher Publishing House, 1938), 146; undated press release, Centennial Press Releases, Texas Centennial Records, 1935–1939, Dolph Briscoe Center for American History, The University of Texas at Austin.

13. Paul M. Lucko, "Hall of Negro Life," *Handbook of Texas Online*; Boswell, "Negro participation," 13; Thomas, *Negro Participation*, 21–22, 73–74.

14. Rosemary Braxton, "Jesse O. Thomas (1885–1972)," Georgia Humanities Council, *New Georgia Encyclopedia*, www.georgiaencyclopedia.org, (accessed Aug. 10, 2015); Thomas, *Negro Participation*, 72–85; "Negroes Are Welcome To Centennial," *Dallas Express*, Aug. 29, 1936. Traditionally, the Texas State Fair accorded one day in October as a special Negro Day with greater access for black Texans. The exposition administration recognized this tradition and expanded it to three days: Juneteenth, August 19, and October 19. "2nd Negro Day Aug. 19th at Centennial," *Dallas Express*, Aug. 22, 1936; "Wiley-PV Grid Classic: To Stress Achievements in Education," *Dallas Express*, Sept. 19, 1936.

15. Tomlinson and Irwin, "Interview with A. Maceo Smith," 10–11; Kevin Mooney, "Texas Centennial 1936: African American Texans and the Third National Folk Festival," *Journal of Texas Music History* 1, no. 1 (2001): 39; Thomas, *Negro Participation*, 79–83.

16. Thomas, *Negro Participation*, 83–84; "History of Negroes from the Jungle Until Now," *Dallas Morning News*, May 14, 1936; "Negroes Stage Big Juneteenth at Centennial," *Dallas Morning News*, June 20, 1936.

17. A. N. Fields, "Dallas Papers Insult Visitors to Exposition," *Chicago Defender*, June 27, 1936; "One Dead as Negroes Celebrate Here," *Dallas Journal*, Oct. 19, 1936.

18. Thomas, *Negro Participation*, 129, 20, 25; Alonzo J. Aden, "Educational Tour Through the Hall of Negro Life," *Southern Workman* 65 (Nov. 1936): 331–32.

19. Thomas, *Negro Participation*, 35–36; W. E. B. Dubois, *What the Negro Has Done for the United States and Texas* (Washington, DC: US Government Printing Office, 1936); Charles E. Hall, *Progress of the Negro in Texas* (Washington, DC: US Government Printing Office, 1936), 2.

20. Thomas, *Negro Participation*, 28–29, 38.

21. Ibid., 39–40; Jesse O. Thomas, *My Story in Black and White: The Autobiography of Jesse O. Thomas* (New York: Exposition Press, 1967), 43–44; Lawrence Daniel Hogan, "Associated Negro Press," *The Encyclopedia of Chicago*, www.encyclopedia.chicagohistory.org (accessed Jan. 8, 2016).

22. Aden, "Educational Tour Through the Hall of Negro Life," 337.

23. Thomas, *My Story in Black and White,* 33–40; Kevin K. Gaines, *Uplifting the Race: Black Leadership, Politics, and Culture in the Twentieth Century* (Chapel Hill: University of North Carolina Press, 1996), 2; "Texas and the Negro," *Dallas Express,* Mar. 7, 1936; Thomas, *Negro Participation,* 87.

24. Cardon, "The South's 'New Negroes,'" 298–304, 317–18; Winton, "Negro Participation in Southern Expositions," 34, 36, 38, 41.

25. In contrast to the Hall of Negro Life, the Juneteenth track meet has been all but forgotten in Texas history. "Champs of Both Races: Title Holders to Shoot at Own Records," *Dallas Express,* June 13, 1936; "Spectators Thrilled—Thinly Clad Athletes; Both Races Perform," *Dallas Express,* June 27, 1936.

26. P. D. Whitted, "Scrappy's Sport Scraps," *Dallas Express,* June 27, 1936.

27. Thomas, *Negro Participation,* 36, 86, 108–9.

28. "Negro Day One of Expo. Most Successful," *Dallas Express,* Oct. 31, 1936; Thomas, *Negro Participation,* 148.

29. "Membership Regular Fee—Way Open for Race Athletes to Participate," *Dallas Express,* Sept. 12, 1936; Thomas, *Negro Participation,* 88–90; "Negro Police Lead Parade," *Dallas Express,* Oct. 17, 1936.

30. Charles H. Bynum II, "The Centennial In Retrospect," *Dallas Express,* Oct. 31, 1936.

31. Thomas, *Negro Participation,* 65, 63–64, 150; Tomlinson and Irwin, "Interview with A. Maceo Smith," 10–11.

32. Thomas, *Negro Participation,* 117–20.

33. Ibid., 121–24.

34. Boswell, "Negro Participation," 41.

35. Lee Park was formerly named Oak Lawn Park. "Board Favors Giving Lee's Name to Park," May 27, 1936, *Dallas Morning News;* Kelly McMichael, *Sacred Memories: The Civil War Monument Movement in Texas* (Denton: Texas State Historical Association, 2009), 46–47; "Stylish Special Events," Arlington Hall at Lee Park, www.arlingtonhallatleepark.com/Venue.html (accessed Jan. 9, 2016); Erin Blakemore, "The Tragic Story of Dallas' First African-American Police Officer," www.smithsonianmag.com, July 12, 2016.

36. Dwonna Goldstone, *Integrating the 40 Acres: The Fifty Year Struggle for Racial Equality at the University of Texas* (Athens: University of Georgia Press, 2006), 3–13, 112, 125–30; D. Keith Luberto, "The Integration Movement: Texas High School Athletic and Academic Contests," *Journal of Sport and Social Issues* 18 (May 1994): 151–68.

37. Boswell, "Negro Participation," 40; Phillips, *White Metropolis,* 112, 116–17; Michael L. Gillette, "The Rise of the NAACP in Texas," *Southwestern Historical Quarterly* 81 (Apr. 1978): 393–416.

38. Phillips, *White Metropolis,* 182, 173, 178.

# Interracialism, Socialism, and William R. Amberson's Vision for the Rural South

ROBERT HUNT FERGUSON

In 1935, in the midst of modest New Deal successes in lowering joblessness, an article appeared in the weekly news magazine the *Nation* that accused the Department of Agriculture of creating "a new unemployment problem." The author of the article, William Ruthrauff Amberson, had witnessed hordes of unemployed rural southerners flooding into Memphis, Tennessee, where he worked as a medical school professor. Amberson, a registered member of the American Socialist Party, blamed the Agricultural Adjustment Act (AAA)—New Deal legislation aimed at leveling agricultural prices—for the rise in unemployment and homelessness among the rural poor. In many communities across the country, New Deal relief programs aided struggling Americans dealing with the economic collapse. The AAA, however, had the opposite effect on poor sharecroppers. This recovery program called for large-scale farmers to participate in acreage reduction that took portions of farmland out of production and allowed it to lie fallow. As compensation, the federal government paid farmers a stipend for reducing their cultivated acreage. President Franklin Roosevelt and Secretary of Agriculture Henry Wallace hoped that when crop production decreased, prices would stabilize. The unintended consequence, however, was that landowners drove sharecroppers off the land and into urban areas or roadside shantytowns. The crop-reduction regulation established by the AAA irrevocably changed the face of agricultural labor in the South, though not in the ways Roosevelt and Wallace anticipated.[1]

The mass eviction of sharecroppers, which began in 1934, spurred a crisis in the rural South. Long hidden from the public eye, sharecroppers became the flashpoint of competing battles for the future of the rural South, a region on the precipice of transformation, its path not yet clear. Any number of avenues stretched out before rural southerners. William Amberson and a small community of likeminded activists stood at the radical vanguard of southern reform. By implementing a cooperative-socialist vision at two interracial, intentional communities in the rural South, they entered a debate that captured the attention of activists and policy makers. Amberson's vision represented an idealistic, nearly utopian plan for rural southerners but one that was not necessarily naïve or untenable. His proposal to reorganize many rural southerners into collective, egalitarian communities was, for a brief period in the 1930s, a viable possibility. Yet many competitors jockeyed for the power to decide the future direction of the region. The entrenched plantation system of labor, the Vanderbilt Agrarians' espousal of individually owned subsistence farms, and the Resettlement Administration (RA), which placed the government in the role of landlord over rural agriculturalists, all competed for the soul of the rural South. Amberson's vision proved to be among the most radical suggestions, although it found wide support among committed reformers across the country.

Amberson's advocacy for the southern sharecropper has heretofore been relegated in scholarly studies to brief, anecdotal references. A decades-long feud between Amberson and H. L. Mitchell, cofounder of the Southern Tenant Farmers' Union (STFU), led Amberson to refuse to allow Mitchell permission to photocopy his correspondence for the now microfilmed STFU papers. As a result, Amberson was almost completely left out of one of the most used archival resources on sharecroppers, and his role in advocating for a radical collectivist future in the South has been largely overlooked.[2]

William Ruthrauff Amberson was born in Harrisburg, Pennsylvania, in 1894. At the age of twenty-eight, he received a PhD in biology from Princeton University. After studying for a brief stint in Germany, the University of Tennessee Medical School in Memphis hired Amberson as chair of the Physiology Department in 1930. He joined the American Socialist Party in Memphis, an affiliation that brought him in direct contact with the unemployed casualties of the Great Depression. In 1932, in conjunction with the Socialist Party local and the Unemployed Citizens League, a group he helped form, Amberson prepared an exposé of dishonest Memphis merchants, particularly grocers, who habitually engaged in deceitful business practices that included overcharging welfare customers. Amberson's report caused a stir in Memphis and was his first taste of the activism that would shape the next decade of his life.[3]

Through his advocacy on behalf of the working class, Amberson noticed that the majority of the unemployed who streamed into Memphis came from rural areas south and west of the city. Throughout the mid and late 1930s, Amberson helped organize labor strikes and relief efforts in the region. His zeal often put him at odds with his university administration, and Amberson gained a reputation as "the angry Prometheus of the sharecroppers' revolt." He published the scathing critique of the AAA in the *Nation,* espoused his interracial collectivist vision for sharecroppers, and cofounded a collectivist farming community south of Memphis in the Mississippi Delta. During this last experiment at community building, Amberson's dream briefly flourished before falling prey to internal disagreements over how to implement the endeavor.[4]

Amberson's article in the *Nation* laid bare the dire situation facing evicted sharecroppers, a class of American laborers already confronting impoverished existences in the best of circumstances. "In the cotton country croppers have been driven from pillar to post for so long and have sunk so low in the human scale," wrote Amberson, "that they cannot imagine any other type of life." Despite feeble attempts by the Department of Agriculture to enforce a stipulation in Section 7 of the AAA that sharecroppers not be forced off the land (what Amberson called "a loophole as wide as the Mississippi River"), planters immediately began serving eviction notices. In mid-January 1934, a sharecropper and his family on Arkansas's Twist Plantation received a terse letter stating, "You are hereby notified that we demand that you quit, and deliver to us the possession of [the plot] now occupied by you on or before January 21 1934." The cropper and his family had only five days to vacate. By booting sharecroppers off their land, landowners were able to comply with the AAA's acreage-reduction program while hoarding the full federal payment they received for keeping the land fallow. By 1935, Amberson and other activists came to hold AAA officials personally responsible for the mass eviction of croppers. "We believe it is fair to say that over the whole cotton belt," Amberson figured, "about one-third of the present rural unemployment can be directly referred to the reduction program." "The plight of these people," he concluded, had become "a national responsibility." What's more, Amberson had little faith that the New Deal agency would be able to do anything to alleviate the wrongs perpetrated against landless farmers. He expressed his displeasure in the *Nation*: "The department can get adequate investigations neither through its county agents, who, though technically competent, are yet unskilled in social relationships and closely bound to the landlords, nor through the hurried trips of harassed minor officials inspecting scattered cases on the run and unfamiliar with local situations . . . In times of economic distress we see the feeble hold of legal forms."[5]

Amberson concluded that the New Deal for sharecroppers had, in practice, been a bad deal. He suggested a number of ways the government could reverse the fortunes of sharecroppers. One of his suggestions was for collective ownership of cooperative farms. Guaranteed tenure of large-scale cooperative farms would "free a whole people from their present shackles," proposed Amberson, "and make possible the education of a more responsible and effective generation than the South has ever known." It was also the only way, Amberson believed, that former sharecroppers could compete economically with large-scale plantation owners. Instead of Roosevelt's New Deal liberalism, however, Amberson based his vision for agrarian collectivism in a leftist-socialist ethos that highlighted economic parity and class-based, interracial cooperation.

William Amberson's activism with sharecroppers reveals a lens through which to view the possibilities and pitfalls facing the rural South in a time when cleavages in the country's economic systems caused many Americans to look for alternative pathways to economic stability. As Jacquelyn Hall, Robin D. G. Kelley, Robert Korstad, Glenda Gilmore, and others have demonstrated, political radicals, labor unionists, agrarian reformers, and hosts of southerners dissatisfied with the status quo possessed bold visions for the South that were consonant with a truly democratic society. These progressive southerners existed alongside segregationists. Southerners who made up this South differed from the racist demagogues who often influenced southern policy—they were leftist and often intensely radical. Amberson was thus one of a legion of activists who embodied the radical essence of the other South in the 1930s.[6]

Highlighting Amberson's vision also reveals three competing agrarian plans for the rural South—three historical contingencies—none of which played out exactly as their supporters had hoped. Like Amberson, intellectuals, activists, and New Deal liberals weighed in on the question of what do to with the southern sharecropper. The three groups discussed here (socialists, New Deal liberals, and the Southern Agrarians) possessed differences in ideology and praxis but were driven by the same social problem: the miserable existence of the southern sharecropper.

The Resettlement Administration, an umbrella bureaucratic program established by executive order in 1935, planned agricultural-based communities throughout the country and placed the government in the role of landlord over rural agriculturalists. The RA's largest project was offering supervised credit to poor farmers, an undertaking known as "rural rehabilitation." Most of the press, however, focused on a far more radical undertaking, the dozens of planned communities built with American tax dollars. As a result, the RA became controversial for its perceived socialist-inspired approaches to resettlement. On the surface, this approach had much in common with Amberson's socialist dream. The RA communities, however, never went so far as to socialize the communities' economies, nor were they racially integrated. Despite being led by the iconoclastic visionary, Rexford Tugwell, the RA found it difficult to manage the communities, and they gradually fell out of favor with the RA and lawmakers responsible for allocating money to New Deal projects. In its place, government reformers would attempt a different solution for destitute sharecroppers, partially inspired by an influential group of southern intellectuals.[7]

Chiefly made up of students and professors at Vanderbilt University—among them historian Frank Owsley, author Donald Davidson, and poet Allen Tate—the Southern Agrarians were a group of social critics who championed a southern pastoral way of life to combat a perceived moral decline hastened by industrial capitalism. Led by Owsley, the Agrarians espoused the idea that small, individually owned subsistence farms were the balm for a sick society and rampant rural poverty. In a 1935 article in the *American Review,* Owsley suggested that the federal government purchase foreclosed or unused land and sell it, at a significant bargain, to poor farmers. In Owsley's solution, the farmsteads would include eighty acres, a dwelling, two mules, two cows, and a small loan to get farmers through the first year. The Agrarian ideology was rooted in romantic ideas of individualism, an imagined idyllic past, and the long-extinct yeoman farmer championed by Thomas Jefferson. Yet their so-called tenant-purchase program found support among Washington politicians. In July 1937, Congress passed the Bankhead-Jones Farm Tenant Act that incorporated many of Owsley's ideas, including the tenant-purchase program. The failure of the bill's solutions, however, and thus Owsley's dream, was nearly immediate. Allocating enough money to help support the new farm owners proved impossible, and most tenant farmers and sharecroppers could not afford the program anyway. "If ever a mountain labored to produce a mouse," complained one congressman, the Bankhead-Jones bill was it.[8]

Amberson had kept abreast of the three-year development of the Bankhead-Jones Farm Tenant Act and found it wanting. Debate over the tenant-purchase program began in 1934, the same year that he became heavily involved with the plight of the sharecropper. Through the fledgling but active socialist community in Memphis, Amberson embarked upon his own mission to alleviate rural poverty and landlessness. On the streets of Memphis and the roadsides of Arkansas, homeless ex-sharecroppers told him of the recent mass evictions throughout the Arkansas and Mississippi deltas. Amberson decided that the best way to search for a solution was to head into the rural South and interview sharecroppers himself. Building on the work of rural sociologists Charles Spurgeon Johnson at Fisk University and Rupert B. Vance at the University of North Carolina at Chapel Hill, Amberson threw himself headlong into the sharecropper research project, traveling throughout the region interviewing landless farmers and coordinating relief efforts. He found that even sharecroppers who still worked the land earned the equivalent of ten cents per day, the lowest wage in the country. Amberson tried many times to get his research in front of officials in the Agricultural Adjustment Administration. Desperate for attention, Amberson wrote chief of the cotton section Cully Cobb and Secretary Wallace that evicted sharecroppers had "just about reached the limit of endurance" and that their talk of "'open rebellion' was therefore no idle threat." His research finally culminated in a report, unflattering toward the AAA—"The Social and Economic Consequences of the Cotton Acreage Reduction Program"—which landed on the desk of Secretary Wallace. Knowing that the survey might have a limited impact on the lives of sharecroppers, and after receiving a terse reply from Cobb defending the acreage-reduction program, Amberson's ideas for a collective solution quickly took shape. He wrote to Mississippi AAA administrator Oscar Johnston that "some of us are reaching out toward new modes of social organization connected with an entirely new set-up. I personally feel that the plantation system must go." Energized by his work, Amberson wrote Socialist Party standard bearer and perennial presidential candidate Norman Thomas of his deepening commitment to assuage the plight of sharecroppers, concluding, "I feel strongly that the socialist groups can do much . . . to aid these dispossessed people."[9]

Compelled by his affection for the working classes and having recently returned from a trip through the South where he saw the destitution firsthand, Thomas collaborated with Amberson on a 1934 pamphlet, "The Plight of the Share-Cropper." The pamphlet called the sharecropper the "most truly forgotten" American and "a man who raises cotton but cannot possibly afford proper underclothes for his children or sheets and towels for the family." Thomas, like Amberson, deployed a socialist critique of the situation and laid much of the blame on the profit system of capitalism. He knew, however, that a wholesale revolution in the market or in American culture was nearly impossible. Instead, the two men advocated for collectivism among sharecroppers. Sharecroppers could use collective organizing to their advantage in two ways. First, they must organize into a viable labor union to take advantage of collective bargaining. Secondly, sharecroppers should join cooperatives "which would get the benefit of expert guidance and a comprehensive plan" and, in turn, pool their production and maximize their buying power. "Social ownership," concluded Thomas, would lead to the "emancipation" of the South's rural laborers.[10]

The widely circulated pamphlet included the fifteen-page report on the "social and economic consequences of the cotton acreage reduction program" that further indicted the Department of Agriculture's local administrators for pocketing government subsidies while denying the laborers "access to the land and to the only labor that they know." Every page of the report contained devastating accusations and statistics, collected from over five hundred interviews with sharecroppers in Missouri, Arkansas, Tennessee, and Mississippi. Amberson wrote: "We have interviewed dozens of families who have been evicted, or in whose hands there are eviction notices. Many other families have been forced to move by pressure and intimidation, without service of papers. Most of these people are still living in the country, some in tents, some in abandoned houses, a few in such miserable shelters as corn-cribs and cotton houses. Many of them have drifted into the cities and towns, where they are dependent upon direct federal relief." The pamphlet concluded that the AAA and plantation owners had colluded to evict sharecroppers. Even as Thomas and Amberson wrote about the travails of sharecroppers, plans were underway to accomplish two of his recommendations: organizing a sharecropper union and establishing cooperative communities.[11]

Amberson was aided in his research by members of the fledgling Tyronza (Arkansas) Socialist Party, led by Clay East and H. L. Mitchell. By the end of 1934, East and Mitchell had organized the first local of the STFU, which would gain thousands of members across the lower South. While East and Mitchell were busy organizing sharecroppers for collective bargaining purposes, Amberson set to work accomplishing Thomas's second suggestion: placing poor farmers into cooperatives.[12]

In January 1936, at the STFU convention in Little Rock, the union approved Amberson's proposal to organize a cooperative farm for displaced sharecroppers. He soon helped convince Thomas's friend, Presbyterian missionary Sherwood Eddy, to fund a project that would relocate hundreds of sharecropping families into communities based on the cooperative method. Eddy, the national secretary of missions for the YMCA, described himself as a Christian socialist and counted Reinhold Niebuhr among his closest friends and most important theological influences. Through his teaching at Union Theological Seminary in New York and his influential book *Moral Man and Immoral Society,* Niebuhr's beliefs in the efficacy of Christian-led social justice movements and socialist-inspired egalitarianism trickled down to some of the most important thinkers and activists of the 1930s, including Vanderbilt religion professor Alva Taylor, Highlander Folk School cofounder Myles Horton, and organizer Howard Kester. Eddy was among Niebuhr's closest associates and brought Christian socialist doctrine to the cooperative plan. Although Eddy and Amberson differed vastly in the roots of their beliefs, they were united by a common single-mindedness on helping the sharecropper out of poverty and shared the belief that collectivism was the answer.[13]

Within two months Amberson and Eddy had secured funds and a small staff. They turned to East and Mitchell to identify potential residents through the STFU. In March 1936, with the aid of a private trust fund, Eddy bought 2,138 acres of land ninety miles south of Memphis in Bolivar County, Mississippi, and the union began aiding over one hundred black and white evicted sharecroppers to relocate to the newly christened Delta Cooperative Farm. There, families worked the land collectively, received medical care, took educational courses, and learned firsthand of the socialist-cooperative model. At the farm, former sharecroppers began living Amberson's vision for the agrarian South. One month after the community's founding, Amberson wrote a leftist collaborator, admiring his own work. "We have great hopes that we have inaugurated a peaceful revolution in the cotton belt," Amberson explained, "which will ultimately destroy the old plantation system."[14]

One of Delta Cooperative Farm's founding tenets was interracial cooperation. Amberson, like the other founders of the farm, believed that racial antagonisms were second only to class differences. In order to truly solve rural poverty and exploitive labor, he believed, white and black sharecroppers would face their future together. Amberson's beliefs were mainly influenced by his adherence to the American Socialist Party platform. "I do not see the race problem as a separate issue," declared Amberson: "I believe that race prejudice is largely economic, and will largely disappear when we have solved the basic economic problems. As a Socialist I believe that their solution must be sought along the line of collectivization in the interest of the whole people.

I am confirmed in my attitude toward the race issue when I see the perfect harmony with which the white and colored croppers work together when once they have seen that their economic interests are identical." Amberson would later admit that his personal interactions with sharecroppers in the fields were quite limited and that he had overestimated the willingness of white and black sharecroppers to work together toward common goals. Yet his early beliefs reflected that of many intellectual activists hoping to help the sharecropper out of abject poverty.[15]

By the spring of 1936, having successfully founded Delta Cooperative Farm, Amberson and scores of southern socialists felt that the tides of labor and (to a lesser degree) race relations in the South were changing. In May 1936 near Chattanooga, Tennessee, delegates from around the region converged for the second meeting of the Southern Policy Committee (SPC), a politically liberal, purely advisory body that hoped to shape the direction of southern politics and labor practices. Some of the most influential southerners of the Depression Era, including sociologists from the University of North Carolina at Chapel Hill as well as the Vanderbilt Agrarians—represented most vocally by Allen Tate—were present at the meeting. William Amberson and officials from the STFU were also present. Discussion at the meeting centered on the debate over small, self-sufficient homesteads versus large cooperative farms as the most viable livelihood for ex-sharecroppers. As had been their position since 1935, the Vanderbilt Agrarians favored small, individually owned homesteads, while the socialist union favored plantation-sized cooperatives. The debate was often heated. The intellectual confrontation between Tate and Amberson that occurred at the meeting led H. L. Mitchell to later write that it was the end of "Southern Agrarianism, which had sought to turn back the pre-Civil War days of moonlight and magnolias." In a clash of ideology, Amberson thoroughly discredited Tate's romantic notions of the agrarian lifestyle as "pretty-poetry foolishness" and "nothing but a plan to reduce the people to peasantry." The Memphis socialist argued that the individual homesteads advocated by the Agrarians and proposed by the Bankhead-Jones Act were unsustainable in the present economy and a naïve throwback to the "Golden Age of the Republic." "Forty acres and a mule," said Amberson, would only produce more tenants in time. Without access to all the modern farming amenities that big planters possessed, small homesteaders would not be able to compete, and the large plantations would eventually take over. "The big planter across the road with his tractor and four row equipment and his superior credit facilities," declared Amberson, "cultivates his cotton at $5 an acre, while the mule, dragging a half-row plow, runs the bill up to over $14." "The frontier is gone," he thundered, "it is gone not only horizontally but vertically." The vertical frontier Amberson declared dead was the mismanaged and deteriorated topsoil that plagued much of the Deep South during the Depression. As sharecropper and union activist John Handcox, an acquaintance of Amberson's from eastern Arkansas wryly put it, "where I was born at, the soil was so poor you couldn't even raise a fuss."[16]

There was, Amberson suggested to delegates of the SPC, a "'middle way' for the agricultural South, steering between plantation exploitation on the one hand and the inefficiency of the small homestead on the other." Amberson suggested that the delegates endorse cooperative endeavors that sought to turn sharecroppers into collectivized landholders. He pointed to early successes by Delta Cooperative Farm in Mississippi as evidence for the feasibility of organizing more farms like it. All Tate could muster, according to journalist Jonathan Daniels, were feeble attempts to paint Amberson as a communist. By the end of the impromptu debate, Amberson had won the crowd over, and Daniels reported that "even Tate's friends grinned" in support of the fiery socialist. Despite Amberson's persuasive arguments, however, the delegates could not come to a consensus on a clear path for the future of the rural South. The SPC chairman, H. Clarence Nixon, sided with Amberson and attempted to push the committee toward more leftist proposals. Yet much of the rank and file membership resisted. The clash of visions led to what amounted to a stalemate. What the committee ultimately recommended was a hodgepodge of all the major suggestions made at the meeting, with the majority of delegates approving the Agrarian-supported individual purchase program while also proposing government-based financial support for ex-sharecroppers and encouraging the formation of cooperatives. That they had gained some ground at the Chattanooga meeting further confirmed to Amberson and his leftist circle that they were riding a rising tide of socialist-inspired collectivism that would remake southern society.[17]

Additional confirmation came just down the road from Delta Cooperative Farm. The New Deal's Resettlement Administration had established a community they called Dixie Plantation not twenty miles from Delta. In 1936, New Deal photographer Dorothea Lange visited the Dixie Plantation community to find it populated with unhappy residents. Former sharecroppers considered their lives there no different than slavery. One resident whispered to Lange that he had been threatened with whipping and said of the government-appointed farm managers, "they think they own us." At Delta Cooperative Farm, however, Lange snapped photographs of residents engaged in interracial cooperation, a founding tenet of the community. Lange's lens captured white and black farmers posing on a new Farmall tractor and the children of sharecropping families sharing watermelon at a Fourth of July picnic. To Amberson, the photographs confirmed that interracial cooperation and a socialized economy could exist and even flourish.[18]

Amberson and his fellow socialists liked to compare Delta Cooperative with the Resettlement Administration's communities and felt certain that farmers at Delta were getting a squarer deal than government-supported residents, who rented the land at a higher rate and complained that they could not get the aid they needed because of government red tape. Amberson took pride in the fact that two families had relocated from the nearby Dixie Plantation to Delta. Sherwood Eddy also bragged that "the Government at Washington" offered to build the houses at $1,000 apiece at Dixie, but because of collective labor, the houses at Delta cost only $33 dollars to build. Amberson concluded that Delta would "ultimately recommend this type of organization to the whole south."[19]

Amberson's belief that interracial cooperation and socialism were revolutionizing the South did not last long. Disillusionment, ideological disagreements, and the quixotic realities of their endeavors soon set in. His fellow socialists in the South, Amberson complained, were "faint-hearts" and not fully committed to the socialist cause. Additionally, pressure from the University of Tennessee Medical School administration also forced Amberson to gradually scale back much of his political activism.[20]

Amberson also soured on the STFU. Disillusioned by the union's protest tactics and wanting more tangible successes for sharecroppers, he felt that striking and marching were empty gestures without serious plans for how to replace the plantation system of agricultural labor. His previous "position was more theoretical than practical." Yet "the experience of the field" made him "not less radical I hope, but less doctrinaire." The union, in his view, gained no political ground and had "no chance whatever to succeed for some years yet." When ex-sharecroppers found economic stability and competed in the agricultural market, Amberson believed, only then could they truly have their voices heard. Instead of the direct political action of the union, he focused all of his energies on the cooperative model at Delta, where he had become a member of the board of trustees. Amberson knew, however, that this would be seen as acquiescence by many leftists. "I have reached the point where I am willing to accept half a loaf," conceded Amberson, "rather than go without bread at all." In this way, Amberson was different than many intellectual socialists of the 1930s. Doctrinaire ideologies often hampered the national party and blocked practical strategies for overhauling capitalism. In 1937, Amberson still had high aspirations for socialism in practice and realized that the endeavor at Delta Cooperative Farm represented a fighting chance for rural socialists to enact their own vision for America.[21]

Gradually, though, Amberson became *persona non grata* with the cooperative's trustees and management. The fallout began when the trustees did not give ownership of the cooperative to sharecroppers in a timely manner. Amberson had written in the *Christian Register* that "our land is held in trust by the trustees. Our members are building an equity in the property through their own labors," he continued, "and they will ultimately own the farm, as a co-operative group, together with all improvements which they make upon it." Sherwood Eddy and the other trustees kept putting off transitioning ownership to the sharecroppers, saying that original overhead costs had not been settled and arguing that the croppers were not yet ready to operate their own cooperative without supervision. If Delta failed, Amberson charged, it was not "because of the antagonism of the planter aristocracy but because of the inexperience and the dishonesty of such men as . . . Eddy." Before his eyes, the collectivist-socialist vision he had dreamed about for years was falling apart.[22]

Interracial cooperation also faltered at Delta Cooperative Farm. Amberson reported to Fisk University sociologist Charles Spurgeon Johnson that only eight months after its founding, the community was "hitting angles of the race problem which have been a revelation to us." He gave no specific account of the "recent indications," although a survey of several white members at Delta revealed that they harbored racist views. The members believed that "Negroes were like brutes" who were unhygienic and sexually promiscuous. One white resident assured the interviewer, "We don't hate the Negro; People in the North think we hate the Negro. We don't. The negro is just different, that's why we don't mix. They don't dance or sing like we do." One volunteer remembered that interracial cooperation was superficial and "didn't go far at all." The main goal, she said, was that the farmers achieve economic equality only. Even the white farm manager, a Christian Socialist who had studied with Reinhold Niebuhr and lived on collectivist farms in Japan, could not overcome his own paternalistic, racist beliefs. "The superstition, ignorance and needs of the colored people are appalling," the manager wrote to a friend in 1936. "We have a woman on the place who tells fortunes with the aid of 'the Holy Ghost, the Virgin Mary, and hoca pocas.'"[23]

In December 1936, African American residents called what Amberson considered an "indignation meeting" to address racial discrimination. Housing was a limited commodity on the farm, and when two African American families vacated Delta, black cooperators felt that the families had been forced out and were concerned that their houses would go to white families. Despite his acute sensitivity to the downtrodden, the incident prompted Amberson to comment that "the race difficulties are much more in the minds of the colored group then in the white. The racial problem is evidently tremendously more difficult than any of us had dreamed," he continued, "yet thereby it becomes an even greater challenge." But Amberson's skepticism of African American residents' complaints belied his hopes for pragmatic interracial cooperation. As his vision was challenged by internal cleavages at Delta Farm, Amberson's commitment to the endeavor wavered.[24]

Finally, at a 1939 meeting of the Delta Cooperative Farm Board of Trustees, Amberson read aloud his six-page resignation letter, stating that he felt the operations in the fields were "a dictated rather than democratic program": "To claim that the procedure actually used was democracy is to trifle with words." It is better to call it a plantation, Amberson scoffed, "than to go through this elaborate hocus-pocus." "Never before have I seen with such blinding clarity," he added, "the essential and irreconcilable conflict over the scientific and ecclesiastical approach to social problems." Christian missionary ideologies, thought Amberson, blinded the trustees to their first purpose of securing land for the rural poor. Condemning the board as a whole, Amberson concluded that while "criticizing absentee landlordism, we have ourselves created its most vicious form." Finally, he asked to be immediately removed from the board of trustees. The board accepted his resignation without discussion. Amberson wrote a cooperative resident after his resignation, summing up his feelings in blunt terms. "I regret more than I can say that this venture, conceived on so high a plane, should have fallen into the hands of a bunch of dishonest ecclesiastics," he lamented. "I loathe them all." Writing of Eddy, he declared that "this colossal fraud brazens his way onward in spite of his own dishonesty." "It is enough," Amberson concluded, "to make the angels weep."[25]

Around the time that Amberson relinquished his position on the board at Delta Cooperative Farm, he relocated to Baltimore, where he accepted a position at the University of Maryland Medical School, and then to Woods Hole, Massachusetts, where he took a full-time research position at the Marine Biological Laboratory. Although Amberson continued to support leftist agendas, he mostly remained on the periphery of political activism.

Like the Vanderbilt Agrarian's vision of small-holding farmers and the Resettlement Administration's government-sponsored communities, the collectivist-socialist dream of cooperative farms died in the wake of the post–World War II boom. Delta Cooperative Farm closed in the early 1940s mainly because the trustees could not keep the operation afloat. Many residents moved to a second cooperative community in Holmes County, Mississippi, where they gradually adopted the far-reaching goals of the civil rights movement. Amberson had been wrong, as had the Agrarians. The future of labor and land in the rural South lay not in socialist collectivism or yeoman independence, but in the emerging Sunbelt, a geopolitical region defined by anti-union regulations and dotted by vertically integrated agribusiness megafarms.

Thirty years after Delta Cooperative Farm closed, former residents took stock of their experience and put the endeavor in perspective. One resident contacted Amberson, a correspondence that allowed Amberson to rekindle some of his accusations against Eddy—namely, that he had engaged in "dubious or completely dishonest handling of money." Amberson also wrote to former STFU organizer H. L. Mitchell to once again complain about the farm. Mitchell, who had had plenty of experience managing difficult personalities while with the union, reminded the former cooperative resident that old wounds should be left alone. "Amberson is old," Mitchell lamented, "and probably a damn sight crankier than he ever was." After several years of communication and nearing the end of his life, Amberson politely ended his correspondence with former cooperative residents. "I cannot embark upon a lengthy correspondence," he wrote in 1973. "I need rest and peace from the problems of the old South."[26]

## NOTES

1. William R. Amberson, "The New Deal for Share-Croppers," *Nation*, Feb. 13, 1935, 186.

2. For a full explanation of the feud that led to Amberson's all but total exclusion from the STFU papers, see correspondence between Mitchell, Amberson, and UNC Chapel Hill archivist Isaac Copeland, William Ruthrauff Amberson Papers, #3862, Southern Historical Collection, Louis Round Wilson Special Collections Library, University of North Carolina at Chapel Hill, (hereafter SHC).

3. "Biographical Sketch," William R. Amberson Papers, Mississippi Valley Collection, McWherter Library, University of Memphis (hereafter, MVC); Jonathan Daniels, *A Southerner Discovers the South* (New York: Macmillan, 1938), 84; "Report on an Investigation of Short-Weighting and Similar Dishonest Practices by Merchants in the City of Memphis," Amberson Papers, SHC.

4. H. L. Mitchell, *Mean Things Happening in this Land: The Life and Times of H. L. Mitchell Cofounder of the Southern Tenant Farmers Union* (Norman: University Press of Oklahoma, 2008), 45–46.

5. Patricia Sullivan, *Days of Hope: Race and Democracy in the New Deal Era* (Chapel Hill: University of North Carolina, 1996), 57; William Amberson to Norman Thomas, Feb. 22, 1934; F. Twist to W. H. Kible, Jan. 16, 1934, Amberson Papers, SHC; Amberson, "The New Deal for Share-Croppers," 185–87.

6. For relevant works on southern progressive reformers and activists, see Glenda Elizabeth Gilmore, *Defying Dixie: The Radical Roots of Civil Rights, 1919–1950* (New York: W. W. Norton, 2008); John Egerton, *Speak Now Against the Day: The Generation Before the Civil Rights Movement in the South* (Chapel Hill: University of North Carolina Press, 1994); David L. Chappell, *Inside Agitators: White Southerners in the Civil Rights Movement* (Baltimore: Johns Hopkins University Press, 1994); Jacquelyn Dowd Hall, *Revolt Against Chivalry: Jessie Daniel Ames and the Women's Campaign Against Lynching* (New York: Columbia University Press, 1993); Robert F. Martin, *Howard Kester and the Struggle for Social Justice in the South, 1904–1977* (Charlottesville: University Press of Virginia, 1991); Robin D. G. Kelley, *Hammer and Hoe: Alabama Communists During the Great Depression* (Chapel Hill: University of North Carolina Press, 1990); Robert Rogers Korstad, *Civil Rights Unionism: Tobacco Workers and the Struggle for Democracy in the Mid-Twentieth Century South* (Chapel Hill: University of North Carolina Press, 2003).

7. Charles Kenneth Roberts, *The Farm Security Administration and Rural Rehabilitation in the South* (Knoxville: University of Tennessee Press, 2015), 56–57; Jess Gilbert, *Planning Democracy: Agrarian Intellectuals and the Intended New Deal* (New Haven: Yale University Press, 2015), 88–89.

8. Paul K. Conkin, *The Southern Agrarians* (Nashville: Vanderbilt University Press, 2001), 113–114; congressmen quoted in Roberts, *The Farm Security Administration,* 68.

9. Michael K. Honey, *Sharecropper's Troubadour: John L. Handcox, the Southern Tenant Farmers' Union, and the African American Song Tradition* (New York: Palgrave Macmillan, 2013), 50–51; Amberson to Paul S. Appleby, Mar. 13, 1934; C. A. Cobb to Amberson, Sept. 18, 1934; Amberson to Oscar Johnston, May 6, 1934; Amberson to Norman Thomas, Feb. 22, 1934, Amberson Papers, SHC.

10. Norman Thomas, "The Plight of the Share-cropper" (New York: The League for Industrial Democracy, 1934), 3, 14–18.

11. Thomas, "The Plight of the Share-cropper," 20.

12. For more on the founding of the STFU, see Donald Grubbs, *Cry from the Cotton: The Southern Tenant Farmers' Union and the New Deal* (Chapel Hill: University of North Carolina Press, 1971); Jason Manthorne, "The View from the Cotton: Reconsidering the Southern Tenant Farmers' Union," *Agricultural History* 84 (Winter 2010): 20–45.

13. Alison Collis Greene, *No Depression in Heaven: The Great Depression, the New Deal, and the Transformation of Religion in the Delta* (New York: Oxford University Press, 2015), 58–59.

14. Amberson to Alice Barrows, Apr. 17, 1936, William R. Amberson Papers, MVC.

15. Amberson to Gertrude Orendorff, undated (c. 1934), Amberson Papers, SHC.

16. Mitchell, *Mean Things Happening in This Land,* 127; Daniels, *A Southerner Discovers the South,* 87; Steve Brown, "Alternative Land Reform Proposals in the 1930s: The Nashville Agrarians and the Southern Tenant Farmers' Union," *Agricultural History* 55 (Oct. 1981): 361–63; William R. Amberson, "Forty Acres and Mule," *Nation,* Mar. 6, 1937, 264–66. Interview with John Handcox, Jan. 15, 1990, William R. Ferris Collection, #20367, Southern Folklife Collection, University of North Carolina at Chapel Hill.

17. Daniels, *A Southerner Discovers the South,* 87; Amberson, "Forty Acres and Mule," 264–66. Historian Paul Conkin, however, has taken a different view of the exchange between Amberson and Tate. "Tate proved an eloquent spokesman," wrote Conkin in the definitive study of the Agrarians, "and helped prevent a collectivist victory." See Conkin, *The Southern Agrarians,* 116–18.

18. Quoted in Jan Goggins, *California on the Breadlines: Dorothea Lange, Paul Taylor, and the Making of a New Deal Narrative* (Berkeley: University of California Press, 2010), 236–37.

19. "*The Delta Cooperative Farm:* First Report of Progress" (Hillhouse, Mississippi, Apr. 19, 1936), folder 3, Delta and Providence Cooperative Farms Papers, SHC; William Amberson, "To Rescue the South," *Christian Register,* Mar. 18, 1937, 23; "Delta Cooperative Farm Review," Delta Cooperative Farms Papers, MVC; William Amberson to Vincent C. Widney, May 6, 1936, folder 5, Delta and Providence Cooperative Farms Papers, #3474, SHC.

20. William R. Amberson to Sam Schneider, Sept. 7, 1937, box VII, A. Eugene Cox Collection, Special Collections Department, Mitchell Memorial Library, Mississippi State University (hereafter AEC); Amberson to Clarence Senior, Nov. 16, 1935, folder 13a, Amberson Papers, SHC.

21. Amberson to Sam Franklin, Feb. 11, 1937, House box 1, AEC; William R. Amberson to Francis A. Henson, May 6, 1936, box VII, AEC.

22. William Amberson to Gene Cox, Jan. 17, 1973, House box 1, AEC

23. Sam H. Franklin Jr., "Early Years of the Delta Cooperative Farm and the Providence Cooperative Farm," (unpublished), 15; Constance Rumbough to Paul Vanderwood, Apr. 11, 1964, folder 1, Delta Cooperative Farm Papers, #3892-z, SHC; Amberson to Charles S. Johnson, Dec. 1936, folder 2-g STFU, box VII, AEC; Sam Franklin to Claibourne Johnson, Aug. 31, 1936, folder 12, Delta and Providence Cooperative Farms Papers, #3474, SHC.

24. William Amberson to Sam Franklin, Dec. 21, 1936, House box 1, AEC; "Report on Delta Cooperative Farm," Delta Cooperative Farms Papers, MVC.

25. William Amberson, "Editorial," *Christian Century,* June 14, 1939; Amberson to A. James McDonald, Dec. 24, 1940, folder 22, Amberson Papers, SHC; H. L. Mitchell to J. R. Butler, May 14, 1940, STFU Papers; "A Statement to the Board of Trustees Cooperative Farms, Inc.," Amberson Papers, MVC; Amberson to J. H. Moody, Sept. 29, 1940, folder 22, Amberson Papers, SHC.

26. Amberson to H. L. Mitchell, Dec. 24, 1970; H. L. Mitchell to Gene Cox, undated; Mitchell to Cox, Dec. 31, 1970; Amberson to Cox, Jan. 26, 1973, House box 1, AEC.

# CONTRIBUTORS

**TED ATKINSON** is associate professor of English at Mississippi State University and editor of the *Mississippi Quarterly*. He is the author of *Faulkner and the Great Depression: Aesthetics, Ideology, and Cultural Politics* (2006) and of several essays that focus on the literature and culture of the 1930s.

**KAREN L. COX** is professor of history at the University of North Carolina at Charlotte. She is the author of *Dreaming of Dixie: How the South Was Created in American Popular Culture* and *Goat Castle: A True Story of Murder, Race, and the Gothic South.*

**LISA DORRILL** is visiting professor of art history at Dickinson College, where she teaches a range of courses, from Modern and Contemporary Architecture to Dutch Seventeenth-Century Art. With degrees from the University of Virginia, Northwestern University, and the University of Kansas, she has spoken widely on her area of research, American art of the 1930s, and particularly art and the environment.

**SARAH E. GARDNER** is Distinguished University Professor of history at Mercer University. She is the author of *Blood and Irony: Southern White Women's Narratives of the Civil War, 1861–1937* and *Reviewing the South: The Literary Marketplace and the Southern Renaissance, 1920–1941.*

**ROBERT HUNT FERGUSON** is an assistant professor of history at Western Carolina University. He is the author of *Remaking the Rural South: Interracialism, Christian Socialism, and Cooperative Farming in Jim Crow Mississippi* (2018).

**BRYAN A. GIEMZA** is Director of the Southern Historical Collection and an adjunct associate professor of English at the University of North Carolina at Chapel Hill. He is author or an editor of six books, including *Irish Catholic Writers and the Invention of the American South* (2013) and *Images of*

*Depression-Era Louisiana: The FSA Photographs of Ben Shahn, Russell Lee, and Marion Post Wolcott* (2017). He is principal investigator of grants from the Andrew W. Mellon Foundation and the National Endowment for the Humanities, among others, for a variety of public humanities projects concerning the history and culture of the US South. He is currently working on a novel set in eastern North Carolina during the 1970s.

**ROBERT W. HAYNES** is professor of English at Texas A&M International University, where he teaches Early British Literature and Shakespeare. His scholarly efforts in recent years have focused on Renaissance humanism and on the American playwright and screenwriter Horton Foote. As R. W. Haynes, he has published poetry in many American and international journals. He edited the collection *Critical Insights: Horton Foote* (2016).

**ELLA HOWARD** is associate professor of history at Wentworth Institute of Technology in Boston, Massachusetts, where she teaches digital history, design history, and the history of technology. Her research focuses on urban history, poverty, and segregation. She is the author of *Homeless: Poverty and Place* (2013).

**STEVEN KNEPPER** is assistant professor in the Department of English, Rhetoric, and Humanistic Studies at Virginia Military Institute. His work has appeared in *Telos,* the *Robert Frost Review, Studies in American Culture,* and the *Cormac McCarthy Journal,* among other places.

**SCOTT L. MATTHEWS** is an assistant professor of history at Florida State College at Jacksonville. He is completing his first book, "The Most Documented Region in America: A History of Documentary Work in the South."

**NICHOLAS ROLAND** is a PhD candidate in US history at the University of Texas at Austin. His dissertation examines political violence in the Texas Hill Country region during the Civil War and Reconstruction era, and he has published in the *West Texas Historical Review,* the *Handbook of Texas Online,* and on the University of Texas public history website *Not Even Past.*

**EMILY SENEFELD** is a PhD candidate in American history at the University of Virginia. Her dissertation examines the cultural programs of the Highlander Folk School as a lens through which to explore networks of radicalism in the mid-twentieth-century South.

**REBECCA SHARPLESS** is professor of history at Texas Christian University. The work of Margaret Hagood and Ruth Allen profoundly influenced her study *Fertile Ground, Narrow Choices: Women on Texas Cotton Farms, 1900–1940.*

**ANTHONY J. STANONIS** is a lecturer of American history at Queen's University Belfast. He is the author of *Creating the Big Easy: New Orleans and the Emergence of Modern Tourism, 1918–1945* (2006) and *Faith in Bikinis: Politics and Leisure in the Coastal South since the Civil War* (2014).

**DOUGLAS E. THOMPSON** is associate professor of history and southern studies at Mercer University. He is the author of *Richmond's Priests and Prophets: Race, Religion and Social Change in the Civil Rights Era* (2017). Doug also serves as editor of the *Journal of Southern Religion.*

**MELISSA WALKER** was George Dean Johnson, Jr., Professor of History at Converse College. She was introduced to Ruth Allen recently by Rebecca Sharpless, but her first encounter with Margaret Hagood occurred in graduate school. Hagood's work helped shaped her book *All We Knew Was to Farm: Rural Women in the Upcountry South, 1919–1945.* She retired from Converse College in 2017.

# INDEX


AAA. *See* Agricultural Adjustment Act
acreage-reduction program, 228, 230, 233–34
Aden, Alonzo, 216
advertising, 2, 26, 39, 211
aesthetics, 47, 61, 72, 88, 91, 100, 125–26, 131–33
African Americans: car ownership, 112–14; discrimination against, 8, 25, 191–206, 210, 240; elites, 195–96; folk culture, 147–48; Hall of Negro Life (Texas Centennial), 211–24; labor exploitation, 13–26; land ownership, 25; newspapers published by, 203, 215–17; participation at Texas Centennial, 211, 214–15, 220–22; respectability, 220, 224; sharecroppers, 16–25, 27n23, 28n29, 161, 165, 167–68; southern world's fairs exhibits on, 212, 214, 218–19, 224; stereotypes about, 16–17, 22–23, 27n12; women, 7, 176–78, 180–81, 188n21. *See also* blackface; interracial cooperation; race; racism; segregation, racial; slavery
"After Winter" (Brown), 24–25
Agee, James, 28n23, 81
Agrarians, 6, 15, 28n33, 88, 97, 100; modernization and, 119, 123–25; support for small-holding farmers, 229, 231, 236, 241, 243n17
agrarian traditions, romanticized, 9, 13–26, 143–44, 151n7, 232, 236
agribusiness, 26, 241
Agricultural Adjustment Act (AAA), 8, 228, 230, 233–34
Alabama, 160; car-related deaths, 117–18; Macon County, 19, 22, 28n26; Montgomery, 192; Muscle Shoals, 76–77, 122; women tenant farmers, 182–86
*Allegory of Chattanooga* (Leech), 76
Allen, Ruth Alice, 7, 172–80, 183, 185–86, 187n19
Allred, James V., 212
Amateur Athletic Union (AAU), 219–20
Amberson, William R., 8, 228–41, 243n17
American Actors Company, 93, 95
American Socialist Party, 228–29, 233, 235
Anderson, Ella, 31
Anderson, Sherwood, 51, 53, 59, 61, 162
Andrews, Garnett, 156–57
Anglo-Saxon culture, 143
antebellum South, 13–26, 89. *See also* slavery
antipastoral critique, 14–16, 18, 25
Antony, Marc, 61
Appalachian folk culture, 7, 141–50
Arent, Arthur, 6, 125–33
aristocracy, southern, 15, 91, 99–101, 185, 239. *See also* elites
Arkansas, 233–34
Arrington, Marvin, 191
artists, 5. *See also* murals; New York theater scene
Associated Negro Press, 217
Atkinson, Brooks, 93, 137n11
Atkinson, Ted, 6
Atlanta, 191–92, 202–5, 219
*Atlanta* (WPA), 204
Atlanta Automobile Association, 116
*Atlanta Constitution*, 154, 163–64
*Atlanta Independent*, 203
*Atlanta Journal-Constitution*, 191
Atlanta Life Insurance Company, 205

Atlanta Zone Plan, 203
Augusta, 191, 194–98
Augustin, Bennett, 52
automobiles, 6, 107–20; affordability, 114–16; deaths from accidents, 117–18; freedom and, 6, 108, 114, 117, 120; modernization and, 110–11; negative attitudes toward, 107–11; race and, 112–13; as status symbols, 112–13, 120

*The Bachelor in New Orleans* (guidebook), 37
backwardness, 82–83, 108, 127, 129–30, 161
Balli, Jose, 39
Baltimore, 63, 168, 191, 205–6, 240
banana boats, 48, 51, 57
Bankhead-Jones Act, 25, 158–59, 232, 236
Barnett, Claude A., 217
Baylor University, 94
Beach Institute, 198
Becker, Jane, 151n7
*Bedford Forrest and His Critter Company* (Lytle), 91
Benítez-Rojo, Antonio, 55
Berger, Michael L., 121n3
Berlin, Irving, 2
Bernasek, Alexandra, 177
Bibb Manufacturing Company, 197
Billings, Henry, 77
Bird, Sam, 31
birth control. *See* family planning
blackface, 14, 22
Blackstone, Gracie, 153n22
Blake, Jeanie, 40
Bloch, Lucienne, 82–83
*Blood and Irony* (Gardner), 3
Blotner, Joseph, 64n3
Blount, J. L., 212
Bolivar County, Mississippi, 8, 235
book fair. *See* National Book Fair
Borden Dairy Company, 79–80
Boswell, Scott, 39
Bourke-White, Margaret, 2, 133, 161
Bowers, Claude, 17
Bradford, Roark, 31
British Broadcasting Corporation (BBC), 7, 141
Bronx post office mural, 76
Brookings Institution, 174
*Brooklyn Daily Eagle*, 93
Brooks, Cleanth, 5, 47–48, 58, 98
Brown, Douglas Edwin, 61
Brown, Jim, 167
Brown, Paul, 154, 163, 165
Brown, Sterling, 4, 15–18, 21–26, 27n12
Buck, Pearl S., 52
Burlingame, Roger, 54
Bynum, Charles H., II, 221

"Cabin in the Cotton" (Crosby), 14
Caldwell, Erskine, 2, 4, 6, 16–17, 59, 161–62; *Tobacco Road*, 54, 110–12, 117
Calhern, Louis, 60
*California Delta*, 48
Callaway, "Put" and Anna, 167
Carawan, Guy, 147, 149, 153n22
Carmer, Carl, 52–54
Carroll, John, 39
*Cartago* (ship), 50, 57
cash-crops, 15, 20, 23–25, 184–85
Charleston, 193, 198
Chase, Stuart, 70, 72, 77, 83
Chatham Savings and Loan Company, 201
Chattanooga, Tennessee, 76
Cheever, John, 59
Chicago, 201
*Chicago Defender*, 215–16
children of sharecroppers, 23–24, 178–86
Children's Bureau, U. S., 187n17
Christian socialism, 119, 235, 239
cities. *See* urban areas; *individual cities*
Citizens Trust Company, 205
Citron, Minna, 69, 78–79
Civilian Conservation Corp (CCC), 70
civil rights movement, 148–50, 150n3
Civil Rights period, 25

Civil War, 94, 133, 195
Clarksdale, Mississippi, 42
Cline, Walter D., 214
Clinton, Bill, 97
Cobb, Cully, 233
Cole, William E., 185
*The Collapse of Cotton Tenancy* (Johnson), 25, 28n35
*Collier's*, 7, 154–70
Columbia, Tennessee, 77
Columbians (white supremacist group), 204
Columbia River (Washington), 127
Columbia University, 212
Columbus, Georgia, 191, 196–97
Columbus, Mississippi, 42
commerce, 132
communism, 142, 146–47, 149, 237
Como, Perry, 40
Confederacy, 88–91, 94, 99; memorialization of, 223
Congress, U. S., 154, 163, 213
*Congressional Record*, 7, 154–55, 165
Congress of Industrial Organizations (CIO), 149
Conkin, Paul, 243n17
consumerism, 128, 130, 135
consumption: of art, 124; automobile, 118 (*see also* automobiles); controlled, 130, 135, 138n26
contraception. *See* family planning
Cooke, Alistair, 143
cotton economy: labor exploitation, 13–26, 167; modernization, 119; poverty in, 154–63, 167; trade and, 132–34; white farmers, 100; women and, 175–78. *See also* plantation culture
cotton gin, 16
courting, 108–9
Cox, Karen, 3
Crosby, Bing, 14
Crossville, Tennessee, 73
cultural erasure, 123–24, 128
Dahl, George L., 214
dairy production, 79–80
Dallas, 210–24
*Dallas Express*, 212–14, 220–21
*Dallas Morning News*, 215
dams, 70–79, 81, 83, 129, 135
Daniel, Pete, 25
Daniels, Jonathan, 118–20, 237
Danish folk schools, 142, 144
dating, 109–10
Davidson, Donald, 6, 71, 100, 123–24, 128, 136n3, 232
Davis, Jefferson, 88
Daykarhanova, Tamara, 95
Decatur Federal Savings and Loan, 191
Deep South, nostalgia for, 1–2, 47–48. *See also* South
Delano, Jack, 158, 168–70
Delta Cooperative Farm, 8, 235–41
DeMille, Agnes, 93
demographics, 175, 178–82
Denning, Michael, 131, 150n2–150n3
Department of Agriculture, 228, 230, 234
Depression. *See* Great Depression
Dettelbach, Cynthia, 111
"Devil in de Cotton" (White), 7, 154–70
Dickson, Amanda, 196
*Diddie, Dumps, and Tot* (Pyrnelle), 13
discrimination: class and sex, 185; racial, 8, 25, 191–206, 210, 240. *See also* Jim Crow laws
Disraeli, Robert, 52
"Dixie," 14
*Dixie Bohemia* (Reed), 48, 61
Dixie Plantation, 237–38
Dixon, W. W., 108
documentary expression, 151n8, 182; controversies over, 7, 154–70; films, 125 (see also *The River*)
Dorrill, Lisa, 5
Douglas, Aaron, 216
Doyle, Thomas, 113–14, 119
*Dreaming of Dixie* (Cox), 4

Driscoll, Charles B., 60
driving tours, 117–20
Dubois, W.E.B., 216–17
Duck, Leigh Anne, 4
Dunning, William, 17

East, Clay, 234
Easton, John and Sarah, 112–13, 115
economic theory, 173–74
economy, 8–9; automobiles and, 107, 114; global, 57; industrial, 56–57 (*see also* industrialization); plantation, 19 (*see also* plantation culture). *See also* cotton economy
Eddy, Sherwood, 234–35, 238–39, 241
Eisen, Kurt, 126–27
Eisenstein, Sergei, 138n26
electrical substations, 77–78
electricity, 69–80, 82, 85n19, 126–27, 130, 135
*Electrification* (Martin), 76
Eliot, T. S., 89
elites: black, 195–96; white, 158–59, 162, 210. *See also* aristocracy, southern
energy management, 71, 74
environmental conditions, 69–74, 134–35, 156–58; exhausted land, 15, 19–20; floods, 125, 131; soil erosion, 20, 70, 73, 122, 157, 160
Evans, Walker, 28n23, 133

family planning, 179, 181–82, 184–85
family wage, 177
*Fancy Free* (Robbins), 100
farms and farmers: acreage-reduction program, 228, 230, 233–34; agribusiness, 26, 241; car ownership and, 112–13; cash-crops, 15, 20, 23–25, 184–85; educational programs for, 70; living standards, 178, 184; modernization, 110, 119, 236–37; small subsistence farms, 229, 231–32, 236, 241, 243n17; women tenant-farmers, 7, 172, 176–86. *See also* agrarian traditions, romanticized; cotton economy; plantation culture; sharecroppers; tenant-farmers
Farm Security Administration (FSA), 25, 131, 133; photographers, 74, 76, 81, 158, 168–69; programs, 154–55, 157–58
Farrell, James, 53, 59
Faulkner, William, 4–6, 16–17, 27n19, 30, 43n2, 48, 54, 64n3, 87, 98, 100, 110–11
Federal Art Project (FAP), 82
federal initiatives: benefits of, 69, 83, 131; local responses to, 154–55, 162–70. *See also* Farm Security Administration (FSA); New Deal; Resettlement Administration (RA); Tennessee Valley Authority (TVA); Works Progress Administration (WPA)
Federal Theatre Project (FTP), 75, 125–27
Federal Writers' Project (FWP), 1, 32, 108, 117, 195
Ferguson, Robert, 8
fertilizers, 77–78
Fields, A. N., 216
Fisk University, 4, 15, 19, 212, 217, 233, 239
Flanagan, Hallie, 126
*Flood* (Warren), 136n3
floods, 125, 131
folk culture: African American, 147–48; Appalachian, 7, 141–50
Foote, Horton, 5–6, 88, 93–101; *Convicts,* 99–101; *To Kill a Mockingbird* (screenplay of Lee's work), 98, 101; *Only the Heart* (earlier, *Mamie Borden*), 96, 100; *The Orphans' Home Cycle,* 95, 97; *Out of My House,* 96; *Tender Mercies,* 101; *Texas Town,* 96; *Tomorrow* (adaptation of Young's work), 98; *The Trip to Bountiful,* 101; "Wharton Dance," 96; *The Young Man from Atlanta,* 101
Ford, Ford Madox, 89
Ford, Henry, 115–16
Ford Motor Company, 115
Forrest, Nathan Bedford, 90–91, 100
Fort Loudon Hydroelectric Dam, 76
*Fortune,* 74, 81, 205–6
Foster, Stephen, 2
Freedmen's Bureau, 198

freedom, 36, 42; artistic, 82, 97; automobiles and, 6, 108, 114, 117, 120; of workers, 148
Freeman, Douglas S., 90
French Quarter (New Orleans), 33–37, 39–42

Gaines, Janet Howe, 2
Gardner, Sarah, 3, 47
Garner, John N., 213, 222
Gasman, Marybeth, 22
Gassner, John, 93
gender, 7, 172–86
General Motors, 115
geography, 47, 58
Georgia: automobiles, 115–17; Columbus, 191, 196–97; Greene County, 7, 154–70; Macon, 114–15, 191, 197; poverty of sharecroppers, 7, 154–70; racial segregation, 8, 191–206; Thomson, 107, 116; women tenant farmers, 182–86
Gershwin, George, 2
Gibson County, Tennessee, 22–23, 28n26
Giemza, Bryan, 5
Gilmore, Glenda, 231
Gilpin, Patrick, 22
Gish, Dorothy, 54, 60
Gish, Lillian, 54
Glasgow, Ellen, 88
global economy, 57
Godchaux, Elma, 59
Goldfield, David, 192
*Gone with the Wind* (Mitchell), 2, 14–15, 53, 99
Gonzalez, Xavier, 73, 76, 81
Gooding, Ella, 108–11, 113, 120
Good Roads movement, 107, 116–17
Gordon, Caroline. *See* Tate, Caroline Gordon
Gordon, Linda, 188n21
government intervention. *See* federal initiatives
*The Grapes of Wrath* (Steinbeck), 131
*The Great Big Doorstep* (O'Donnell), 5, 47, 52, 54–55, 60, 63–64
Great Britain, 143
Great Depression, 1, 3, 8, 52, 108
Greater Texas and Pan American Exposition, 222
Great Migration, 25
Green, Paul, 95
Greene, Felix, 141–43, 147, 149, 150n1
Greene County, Georgia, 7, 154–70
*The Green Pastures* (film), 31
*Greensboro Herald-Journal*, 154, 163–64
Greenwood, Grace, 75–76, 81
Greenwood, Marion, 73, 75, 81
Greeson, Jennifer Rae, 2
Group Theatre, 126
Grundtvig, Nikolai, 142
Grundy County, Tennessee, 141–42
*Guide to Augusta* (FWP), 195
Gussow, Mel, 33
Guthrie, Woody, 142
Gutierrez, Elena R., 187n19

Hagood, Margaret Jarman, 7, 27n23, 172–75, 180–86, 188n21
Hall, Charles E., 217
Hall, Jacquelyn, 231
Hall of Negro Life, at Texas Centennial, 211–24
Hammett, Dashiell, 60
Hanchett, Thomas, 194
*The Handbook of Texas*, 211
Handcox, John, 142, 147–49, 152n22, 237
Handman, Max, 173
Harris, Joel Chandler, 2, 22
Harvey, David, 155
Haselton, Johny, 109–11, 113, 120
Hayes, Gabby, 95
Haynes, Robert, 5
Hays, Lee, 142, 147–49
Hearn, Lafcadio, 49
Hemingway, Ernest, 50–51, 87
Highlander Folk School, 7, 141–50, 235; labor movement and, 7, 141, 144–50, 229
Hillhouse, 119
Hillier, Amy, 194

Hindman School, 144, 151n6
Hiss, Alger, 59
historical fiction, 1
historic preservation, 194, 199
Holmes, D. H., 39
Holmes County, Mississippi, 241
home ownership, 191–206
Home Owners' Loan Corporation (HOLC), 191, 193–94, 196–97, 199–203
homosexuality, 30, 36–37, 52
Hopkins, Harry, 75
Horing, Allan, 38
Horton, Myles, 141–42, 145–46, 148, 235
Horton, Zilphia, 141, 144–47, 149–50, 152n22
housework, 178
Howard, Ella, 8
Hughes, Langston, 59
Hughes, Sarah T., 212, 226n8
humor, southwest, 54
Hurston, Zora Neale, 4
Huxley, Julian, 60
hydroelectric dams, 70–79, 81, 83, 129, 135
Hyer, Jack, 39
hymns, 146, 148

Ibsen, Henrik, 97
"I Hear America Singing" (radio program), 143
*I'll Take My Stand* ("Twelve Southerners"), 15, 28n33, 88–89, 99
imperialism, 57–58
*The Indicted South* (Maxwell), 4
industrialization, 6, 9, 56–57, 75, 78, 181, 197–98, 200; critiques of, 15, 89, 134, 232. *See also* labor movement; modernization
inequality, 89, 97, 203. *See also* discrimination; Jim Crow laws; racism
*Injunction Granted* (1936), 126
institutionalism, 173–74
International Ladies Garment Workers Union, 146
International Workers of the World (Wobblies), 141, 146
interracial cooperation: in athletics, 21, 219, 223, 227n25; Christianity and, 146; on collective farms, 8, 228, 231, 235–36; unionism and, 147–48
interracial neighborhoods, 200–201
*In the Land of Cotton* (Scarborough), 13–14
Ipcar, Dahlov, 71–73
*Item-Tribune,* 61

Jackson, Thomas Jonathan "Stonewall," 88
Jefferson, Thomas, 232
Jilinsky, Andrius, 95
Jim Crow laws, 180, 188n21, 193–95, 198–99. *See also* segregation, racial
John C. Campbell School, 144, 151n6
John P. King Manufacturing Company, 196
Johnson, Charles Spurgeon, 4, 15, 19–26, 27n23, 28n26, 233, 239
Johnson, James Weldon, 53
Johnston, Oscar, 119, 233
Josset, Raoul, 216
Julius Rosenwald Foundation, 182
Juneteenth celebrations, 215, 219, 221, 227n25

Kazin, Alfred, 162
Kelley, Robin D. G., 231
Kennedy, John Pendleton, 19
Kentucky, 117–18
Kester, Howard, 146, 235
King, Mary, 60–62
King-Smith School, 100
Kinnear, Douglas, 177
Kinney, Alberta, 61
Knepper, Steven, 4
Korstad, Robert, 231
Kraft, Stewart, 201
Kroll, Lucy, 95
Krutch, Charles, 137n23
Ku Klux Klan, 90, 108, 204

labor exploitation, 13–26, 57, 167
labor movement, 7, 141, 144–50, 229. *See also* Southern Tenant Farmers Union
La Guardia, Fiorello, 53

Lake, Devereaux, 168
Lamar, Henry J., 114
land, exhausted, 15, 19–20
Land, Lucy Rosengardt, 95
land management, 74, 131, 134–35
*Land of Plenty* (Bloch), 82
Lange, Dorothea, 158, 237–38
Laura Spelman Rockefeller Memorial (LSRM), 174
Leadbelly, 147
Lechay, Myron, 61
Lee, Harper, 98
Lee, Robert E., 89–91, 223
Lee, Russell, 158
Leech, Hilton, 76
leftist activists, 228–41
Le Gallienne, Eva, 97
leisure, 13–15, 18, 20
Lenoir City, Tennessee, 76–77
Leverich, Lyle, 36
Lewis, Joe, 219
Lexington, Tennessee, 75
Liberty Loan and Investment Company, 197
Lieber, Maxim, 59
*Life,* 38, 74, 155
Lilienthal, David, 72, 78, 82, 125, 136n7
literary culture, southern, 5, 47–48, 54; New York theater scene and, 87–101; renaissance, 16; "renascence," 124, 136n5
Living Newspaper Unit, 125–26
local-color writing, 54
local governmental power, 154–55, 162
Logan, Trevon, 192
Lomax, Alan, 142–43, 147
Lomax, John, 147
Lonigan, Studs, 59
*Look,* 155
Loomis, Homer, 204
Lorentz, Pare, 6, 74–75, 130–35
Losey, Joseph, 126
Louisiana, 55. *See also* New Orleans
Louisiana Farmers Union, 59
Louisiana State Museum, 40
*Louisiana Story* (documentary), 56
Louisiana Tourist Commission, 39–40
Lumpkin, Grace, 16
lynchings, 193, 210
Lytle, Andrew, 91, 100

MacLeish, Archibald 53
Macon, Georgia, 114–15, 191, 197
Macon County, Alabama, 19, 22, 28n26
*Man Power* (Zorach), 73
*March of Time* (1933), 74
Marcus, Stanley, 210
Mardi Gras, 34
marriage, 109–10, 176, 181
Marshall, Don, 41
Martin, Bill, Jr., 48
Martin, David, 76
*Mary Poppins* (Travers), 53
Massey, Douglas, 191
"Master and Man" (Brown), 17–18, 28n28
Masters, Edgar Lee, 53
materialism, 134–35
Mathews, Jane de Hart, 126
Matthews, Scott, 7
*Maury County Landscape* (Billings), 77–78
Maxwell, Angie, 2, 4
Mazzari, Louis, 165
McCullers, Carson 43n2, 59
*McDuffie Progress,* 116
McPherson, Tara, 4
Memphis, 201, 229, 232
Metcalfe, Ralph, 219
Mexican laborers, 179
Mexican women, 7, 176, 178–79, 187n19
Meyerhold, Vsevolod, 126
Middle Georgia Saving and Investment Company, 197
milking machines, 79–80
Millet, Clarence, 61
Millis, Harry A., 176
Milton, L. D., 205
minstrelsy, 14, 19, 22, 54
Mississippi, 234–35, 241
Mississippi Delta, 230, 233
"Mississippi Mud" (Rhythm Boys), 14

Mississippi River, 56, 125, 131–32, 134–35
Missouri, 234
Mitchell, H. L., 229, 234, 236, 241
Mitchell, Margaret, *Gone with the Wind,* 2, 14–15, 53, 99
mobility, 108–10, 133, 135
modernism, 3, 6, 61, 122–36
modernization, 6, 9, 80–83; agricultural, 110, 119, 236–37; automobiles and, 110–11; of housing, 199. *See also* electricity; industrialization; technology
Monahan, Lawrence, 154–55, 158–66
Monsanto Chemical Company, 77–78
Montgomery, Alabama, 192
Morgan, Arthur, 81–82, 136n7
Morgan, Harcourt, 136n7
mortgages, discrimination in, 8, 191–206
*Mothers of the South* (Hagood), 27n23, 181–85
murals, 5; Hall of Negro Life (Texas Centennial), 216; Tennessee Valley Authority (TVA), 5, 69, 71–80, 84n1, 85n21
"Murder Ballad" (Jelly Roll Morton), 50
Murdock, Arthur, 54
Muscle Shoals, Alabama, 76–77, 122
*Music in the Old Bones* (Gaines), 2
Mutual Federal Savings & Loan Association of Atlanta, 205

NAACP, 223–24
Nashville, 192, 219
Nashville Fugitives, 91, 98
Nathan, George Jean, 53–54
*Nation,* 230
National Book Fair, 47, 52–54, 64
National Fertilizer Development Center, 77–78
National Negro Business League, 212
national progress, 122–36
National Youth Administration, 216
*The Nation's Region* (Duck), 4
"Negro Character as Seen by White Authors" (Brown), 16
"Negro Days" (at Texas fairs), 215, 226n14
"The Negro's New Economic Life" (*Fortune*), 205–6
Neisser, Pat, 40
Newark, 201
New Deal, 25; criticism of, 123–24, 163; legislation, 8; liberals, 231; modernism, 131; murals, 5, 69; propaganda, 74–75, 126; public housing, 194. *See also* Farm Security Administration (FSA); Federal Art Project (FAP); Federal Theatre Project (FTP); Federal Writers' Project (FWP); Resettlement Administration (RA); Tennessee Valley Authority (TVA); Works Progress Administration (WPA)
New Orleans: E. P. O'Donnell and, 50–52, 58, 61–64; French Quarter, 33–37, 39–42; nightlife, 37; Tennessee Williams and, 30–43; tourism industry, 5, 30–43; World's Industrial and Cotton Centennial, 212
New Orleans Public Service Incorporated (NOPSI), 39–40
Newport, Tennessee, 69, 78–79
"The New Provincialism" (Tate), 124
New South city, 202–3
*New York Magazine,* 38
New York theater scene, 6, 87–101
*New York Times,* 74, 79, 93; National Book Fair, 47, 52–54, 64
New York World's Fair of 1939, 79
Nicholson, Eleanor, 37
Niebuhr, Reinhold, 146, 235, 239
Nixon, H. Clarence, 237
"The No 'Count Boy" (Green), 95
"No More Mourning," 146–47, 149
*None Shall Look Back* (Gordon), 91
Norris Dam, 71–73, 76, 78–79, 129
North, Sterling, 56
North Carolina: car ownership, 112; Raleigh, 192; Wilson County, 112; women tenant farmers, 7, 172, 182–86. *See also* University of North Carolina
nostalgia, 1–2, 14, 17, 21–22, 99, 123, 128. *See also* romanticized images of the South

O'Brien, Alice, 49
O'Connor, Flannery, 63
Odets, Clifford, 96–97
O'Donnell, Daniel, 63
O'Donnell, E. P. "Pat," 5, 47–64; *The Great Big Doorstep,* 5, 47, 52, 54–55, 60, 63–64; *Green Margins,* 52–53, 59; "Lines to Jules Petit," 49, 62; "Plowshares Are Swords," 59
O'Donnell, Gertrude, 49–51, 63
O'Donnell, Patrick, 63
Odum, Howard, 17, 27n21, 28n33, 137n19, 157, 174, 182, 192
"Old King Cotton" (Brown), 21
"Old Lem" (Brown), 17
Old South, 1–2, 9, 13–26, 128, 232, 236. *See also* South
*Ol' Man Adam an' His Chillun* (Bradford), 31
Olmstead, Harry, 214
O'Neill, Eugene, 17
*On the Shores of the Lake* (Ipcar), 72
*Opportunity* (journal), 15, 19
Owsley, Frank, 232

Page, Thomas Nelson, 22
Park, James, 155, 161, 163–65, 169–70
Parman, John, 192
Pasadena Playhouse, 95
paternalism, 17, 107, 119–20, 155, 158, 162–64, 166–68, 214, 240
Patman, Wright, 213
*Penhally* (Gordon), 89
People's Songs, Inc., 148–49
Peterkin, Julia, 17
Phidelah Rice Institute, 95
Philadelphia, 194
Phillips, Michael, 224
phosphate-mining companies, 77–78
photography, 137n23
Pilkington, John, 91
plantation culture, 55, 57, 99–101; cotton and, 19, 156–57; critiques of plantation myth, 4, 13–26; mechanization and, 119–20, 236–37; novels about, 2, 14–15. *See also* cotton economy
"The Plight of the Share-Cropper" (1934), 233–34
*The Plow That Broke the Plains* (Lorentz), 130
Pollock, Arthur, 93
popular culture, 1–3, 9
population growth, 181; urban, 192, 195
Porter, Katherine Anne, 43n2
Porter, Russell, 81
Post-Wolcott, Marion, 158
poverty: rural, 232; of southern whites, 59, 70, 99–101, 133, 144–45; urban, 87; of women tenant farmers, 7, 172, 176–86. *See also* sharecroppers
*Power* (1937), 6, 75, 125–35
*The Power of Progress* (Greenwood), 75–76
*Preface to Peasantry* (Raper), 27n23, 157–58, 160, 166
prejudice: against poor southern whites, 81; against the South, 89. *See also* racism
Price, Theodore H., 211
Prince, K. Stephen, 2
"Problem South," 2, 127–28, 132
Prohibition, 50
propaganda, 74–75, 126
prostitution, 35–36
Pyrnell, Louise Clarke, 13

Quinlan, Gertrude, 50

Rabinowitz, Howard, 192–93
race, 8–9, 155, 211–24; racial uplift, 218–21, 224. *See also* African Americans
race riots, 202, 210
racism, 25, 179, 188n21; institutional, 191–206; white attitudes toward blacks, 215–16, 219, 223, 239–40. *See also* discrimination; segregation, racial
radical activists, 97, 228–41
Raleigh, 192
Ransom, John Crowe, 15

Raper, Arthur, 16, 27n23, 28n33, 156–58, 160–61, 163, 165–66, 168–70
Ray, Nicholas, 126
Rayburn, Sam, 213
*Reconstructing Dixie* (McPherson), 4
Reconstruction, 17, 25, 198
redlining, 8, 191–206
Reed, John Shelton, 48, 61
regionalism, 137n19, 175
Regionalists, 28n33
Resettlement Administration (RA), 130–31, 229; planned communities, 231–32, 237–38. *See also* Farm Security Administration (FSA)
*Reviewing the South* (Gardner), 3
Rhythm Boys, 14
Rice, T. B., 155, 161, 163–70
*Rich Land, Poor Land* (Chase), 77
Richmond, 193
Rieger, Chris, 26n9
Ring, Natalie J., 2, 127–28
*The River* (Lorentz), 6, 74–75, 125, 130–35
*River of Romance* (film), 2
road construction, 107, 116–18, 144
Robbins, Jerome, 100
Rockwell, Norman, 53
Roland, Nicholas, 8
Rollins, Peter, 132, 138n26
"Roll the Union On," 148
romanticized images of the South, 1–3, 9, 13–26, 39–40, 42, 143–44, 151n7, 232, 236
Romero, Rolland, 219
Roosevelt, Eleanor, 28n35
Roosevelt, Franklin Delano: AAA program, 228; Foote and, 97; on rural southerners, 80; Technical Committee on Farm Tenancy, 25; at Texas Centennial, 223; TVA and, 69–70, 74, 76, 81–82, 122–23, 136n7
Roosevelt, Teddy, 57
Rotolactor milking machine, 79–80
Roy, William, 150n3
rural areas: depopulation, 25, 110, 114, 186; identity, 3, 6–7; poverty, 232. *See also* agrarian traditions, romanticized; farms and farmers; plantation culture; sharecroppers
Rural Electrification Administration (REA), 85n19
Rust Brothers Picker, 119

Sandburg, Carl, 53
*Saturday Review*, 52–53, 58, 61; "The Deep South Issue," 47–48
Savannah, 191–92, 194, 198–202, 204
Saxon, Lyle, 32
Scarborough, Dorothy, 13–14
Schmeling, Max, 219
Scott, Mississippi, 119
Scott, Randolph, 99
sectionalism, 133, 137n19
Seeger, Pete, 142, 149, 152n22
segregation, racial: in exhibitions, 211, 215, 218–19, 221–22; residential, 8, 191–206. *See also* Jim Crow laws
Senefeld, Emily, 7
sexuality, 184–85
*Shadow of the Plantation* (Johnson), 15, 19–22, 27n23, 28n29
Shahn, Ben, 76, 81
sharecroppers, 2, 15; black, 16–25, 27n23, 28n29, 161, 165, 167–68; car ownership, 112; collective farms, interracial, 8, 228–31, 234–41; eviction of, 8, 228, 230, 233–35; poverty, 154–70; research on, 233
Sharp, Cecil, 143, 147, 151n6
Sharpless, Rebecca, 7
Sheldon, Porter ("Pote") and Lily, 154, 161, 164, 166–68, 171n13
Sherman, William Tecumseh, 90, 195
Sibley Mills, 196
slavery, 13–14, 16–17, 87, 89, 97, 156
Smith, A. Maceo, 212–13, 215–16, 218–19, 221–24
social demography, 175
social engineering, 80–83
socialism, 8, 228–41; Christian, 119, 235, 239

social norms, 108–11
social science research, 172–86
soil erosion, 20, 70, 73, 122, 157, 160
*So Red the Rose* (Young), 2, 90, 99
South: antebellum, 13–26, 89; Deep South, 1–2, 47–48; Old South, 1–2, 9, 13–26, 128, 232, 236; pathologized images of, 2–3, 82–83, 108, 127–30, 132, 161; romanticized images of, 1–3, 9, 13–26, 39–40, 42, 143–44, 157, 232, 236
Southern Agrarians. *See* Agrarians
*A Southerner Discovers the South* (Daniels), 118–20
Southern Historical Association, 3
Southern Policy Committee (SPC), 236–37
southern studies, 3–4
Southern Tenant Farmers Union (STFU), 147–49, 229, 234, 238, 241
spirituals, 146
Spring Fiesta, 35–36
square dances, 142
Stanonis, Anthony, 4–5
State Guide Book series, 1, 32, 72, 108, 117
steamboats, 47–48
Steinbeck, John, 131
Stevens, Wallace, 87
STFU. *See* Southern Tenant Farmers Union
St. Louis, Missouri, 41–42
Stokely Brothers Canning Company, 79
Stoll, Steven, 27n20
Stott, William, 151n8, 159–60
strangers, fear of, 107, 109–10
*A Streetcar Named Desire* (Williams), 33–35, 37–41
Stryker, Roy, 169
Sullavan, Margaret, 99
Supreme Court, 126
Szalay, Michael, 124–25

Tallant, Robert, 35
Talmadge, Eugene, 163
Tate, Allen, 6, 88–89, 91, 100, 124, 232, 236–37, 243n17
Tate, Caroline Gordon, 88–89, 91, 98, 100
*Tatty Mae and Catty Mae* (Martin), 48
Taueber, Karl and Alma, 193
Taylor, Alva, 235
Taylor, Paul, 158
Technical Committee on Farm Tenancy, 25
technology, 6, 107, 126, 128, 135
Tefferteller, Ralph, 141, 144–45, 149–50, 150n1, 152n13
Temple, Shirley, 2
tenant-farmers: purchase program (Bankhead-Jones Act), 25, 158–59, 232, 236; women, 7, 172, 176–86. *See also* sharecroppers
*Tenants of the Almighty* (Raper), 161, 166, 169–70
Tennessee, 69, 234; car ownership, 115–16; Chattanooga, 76; Columbia, 77; Crossville, 73; Grundy County, 141–42; Lenoir City, 76–77; Lexington, 75; Newport, 69, 78–79
Tennessee Valley: environmental conditions, 69–74, 134; socioeconomic conditions, 70, 80–83
*Tennessee Valley Authority* (Gonzales), 73
Tennessee Valley Authority (TVA): authorization of, 122; constitutionality of, 126; criticism of, 123–24; modernism, 6, 122–36; murals, 5, 69, 71–80, 84n1, 85n21; overview, 69–71; photography, 137n23; social engineering, 80–83
Texas, 7; car ownership, 115–16; car-related deaths, 118; race relations in, 8; women tenant farmers, 172, 176–80, 183
Texas Centennial Exposition (1936), 8, 210–24
Texas Negro Centennial Committee (TNCC), 214, 216
Texas State Fair, 226n14
Textile Workers Organizing Committee (TWOC), 141, 145
Thacher, Molly Day, 93
theater: marketing and, 30; New York scene, 6, 87–101; TVA modernism and, 125–30

*These Are Our Lives*, 112
Thomas, Jesse O., 214–23
Thomas, Norman, 233–34
Thompson, Douglas, 6
Thomson, Georgia, 107, 116
*Time*, 74
*Times-Picayune*, 37–38, 41, 51–52, 55, 58–59, 62–63
Tindall, George, 13, 158
Tin Pan Alley, 2
*Tobacco Road* (Caldwell), 54, 110–12, 117
*To Kill a Mockingbird* (Lee), 98, 101
Tolan, Eddie, 219
Torrance, Jack, 219
tourism, 3; Augusta, 196; automobiles and, 117; New Orleans, 30–43; Norris Dam, 72–73
Travers, Pamela, 53
Treasury Department, Section of Painting and Sculpture, 69, 82
*Triple-A Plowed Under* (1936), 126
Tubb, Vincent, 38
Tugwell, Rexford, 232
Turner, Gracie, 112–13, 115
TVA. *See* Tennessee Valley Authority (TVA)
*The TVA at Work* (1935), 74
*TVA: Democracy on the March* (Lilienthal), 125
*TVA Power* (Citron), 78–79
"Twelve Southerners," 15, 28n33, 88–89, 99
Tyronza (Arkansas) Socialist Party, 234

Uncle Remus tales, 2, 22
unemployment, 229
unions. *See* labor movement
United Fruit Company, 57
University of Chicago, 173–74, 180
University of North Carolina, 174, 233, 236
University of Texas, 173–74, 179–80
urban areas, 110, 129, 134; development, 192, 195; New South cities, 202–3; poverty, 87
utility companies, 71, 74, 123; public, 128; rural/urban alliance against, 129. *See also* electricity

Vallish, Lillian, 97, 100
Vance, Rupert B., 16, 27n21, 28n33, 233
Vanderbilt Agrarians. *See* Agrarians
Vanderbilt University, 232
Veblen, Thorstein, 173–74
violence, racial, 193, 202, 210
Virginia, 112, 117–18

wage labor, 145, 233; women and, 177, 179
*Waiting for Lefty* (Odets), 97
Walker, Melissa, 7
Wallace, Henry, 166, 228, 233
Warren, Brett, 126
Warren, Robert Penn, 136n3
Washington, Booker T., 212, 218
Watson, Thomas E., 107, 110, 120n1
wealth, 101
Webb, Jon Edgar, 61–62
Webb, Louise, 61
Webb, Walter A., 214
Wells, Ammon S., 213
Wells, Jeremy, 2
Welty, Eudora, 31, 43n2, 55, 63
"We Shall Not Be Moved," 148–50
West, Don, 141, 146
West End Cooperative Corporation, 204
"We Will Overcome," 150
Wharton, Texas, 93, 96
White, Owen P., 154–55, 158–70
Whiteman, Paul, 14
whites: car ownership, 112–13; elites, 158–59, 162, 210; poverty, 59, 70, 99–101, 133, 144–45; prejudice against "white trash," 81, 100; women tenant-farmers, 172, 176–86
white supremacy, 164, 193, 204, 218, 224. *See also* racism
Whitney, Eli, 16
Wilder, Thornton, 93–94
Williams, Carey, 163
Williams, Claude, 142, 146, 148
Williams, Tennessee: festivals celebrating, 40–42; in New Orleans, 30–43; New York

theater scene and, 5–6, 91–93, 96, 99–100; reputation, 87–88, 101
—Works: "The Angel in the Alcove," 43; *Auto-Da-Fé*, 33, 35; *Battle of Angels*, 37; *Camino Real*, 34; *Cat on a Hot Tin Roof*, 40; *The Eccentricities of a Nightingale*, 32; *The Glass Menagerie*, 93, 99; *The Lady of Larkspur Lotion*, 35; "The Long Goodbye," 93; *Memoirs*, 37; *The Mutilated*, 33, 35; "One Arm," 35; *Orpheus Descending*, 37; *The Rose Tattoo*, 34; *Small Craft Warnings*, 33; *A Streetcar Named Desire*, 33–35, 37–41; *Suddenly Last Summer*, 33–34; *Sweet Bird of Youth*, 33–34; *Vieux Carré*, 31, 33, 35–36; "The Yellow Bird," 35–36
Willkie, Wendell, 123
Wilson, T. A., 166
Wilson County, North Carolina, 112
Wilson Dam, 73, 76, 78–79
Wise, Claire, 39
Wolfe, A. B., 173
Wolfe, Thomas, 51, 59, 62, 65n9
women: African American, 7, 176–78, 180–81, 188n21; childbearing and, 178–86; Mexican, 7, 176, 178–79, 187n19; tenant farmers, 7, 172, 176–86; wage labor, 177, 179
"Wondrous Love," 145–46
Wood, Audrey, 92–93
Wood, Grant, 73
Works Progress Administration (WPA), 75, 82, 204, 216; interviews with southerners, 108–15. *See also* Federal Writers' Project (FWP)
World War II, 56, 185
Wright, Gavin, 27n20

*You Have Seen Their Faces* (Caldwell and Bourke-White), 28n23, 161
Young, Stark, 5–6, 83–91, 94, 98–99, 101; "Not in Memoriam but in Defense," 89; *So Red the Rose*, 2, 90, 99; *The Street of the Islands*, 88; *Tomorrow*, 98
"The Young Ones" (Brown), 23–24, 28n29

zipper songs, 148
zoning laws, racial, 203
Zorach, William, 72–73, 81